The Economic Roots of the Umbrella Movement in Hong Kong

In the autumn of 2014, thousands of people, young and educated in their majority, occupied the chief business district and seat of the government in Hong Kong. The protest, known as the Umbrella Movement, called for 'genuine democracy', as well as a fairer social and economic system.

The book aims to provide a dynamic framework to explain why socio-economic forces converged to produce such a situation. Examining increasing inequality, rising prices and stagnating incomes, it stresses the role of economic and social factors, as opposed to the domestic political and constitutional issues often assumed to be the root cause behind the protests. It first argues that globalization and the increasing influence of China's economy in Hong Kong has weighted on salaries. Second, it shows that the oligopolistic nature of the local economy has generated rents, which have reinforced inequality. The book demonstrates that the younger generation, which is still finding its place in society, has been particularly affected by these phenomena, especially with social mobility at a low point.

Offering a new approach to studying the Umbrella Movement, this book will appeal to students and scholars interested in Hong Kong's political landscape, as well Chinese politics more broadly.

Louis Augustin-Jean is Research Fellow in the Centre for Economic Research, the University of Paris-North (CEPN).

Anthea H.Y. Cheung is Visiting Lecturer in the Department of Chinese and Bilingual Studies at Hong Kong Polytechnic University, Hong Kong.

Routledge Contemporary China Series

For our full list of available titles: www.routledge.com/Routledge-Contemporary-China-Series/book-series/SE0768

179 The Politics of Memory in Sinophone Cinemas and Image Culture
Altering Archives
Edited by Peng Hsiao-yen and Ella Raidel

180 China's Soviet Dream
Propaganda, Culture, and Popular Imagination
Yan Li

181 Deng Xiaoping and China's Foreign Policy
Ronald C. Keith

182 Corporate Social Responsibility Reporting in China
Evolution, Drivers and Prospects
Jieqi Guan and Carlos Noronha

183 China's Generation Gap
Jiaming Sun and Dongmei Cheng

184 China Reclaims World Power Status
Putting an end to the world America made
Paolo Urio

185 The Economic Roots of the Umbrella Movement in Hong Kong
Globalization and the Rise of China
Louis Augustin-Jean and Anthea H.Y. Cheung

186 China's Hydro-politics in the Mekong
Conflict and Cooperation in Light of Securitization Theory
Sebastian Biba

The Economic Roots of the Umbrella Movement in Hong Kong

Globalization and the Rise of China

Louis Augustin-Jean and Anthea H.Y. Cheung

Routledge
Taylor & Francis Group
LONDON AND NEW YORK

First published 2018
by Routledge

2 Park Square, Milton Park, Abingdon, Oxfordshire OX14 4RN
52 Vanderbilt Avenue, New York, NY 10017

Routledge is an imprint of the Taylor & Francis Group, an informa business

First issued in paperback 2019

British Library Cataloguing in Publication Data
A catalogue record for this book is available from the British Library

Library of Congress Cataloging in Publication Data
Names: Augustin-Jean, Louis, author. | Cheung, Anthea H. Y., author.
Title: The economic roots of the umbrella movement in Hong Kong : globalization and the rise of China / Louis Augustin-Jean and Anthea H.Y. Cheung.
Description: Abingdon, Oxon ; New York, NY : Routledge, 2018. | Series: Routledge contemporary china series ; 185 | Includes bibliographical references and index.
Identifiers: LCCN 2017048637| ISBN 9780815368236 (hardback) | ISBN 9781351255516 (ebook)
Subjects: LCSH: Democracy–China–Hong Kong. | Protest movements–China–Hong Kong. | Hong Kong (China)–Economic conditions. | Hong Kong (China)–Politics and government–1987–
Classification: LCC JQ1539.5.A91 A94 2018 | DDC 322.4/4095125–dc23
LC record available at https://lccn.loc.gov/2017048637

ISBN: 978-0-8153-6823-6 (hbk)
ISBN: 978-0-367-35584-5 (pbk)

Typeset in Times New Roman
by Wearset Ltd, Boldon, Tyne and Wear

Contents

Tables

Preface and acknowledgements

When, in autumn 2014, students occupied Admiralty – the business district and the location of the Chief Executive office – and started what was not yet known as the Umbrella Movement, journalists and scholars focused mainly on the demands of the protesters – namely: the withdrawal of the 31 August 2014 Decision of the National People's Congress Standing Committee to grant universal suffrage to Hong Kong, but under a restrictive framework, and the implementation of 'genuine democracy'. These demands were first and foremost political.

However, this focus left many questions remaining. It was not asked what people did expect from the universal suffrage, if it was hypothetically granted? What would be their next step after the implementation of democracy? And so on....

Our motivation to write this book was, for a part, directed by these interrogations. As the Hong Kong society has diversified and its demands proliferated in recent years, it is difficult to fully address these points. However, we believe that at least three types of answers are shared by most, if not all, the protesters. First, people fought for democracy because they wanted to make decisions on their own future; second, they wanted to protect the freedoms and civil liberties that are guaranteed by the Basic Law, but that they felt jeopardized (what we call a 'protective attitude'). And third, they were guided by the desire to have a society and an economic model that provides more equal opportunity to everyone – which supposes that the current system does not (this is a 'proactive behaviour'). While the ensuing chapters of this book mainly centre on this last point, a few words for each of these three attitudes are presented below.

The first point – the wish of the people to make their own choice – may not be as trivial as it may first seem. To start with, Ortmann has highlighted some existing contradictions between the 'liberal democratic' principles and the way the Basic Law frames the political system. For the author, these contradictions are not due to the absence of an independent state – the example of Taiwan negates this classic hypothesis – but to the lack of two other elements of sovereignty: 'a polity [which] must be able to determine its own political structures without the intervention from the outside'; and (...) 'a polity [which] must also be free from external intervention in its decision-making' (Ortmann 2016: 115–116). None of these conditions is fulfilled in Hong Kong, since, in the eyes of the Mainland authorities, the 'Hong Kong's system is entirely dependent on the Beijing government' (ibid.: 117). For the Central government, thus, the introduction of the liberal democracy (the 'genuine democracy', in the language of the protesters) in Hong Kong would threaten the current political order in the Mainland because 'it would serve as a basis for subversion of the one-party state' (ibid.). And, within Hong Kong itself, it would stimulate the demands for more autonomy and thus, compromise the unity of the country. For Beijing, then, the 'genuine democracy' requested by the protesters were conflicting with the 'One Country, Two Systems' principles – even though they were not in opposition to the Basic Law. The ambiguity between the introduction of democracy in Hong Kong and China's sovereignty over Hong Kong may not be apparent at first, but for the Mainland authorities it is real.

There is thus a real divergence between the analyses of the central leadership and the aspiration of the people to access the liberal democracy – and to make their own choice for their future under the Basic Law framework. This rationale, however, does not explain why people really desire the implementation of this democracy. On this topic, Ortmann only added that, in accordance with the principles of the modernization theory, this desire is stimulated by the evolution of the economic conditions in the last decades: when a country grows economically, its middle class also enlarges and inevitably asks for more democracy. At first, this thesis seems to contradict the seminal analysis of Lau Siu-kai, who stated that Hong Kong people were not interested in democracy during most of the colonial era, because, as they were mainly political or economic refugees who fled China, they were more concerned by good governance (Lau 1984; Lau and Kuan 1995). In recent years, this theory has been nuanced, and it was shown that Hongkongers were not as apathic as Lau Siu-kai thought. Finally, Ma Ngoc proposed common ground between these two theories:

> (…) Hong Kong people supported democracy not because of its intrinsic value or as a principle of societal or political organization, but because they believed it could deliver good governance and defend their way of life. Even if they supported democracy, they considered their participation inconsequential in bringing about its fruition, and many preferred to stay away and free-ride.
>
> (Ma 2011: 687)

In recent years, this paradigm has evolved, and the call for democracy came to the forefront. It has been, for a part, stimulated not by the growth of the middle class, but by its difficulties – especially the lack of opportunities and the rise in inequality. In relation to it, Ma added that, since the handover, values have become less instrumental and 'more and more people in Hong Kong conceive democracy in terms of political rights or equality' (ibid.: 695). As we will see below, these political and economic dimensions are completely embedded.

This argumentation is, of course, only one element of answer among many others. Participants to the Umbrella Movement had also a 'protective attitude', which was generated by their wish to obtain stronger safeguards to the civil liberties which are, in principle, protected by the Basic Law (mainly from Article 25 to 42). Article 39, in particular, specifies that 'the provisions of the International Covenant on Civil and Political Rights [ICCPR], the International Covenant on Economic, Social and Cultural Rights, and international labour conventions as applied to Hong Kong shall remain in force (…)', while Article 27 guarantees the freedom of speech, of assembly, of the press, etc.

However, more and more people feel this legal and institutional protection has weakened in recent years and these rights have eroded. The attempt to implement an anti-subversion law (in accordance to Article 23 of the Basic Law) in 2003, and a 'Moral and National Education', in 2010–2011, contributed to this feeling. Both were opposed by massive protests (half a million people, or 7 per cent of the population, joined the 2003 protest), and prompted the government to shelve (but not abandon) the two proposals. Similarly, a year after the end of the Umbrella Movement, the alleged kidnapping of five staff members of Mighty Current, a local publishing house considered subversive by Beijing, did nothing to reassure the people. To push the argument further, the fight for democracy, then, can also be understood as a fight to gain the missing freedom – the freedom to choose one's own leader, as specified in Article 45 of the Basic Law. In fact, local democrats have long pointed out that the ICCPR, which sees universal suffrage as a basic right, is not respected in the absence of democracy.

In the end, as 'protective' as this strategy may be, it can rapidly shift into a more offensive one if the plea for democracy is not satisfied. During the Umbrella Movement, most protesters were quite legalistic and referred to the Basic Law. However, the apparent failure of the Movement has stimulated the development of more radical forms of action, most notably the spread of indigenous or localist movements. These groups have an easy task in criticizing the traditional democratic parties for failing to achieve any tangible results since the 1980s. Some of their members have also found their way to be elected in the Legislative Council (LegCo), even though some have been disqualified in court for failing to take oath properly. In brief, the refusal of the Central and Hong Kong governments to introduce (more) democracy resulted in exactly what they were trying to avoid.…

The last type of demand of the Umbrella Movement's participants was much more proactive. It is supported by the ideal that democracy should bring equal opportunity to all. This attitude was triggered by the decrease in the support for the prevalent economic system. According to Ma Ngoc:

> For decades, neoliberal ideology in Hong Kong was justified on the grounds that it provides 'equal opportunity.' Surveys in the 1980s showed that the Hong Kong people in general, and the middle class in particular, bought into the dictums of equal opportunity, upward mobility, and self-reliance within the Hong Kong capitalist order.
>
> (Ma 2011: 688)

But, in recent years:

> More people began to question neoliberal dictums. In 1988, surveys found 58% agreed with the laissez-faire policy, while only 42% did in 1994. The 1999 SIS (Social Indicators Surveys) showed that 45% supported maintaining the 'positive noninterventionist policy,' while 23% were opposed. More people began to question the fairness of the system.
>
> (Ibid.: 702–703)

Thus, there is a growing trend of people who do not believe that the economic system is fair. And that was especially the case among the educated youths who protested during the Umbrella Movement. Conceptually, therefore, this new behaviour is characterized by a mixed of a pragmatic attitude (i.e. the rejection of a system which does not provide suitable opportunities to all – especially to them) and of a democratic ideal.

This trend is fuelled by indicators showing that the current system provides more inequality than opportunities. Hong Kong has become one of the most unequal places of the developed world, with the Gini coefficient based on original monthly household income reaching 0.539 in 2016; more and more citizens can see that working hard is not sufficient to bring them wealth, when the minimum salary is set at HK$34.5 (which is already an improvement); they also see that opportunities are declining, as well as the social mobility. Even though their demands were not especially targeted to their own situation, they can clearly see that their access to good jobs and comfortable housing is limited.

Our book concentrates on this latest perspective. While we fully concur to the first two viewpoints, we believe this economic analysis has been insufficiently tackled: it is one thing to show that more and more people think the economic system does not fulfil its promises; it is another to analyse why this is actually the case. For years, Hong Kong economy has been ranked as the most liberal in the world. Since 1971, the colonial authorities have stood by the 'positive non-interventionism' principle, by which the government should theoretically refrain from intervening in economic affairs. This ideology was even incorporated into the Basic Law. Based on these mainstream economic principles, the low level of government intervention and the 'free market' should be conducive to higher economic growth and equal opportunity to everyone; the institution of the market is neutral, and just helps sellers and buyers to solve their contradictions.

So, what went wrong? Why has this system generated so much inequality? Why have the opportunities declined so much for the younger generation, even though families have invested greatly to allow their kids to get a university degree? Why did salaries increase so little, even though the GDP per capita has progressed steadily since the handover?

This book addresses these questions. The paradigm it develops presents the idea that the economic organization, as it has evolved since the 1960s, generated rents – meaning that a tiny portion of the population (whom we called the 'economic élites') has extracted a significant economic surplus from the rest of the population. Over the years, these rents, which started in the housing sector but extended to other sectors, accumulated until today, when inequality reached a historical high. The influence the economic élites have exerted in Hong Kong's governance, as well as historical circumstances (decolonization, Beijing's support to the existing system, the development of an 'economic ideology', etc.) has been influential in this process. Interestingly, the educated youths, who are supposed to become the driving force of the future – and who are the ones who should supposedly benefit the most from globalization –, have been particularly affected, as they have seen their salaries stagnated since the handover, while opportunities and social mobilities have declined.

Most Hong Kong people are well aware of the consequences of this economic organization, including the role the economic élites have played in the economy, the difficulties to access decent housing, the rise in inequality, and so on. However, beyond these factors, we aim to show that all these elements are connected, and are the consequence of this specific economic organization. In other words, if (young) people are less supportive to the neoliberal system, it is because they feel this system is biased in favour of the happy few. But, contrary to what the protesters of the Occupy Wall Street movement demanded, they do not want to remove this system: they just want to amend it, since they don't see any credible alternative.

Having said that, *the purpose of this book is first and foremost to create the conditions for a discussion, not to present a definitive analysis.* For this reason, we have analysed data in the most straightforward form, so that the book can be accessible to most, from confirmed scholars and journalists to undergraduate students. We have also tried to present them in the most objective fashion we can, so that further debates can nurture and unnecessary polemics be avoided.

Finally, we would like to conclude this Preface by adding a few words on two important events that occurred since the completion of this book. The first is the publication of new set of statistics by the Census and Statistics Department (C&SD), and the second is the nomination of Carrie Lam Cheng Yuet-ngor as Chief Executive on 1 July 2017.

The first issue concerns the publication of the new *Household Distribution Income Report* by the C&SD in 2017. If this document mainly confirms the observations made in this book, a caveat regarding the gap between the highest and the lower individual incomes is necessary. On the contrary, the report fully confirms the current difficulties of the educated youths, whose salary has mostly stagnated since 1997.

In more detail, in line with the theory of polarization, Chapter 3 shows that both globalization and the development of China's economy (the two phenomena are difficult to separate) have pushed up salaries of professionals and pressured downward the incomes of individuals with low educational achievements. Consequently, the gap between the highest and the lowest deciles (for personal income) has grown constantly.

The new C&SD report does not confirm this phenomenon. On the contrary, it indicates that the gap between the highest and the lowest deciles for personal incomes has actually *decreased* from 2011 to 2016. In 2006, the median income for the highest decile was 15 times higher than the one of the lowest; in 2011, this ratio increased further to 15.36. But, in 2016, it reduced to only 12.95 (C&SDa 2017: 25, Table 2.3). While this seems counterintuitive, the government explained this welcome evolution by the introduction of a Statutory Minimum Wage (SMW) in 2011, as well as by the situation of full employment (C&SDb, 2017). However, at this stage, it is difficult to know if this evolution will last, or if it is just a short-term effect following the implementation of the SMW. An OXFAM study leans towards the second hypothesis, as it emphasizes that the positive effect of the SMW for poor households is progressively wiped out, because the regular increase of the hourly rate does not match the inflation rate:

> Under the current biannual review system, the increase in minimum wage has continued to lag behind the rate of inflation. When the Minimum Wage Commission suggested the first minimum wage level of $28/hour in October 2010, the Composite CPI [Consumer Price Index] was 82.9 (using 2014/15 as the base year); in August 2016, the Composite CPI rose 24% to 102.8. With this inflation rate, the actual purchasing power of the current minimum wage level ($32.5/hour) is only equivalent to $26 in October 2010, which is even lower than the original minimum wage level.
>
> (OXFAM 2016: 13)

It is therefore possible that the gap between the highest and the lowest deciles will soon increase again, but it is too early to give a definitive answer on this point.

Concerning the second element – the evolution of the salaries of young graduates – the conclusions reached in the book are fully confirmed. From 1997 to 2016, the 'median monthly employment earnings of employed persons aged 20–24 who had attained a post-secondary level' has only increased from HK$10,500 to HK$11,700 (or, about 10 per cent). Since these data are in current prices, the increase does not even make up for the inflation rate. While most of this rise occurred in the last few years (the earnings were only HK$8,500 in 2010), the new data pinpoint that the educated youths did not benefit at all from the economic growth.

This is certainly an issue that Carrie Lam, the new Chief Executive (CE), has to tackle during her tenure. During her election campaign, she showed sympathy for young people, and promised to include some of them into the government apparatus. She also indicated that her first efforts would be directed to improve the education system. A few days after she started her term as CE, she confirmed these intentions and provided an additional HK$3.6 billion to the education sector, including grants for some self-financed students. Other proposals for small and medium enterprises (SMEs) and the welfare system are in the pipeline.

The reinjection in the economy of some of the money that has been withdrawn from it by the previous administrations is certainly a positive sign. Long-term effects and spillovers may be expected and the different projects, if well designed, will certainly help recipients. Carrie Lam herself may also benefit from this policy, with an improved popularity, at least in the short term.

However, the distribution of funds from the reserve leaves the core of the economic system untouched. In other words, it does not aim to address the underlying causes of the inequality, and the economic system will remain intact. As the book shows, possible reforms in the tax system or the extension of the scope of the newly introduced competition law will be difficult to implement, because of the opposition coming from both the economic élites and the Chinese government. In addition, it would need an ideological shift from government officials, including Carrie Lam, and this is not likely for people who spent most of their career as civil servants. In short, the necessary economic reforms may be as difficult to implement as the institutional ones.

To conclude, this project led us much farther than we first foresaw. Several issues that surprised us have been discussed at length with colleagues and led to discussions, which, at times, have been animated. This book benefited a lot from these debates, as well as from the comments we received from friends who have read the different versions of the manuscript.

Our thanks go first to Pascal Petit, Professor Emeritus at the Centre d'Economie de Paris Nord (University of Paris XIII) who carefully read the first draft of the manuscript and suggested several adjunctions and reorganizations. Further strong support was provided by Doctor Gavin Ure, Louis' colleague at the Hong Kong Polytechnic University. Gavin made strong recommendations and provided important references that led to significant rewritings of Chapter 1. This book also benefited greatly from discussions with Professor Tsui Ming-sum and Doctor David Herold, respectively Professor of Social Work and Assistant Professor of Anthropology at the Hong Kong Polytechnic University. We also discussed several points with our friends Professor Philippe Steiner, from the University of Paris Sorbonne, Professor John Lagerwey from the Chinese University of Hong Kong and Professor Hélène Ilbert, from the Institut Agronomique Méditerranéen in Montpellier. We also would like to thank two anonymous reviewers who, by their justified criticisms, stimulated important changes, especially in the Introduction and the Conclusion. Of course, any mistake and shortcoming remain ours.

Finally, the last words go to Choi Cho-hong, who had the irksome task of editing the first two drafts of the manuscript. We would like to thank him for his hard work and for his care in improving the style of the original text.

Louis Augustin-Jean and Anthea H.Y. Cheung

Bibliography

Census and Statistics Department (2017a) 'Population By-Census 2016. Thematic Report. Household Distribution Income', Hong Kong: General Statistics Section Census and Statistics Department.

Census and Statistics Department (2017b) 'Census and Statistics Department Announces Results of Study on Household Income Distribution in Hong Kong', www.censtatd.gov.hk/press_release/pressReleaseDetail.jsp?charsetID=1&pressRID=4180, accessed 25 June 2017.

Lau, S.K. (1984) *Society and Politics in Hong Kong*, Hong Kong: Chinese University of Hong Kong Press.

Lau, S.K. and Kuan H.C. (1995) 'The attentive spectators: Political participation of the Hong Kong Chinese', *Journal of Northeast Asian Studies*, 14(1): 3–24.

Ma, N. (2011) 'Value Changes and Legitimacy Crisis in Post-industrial Hong Kong', *Asian Survey*, 51(4): 683–712.

Ortmann, S. (2016) 'The Lack of Sovereignty, Umbrella Movement and Democratisation in Hong Kong's', *Asia Pacific Law Review*, 24(2): 108–122.

OXFAM Hong Kong (2016) 'Hong Kong Poverty Report (2011–2015)', www.oxfam.org.hk/content/98/content_31062en.pdf, accessed 22 June 2017.

Abbreviations

AEOI	Automatic Exchange of Financial Account Information
AMLO	Anti-Money Laundering and Counter-Terrorist Financing (Financial Institutions) Ordinance
BVIs	British Virgin Islands
CE	Chief Executive of the HKSAR
CEPA	Mainland and Hong Kong Closer Economic Partnership Arrangement
CPI	Consumer Price Index
C&SD	Census and Statistics Department
DAB	Democratic Alliance for the Betterment and Progress of Hong Kong
DI	Direct Investments
DTA	Double Tax Agreement
ExCo	Executive Council
FDH	Foreign Domestic Helpers
FDI	Foreign Direct Investments
GDP	Gross Domestic Product
GST	Goods and Services Tax
G20	Group of Twenty
HKIEd	Hong Kong Institute of Education
HKSAR	Hong Kong Special Administrative Region
HKU	The University of Hong Kong
ICCPR	International Covenant on Civil and Political Rights
IVS	Individual Visit Scheme
LegCo	Legislative Council
NPM	New Public Management
NPCSC	The Standing Committee of the National People's Congress
OCLP	Occupy Central with Love and Peace
OECD	Organisation for Economic Co-operation and Development
PMR	Persons from the Mainland Having Resided in Hong Kong for Less Than 7 Years
PolyU	The Hong Kong Polytechnic University
PRC	People's Republic of China

RMB	Renminbi
RVD	Rating and Valuation Department
SAR	Special Administrative Region
SARS	Severe acute respiratory syndrome
SCMP	*South China Morning Post*
SMEs	Small and Medium Enterprises
SMW	Statutory Minimum Wage
TEU	Twenty-Foot Equivalent Unit
US	United States of America
WTO	World Trade Organization

Introduction

At 1:30 AM on Sunday, 28 September 2014, Benny Tai, one of the three architects of 'Occupy Central with Love and Peace' (Occupy Central or OCLP hereinafter) formally launched the Movement. Its original kick-off date was 1 October 2014, but Tai was upstaged by class boycotts and mass protests initiated by university and high school students almost a week earlier on 22 September. The two movements finally 'merged' into the 'Umbrella Movement', which attracted, at its peak, over 100,000 people and blocked some of the main arteries of the Admiralty business district on Hong Kong Island for almost 80 days.[1] According to one survey, a great majority of the protesters were young (over 75 per cent were between 18 and 39 and 37 per cent under 24), 26 per cent of them were students (with another 58 per cent white-collared workers or self-employed), and more than half (56 per cent) held a university education.[2]

The protesters justified their action by questioning the decision made by the Standing Committee of the National People's Congress (NPCSC) on 31 August 2014 to grant 'universal suffrage' to the Hong Kong people (as stated in the Basic Law, the de facto mini constitution of Hong Kong; see below), but in a very restrictive way. Hence, they demanded the withdrawal of the 31 August Decision and the implementation of what they considered 'genuine' democracy and universal suffrage. But beyond these demands, the question remains: why did so many young, educated Hongkongers – some of them born after 1 July 1997 and, hence, had only lived under Chinese rule and the Basic Law – decide to take to the streets to voice their demands?

The 'classic' answer to this question emphasizes the continuity of the call for democracy since the 1970s (Ortmann 2015a, 2015b) or even earlier (Pepper 2008). For example, Ortmann provided a historical account of Hong Kong's democratic movement since the 1970s. The author documented how the democratic seeds germinated in the 1970s, grew in strength in the 1980s and, in 1989, turned to reach a first climax, which was actually in alignment with the protest movement of the Tiananmen Square in Beijing. This led to the rise of democratic parties in Hong Kong, which started to compete for the few directly elected seats at the Legislative Council (LegCo) since 1991. In 2003, attempts by the government to introduce an anti-subversion law in Hong Kong prompted half a million people to join a mass protest, leading to another climax – the law was drafted in a way that many Hongkongers felt being threatened with deprival of civil liberties (see below, Chapter 1).

In these movements, students and, more generally, young people did not have the driving seat, even though some were active participants. From the end of the 2000s, however, such a pattern started to evolve and many educated young people became more involved in social actions. Thus, in May 2011, 'secondary-school students were at the forefront of a movement against the introduction of Moral and National Education, which was proposed by the Education Bureau' of the Hong Kong government (Ortmann 2015: 44). Through their actions, students succeeded in getting rid of the proposal, which, according to them, was not objective – even though the idea to reintroduce 'national education' resurfaces regularly. This action steered them well to the leadership they took in 2014 during the Umbrella Movement.[3]

This historical approach is perfectly suitable to analyse the political factors behind the development of democracy forces in general, and the Umbrella Movement in particular.[4] But this type of analysis, only briefly outlined above, hides the fact that the political and the economic factors are intricately embedded. An important reason for not introducing democracy in Hong Kong in the 1980s, in addition to the opposition of Beijing, was also the veto of the economic élites (see Chapter 1). And, as the subsequent chapters of this book will demonstrate, this created a certain paralysis of both the political and economic systems. In this sense, the Umbrella Movement can be seen as a consequence of the contradictions that accrued from this paralysis. This is especially the case since young people, if they are not fully aware of the structure of the system, are totally obsessed by some of its consequences, such as the rise in inequality, the difficulties in accessing a decent lodging, the lack of upward-mobility for young graduates, and so on. In short, the fight for democracy is *also* the fight for equal opportunities.

Thus, the purpose of this book is not to depict the Movement or show the divergent analyses of it that were published when it occurred. On the contrary, it intends to provide a dynamic framework that analyses the economic and social forces that have converged to produce such a situation. While a large part of the existing literature is centred on domestic factors (including the intricate relations between Hong Kong and China) and has favoured political (the democratization process) and constitutional (divergent readings of the 'Basic Law') issues, this book stresses the role of economic and social factors in the context of globalization as parameters behind the Movement. As this book is more concerned by an analysis of the system which has produced these inequalities – and diminishing opportunities for the educated youth – it also departs from previous studies, which mainly concentrated on measuring the level of dissatisfaction of what used to be called, ten years ago, the 'post-1980s generation' (Hong Kong Transition Project 2010; Wu 2010).[5]

Back in 2010, two surveys from the Hong Kong Transition Project and from Wu Xiaogang, while focusing on the perception of the young generation on the government's policies or on China, already included economic and social data.

The Transition Project, in particular, showed that, in comparison to their elders, people under 30 were much more concerned by economic problems and less by political ones.[6] The report also insisted that, for young people, direct elections were the best tool to settle these problems:

> This perception gap [between generations] may also account for some of the frustration felt among younger cohorts, for to the majority of the under 30s, direct election and political parties and protests are obvious means to address problems and press for solutions. For those over 60, the same means appear either useless or have a negative impact on the problem, or worst of all to many of them, risk causing political instability.
>
> (Hong Kong Transition Project 2010: 61)

This is not to say, of course, that these economic and social factors *alone* would have been sufficient to trigger a mass protest of such a scale, but they did provide a favourable bedrock for the Umbrella Movement to nurture. In this respect, it is noticeable that even scholars who placed political factors at the forefront of their analyses still pointed out the paramount role played by the economic situation for both the post-1980s generation 'which cares less about materialistic values and seeks more fulfilling goals' (Ortmann 2015: 44) – but promotes a fairer economic system – and the government and economic élites, who worry that more democracy may bring more resources redistribution (and tax increases). Thus, since the 1980s, the debate over the introduction of democracy in Hong Kong has always been tainted by economic factors. The opposition to democracy by both the Chinese authorities and the economic élites prompted the formation of an unlikely alliance between these two forces.[7]

The ensuing chapters will develop these points further. More precisely, this book argues that the Umbrella Movement was, in part, triggered by the changing position of Hong Kong in global capitalism – its international openness reinforcing its sensitivity to the ever-evolving global environment. Thanks to its proximity to Mainland China, Hong Kong benefited from globalization during the first stages of China's reforms (up to the mid-1990s), but now a significant part of its population seems to be negatively affected similarly to other global metropolises. This phenomenon was further aggravated by two related factors: its own history, including the rise of a business community that dominates politics and has been able to create an oligopolistic market for many goods, and the difficulty of integrating Hong Kong into China after the handover, which ambiguities in the Basic Law have highlighted.

In this context, the fight for democracy and universal suffrage reveals deeper contradictions that exist in the city's social and economic order, including the growth in inequality and the decreasing opportunities for (relatively) educated youth and the middle class. In other words, the recent evolution of the Hong Kong economy is another illustration of the Polanyian framework, in which the development of capitalism and the deepening of market relations generate social conflicts (Polanyi 1944/1957). Quark (citing Silver 2003: 18) has put it in a very different context, 'actors marginalized by liberal market projects are compelled to defend 'established and widely accepted social compacts in the right to livelihoods – in other words, [they are] in part fueled by a sense of "injustice"' (Quark 2013: 16). In Hong Kong, the young protesters may not be 'marginalized actors', but this book will show that they do not really benefit from the existing economic system and thus, they are, for a part, displacing the issues in political and social arena – as it will be emphasized in the course of this book's writing. Related to it, Hongkongers are still trying to find their new roles not only in China, but in the world as well (Augustin-Jean 2005; Augustin-Jean and Padovani 2007), which add to their anxieties. Therefore, even though the current political and social crisis has multiple origins,[8] the authors contend that these two forces have played the role of catalysts.

The aim of this book is to develop these central arguments. It will be shown that three dynamics have converged to provoke subtle changes in the economic system that impacted on the situation of the (educated) youth and the middle class. These three dynamics are: the influence of China in the domestic economy; the forces of globalization; and the evolution of the domestic economy itself since the 1960s. This evolution led to a new economic system in which young people receive declining opportunities and which they perceived as biased.

The first two chapters will introduce a metacontext, which is characterized by uncertainties regarding Hong Kong's future in the political and economic fields. Consequently, this creates a sentiment of unease for many people, in particular younger folks who have yet to find their places in society. More precisely, the first chapter will present the specificities and the main principles that have shaped the reunification of Hong Kong with the People's Republic of China (PRC). It will also review the changes and continuities from the colonial period, in particular the role played by the economic élites: while the Chief Executive (CE) of Hong Kong (like the governor before him) has, in theory, large powers, he is often not able or unwilling to exert them due to his dependence on these economic élites and to the fact that he is appointed by the Central government after being elected by a tiny minority of people. Hence, he cannot be fully legitimate. For that purpose, the principle of 'One Country, Two Systems' and its concrete incorporation into the Basic Law will be reviewed, although it is already well known and has been discussed in-depth: its presentation will help one see why it was not obvious that the proposed NPCSC reform could give extra legitimacy to the CE. In the second section, the reason why the CE not only lacks more legitimacy, but also has even less than governors before him, will be shown. There are at least three parameters with which to justify this statement. The first is the degrading economic situation immediately following the handover. The second is the disarticulated nature of the political system since the handover. The third is the lack of flexibility in this political system, which was partly caused by the Basic Law, the action of the business élites and Beijing. This stands in sharp contrast to the colonial era, when the government compensated for its lack of legitimacy by co-opting new élites, introducing new social welfare programmes, and, in the very last decade, launching political reforms.

The second chapter will extend this theme by introducing some issues related to the relations between Hong Kong, the global economy and China. It will show that these relations are changing, but in a direction that is difficult to define, and hence creates additional worries and ambiguities for many Hongkongers. Once again, the purpose of this book is not to present a general perspective of the economic system, but to show, through selected examples, that Hong Kong's traditional role as a bridge between the Chinese economy and the rest of the world is evolving while its position within the Chinese economy has to be reinvented. The examples that the authors have selected are foreign direct investments (FDIs) and international trade, as well as some of the industries picked as 'pillars' by the Hong Kong government: logistics and trading, finance, and tourism. As it can be inferred, these economic sectors are traditionally at the forefront of the globalization process, but in Hong Kong, their development is also strongly conditioned by the growing influence China's economy is exerting on the Territory. This is especially the case with tourism. Accordingly, a special emphasis will be given to it as it has raised a lot of controversies in recent years. It is necessary to insist here that the aim of this section is not to bring (pessimistic or optimistic) perspectives to the future of the Hong Kong economy. Rather, it argues, by means of statistics, that the recent evolution of the Hong Kong economy has cast doubts over its future role in China and throughout the world. For Hongkongers, a consequence of such doubts is the declining support for Hong Kong's liberal economy and globalization, especially among the more educated youth – which the authors call the 'disenchantment of youth'. This is not to say that (younger) people are bluntly rejecting capitalism or globalization (especially since they don't see a credible alternative), but they do not believe any more that the current economic system in Hong Kong is helping or benefiting them. In other words, Hong Kong is no longer (seen as) a land where everybody has a chance to succeed as in the past.

Chapters 3 and 4 will elaborate on this topic by analysing the reasons for this disenchantment – namely, the decline in (economic) opportunities, income stagnation, growing inequality, housing problems, etc. All in all, it appears that even for those of its members equipped with university degrees (which have now become indispensable), the younger generation is not guaranteed a better future. At the same time, increased inequality, triggered by the growing concentration of capital and wealth at the top, has jeopardized opportunities for those even lower on the social ladder in Hong Kong.

Chapter 3 will show that globalization forces are unlikely to generate sufficient positions at the managerial or professional levels vis-à-vis the increase in the number of university graduates. Rather, these forces may create more opportunities for 'associate professionals', whom some scholars have grouped into a 'new middle class'. Whether or not one accepts such terminology is a matter of opinion; but what is more important is that the opportunities to climb the social ladder for these associate professionals are getting slimmer and slimmer while salaries stagnate and/or progress at a slower speed than the city's gross domestic product (GDP) growth.

Chapter 4 will show that the effects of this lack of social mobility and increased inequality have been reinforced by local forces. More specifically, the extreme concentration of capital and the oligopolistic nature of the Hong Kong economy do not only reinforce inequality, but also impact prices, especially for housing. The consequence is that younger people have not only diminished opportunities, but also difficulties in accessing decent lodging. In this context, the recent introduction of the Competition Ordinance in December 2015 appeared to be a missed opportunity to fix some of these issues, most of which are not specific to Hong Kong. Similarly, while the government was eager to modify the tax system at the beginning of the 2000s, its main propositions – the creation of a goods and services tax (GST) and, simultaneously, a lowering of the income tax – would not have reduced inequality or provided more affordable housing and opportunities to the middle class and young people (in any case, that was not its aim). Yet these social and economic issues and the way the government tackled them laid the foundation for a climate of protest that sees (relatively educated) youth demanding a larger say in the political arena. But the demise of the Umbrella Movement has extinguished their hopes in this sector – at least for the time being.

Finally, the conclusion will show how this changing framework can be related to the Umbrella Movement. It will be highlighted that, from the top, the economic élites have always managed to impede or, at least, to considerably slow down democratic evolutions in order to maintain the existing economic system. This created a situation in which young people feel trapped. Second, even though protesters did not clearly demand economic changes during the protest, there are evidences that participants in the Umbrella Movement were also concerned by economic and social criteria such as the wealth gap, as mentioned earlier. All in all, in linking democracy and equality of opportunity, young people were, directly or indirectly, promoting economic changes.

Before presenting all these different points, the authors should emphasize, first and foremost, that the objective of this book is to present an analysis that explains why so many younger people who participated in the Umbrella Movement are disillusioned with Hong Kong's existing economic and social system. Thus, the authors will introduce a framework which incorporates elements that are usually analysed separately and illustrate, as precisely as possible, the role of certain institutions or groups of people in the current social crisis. In other words, while some elements of the puzzle may already be known and well documented, others have not led to deep analysis: if most academic work generally centres on one specific issue, this book will present a more comprehensive picture of the situation. This does not mean, however, that the authors aim to give an exhaustive analysis of the economic and social situation; for example, they have not examined all the elements of the current overhaul of Hong Kong's economy, which has enlarged the stakes in it for many Mainland companies while local companies have had to evolve by changing their leadership. But, through a careful analysis of the existing data – published and unpublished – the authors hope to provide a new and unique interpretation of the Umbrella Movement by highlighting some of its economic causes. More importantly, the authors expect this work and its conclusion – that the younger generation holds little hope for the existing economic and social framework – will enrich the debate over Hong Kong's future without offering definitive answers.

Notes

1 In reality, the two movements did not really 'merge' and the whole movement remained quite decentralized, with prominent figures, but without real leader(s). The term, 'Umbrella Movement', was coined in reference to the umbrellas protesters used to protect themselves from tear gas fired by the police on 28 September 2014.

2 These statistics only give a rough indication of the protesters' demographics because the survey was done on the spot from 20–26 October 2014. On the one hand, the sampling could not be controlled, while on the other hand, the participation rate changed during the 79-day occupation. See Cheng and Yuen (2014).

3 In fact, the Umbrella Movement was, at times, misunderstood by the Western media, which referred to it as the 'Umbrella Revolution'. See, among many examples in the foreign press, Kayman (2014) and Hilgers (2015). It fact, the Movement had nothing to do with a revolution, as the protesters themselves stated. The Federation of Students stressed that 'the Occupy movement is 'absolutely not a revolution,' but rather a drive initiated by Hong Kong's civil society (see *SCMP*, www.scmp.com/news/hong-kong/article/1609580/live-chinese-university-urges-students-leave-thousands-gather). The protesters insisted on the fact that, even though the occupation can be considered illegal, the demand for universal suffrage and democracy are far from 'radical', since they are clearly stated in the Basic Law. In that sense, the protesters did not aim to change the system, but rather wanted to implement what is already stated in Hong Kong's constitution (see below).

4 For an analysis of the political roots of the Umbrella Movement, see, among others Ortmann (2015, 2016) and Veg (2015).

5 This 'post-1980s' generation reached roughly 34 years old or below in 2014; it formed the core of the people who protested during the Umbrella Movement (75 per cent of the protesters were 18–39 years old), as shown above.

6 61.4 per cent of the interviewees under 29 were most concerned by economic issues, in comparison to 9.4 per cent who placed political issues on the top. In fact, the economic factors are even more important for the age range 30–59 (65.4 per cent), but this difference is mainly due to the fact that 29 per cent of them have listed employment/unemployment as their most concerned problem versus 17 per cent for the younger generation. Interestingly, the wealth gap is listed as the No. 1 problem by 20 per cent of the younger generation, but only 17 per cent by the 30–59 generation and 10 per cent by people over 60 years old (Hong Kong Transition Project, 2010: 59, Table 76).

7 This point will be discussed in depth in Chapter 1. See also Goodstadt (2000) and Fong (2014).

8 Again, this book does not deny that other forces – especially cultural values and identity – played an important role in the protest. Also, as in economics, the future of the Hong Kong identity depends on its place within China and the globalization process. A recent example that has been recurrent since the handover – and which could be multiplied at will – is the use of English in the Territory. The title and headline of an article published on the *SCMP* (8 June 2015) illustrated this issue well: 'Official use of English being 'neglected' by [the] Hong Kong government. Critics say government contravenes own laws by favouring Chinese in communicating with [the] public and media, despite both being official languages' (Yau 2015). The article

pointed out the fact that senior officials (such as the Finance Secretary, John Tsang Chun-wah) only published blogs in Chinese, while the Chief Executive Leung Chun-ying seldom delivers speeches in English. Claudia Mo Man-ching (a Pan-Democrat LegCo member) said,

> there was a clear problem the government was refusing to acknowledge. I have a feeling that the government is trying to shut down the use of English in order to emphasize the fact that Hong Kong is a Mainland city and English is just a second language for Hongkongers. But this is not right, since English shares an equal status with Chinese.
>
> (Ibid.)

Bibliography

Augustin-Jean, L. (2005) 'Urban Planning in Hong Kong and Integration with the Pearl River Delta: An Historical Account of the Local Development?' *GeoJournal*, 62(1–2): 1–13.

Augustin-Jean, L. and F. Padovani (2007) *Hong Kong: Economie, Société, Culture*, Paris: L'Harmattan.

Cheng, W. and W.H. Yuen (2014) 'Post Umbrella Movement: To Say Goodbye to the Era of Political Apathy' 後雨傘運動：告別政治冷感的年代, *Ming Pao*, 29 November.

Fong, B.C.H. (2014) 'The Partnership between the Chinese Government and Hong Kong's Capitalist Class: Implications for HKSAR Governance, 1997–2012', *The China Quarterly*, 217: 195–220.

Goodstadt, L.F. (2000) 'China and the Selection of Hong Kong's Post-Colonial Political Elite', *The China Quarterly*, 163: 721–741.

Hilgers, L. (2015) 'Hong Kong's Umbrella Revolution Is Not Over Yet', *New York Times*, 18 February, www.nytimes.com/2015/02/22/magazine/hong-kongs-umbrella-revolution-isnt-over-yet.html?_r=0, accessed 25 May 2015.

Hong Kong Transition Project (2010) 'Protest and Post-80s Youth. Sources of Social Instability in Hong Kong', the Baptist University, February, http://hktp.org/list/protest_and_post_80s_youths.pdf, accessed 12 July 2017.

Kayman, J. (2014) 'Hong Kong Umbrella Revolution – The Guardian Briefing', *Guardian*, 30 September, www.theguardian.com/world/2014/sep/30/-sp-hong-kong-umbrella-revolution-pro-democracy-protests, accessed 24 May 2015.

Ortmann, S. (2015) 'The Umbrella Movement and Hong Kong's Protracted Democratization Process', *Asian Affairs*, 46(1): 32–50.

Ortmann, S. (2016) 'The Lack of Sovereignty, Umbrella Movement and Democratisation in Hong Kong's', *Asia Pacific Law Review*, 24(2): 108–122.

Pepper, S. (2008) *Keeping Democracy at Bay. Hong Kong and the Challenge of Chinese Political Reforms*, Lanham: Rowan & Littlefield.

Polanyi, K. (1944/1957) *The Great Transformation: The Political and Economic Origins of Our Time*, Boston: Beacon Press.

Quark, A.A. (2013) *Global Rivalries. Standards Wars and the Transnational Cotton Trade*, Chicago and London: Chicago University Press.

Silver, B. (2003) *Forces of Labour: Workers' Movement and Globalization since 1870*, Cambridge: Cambridge University Press.

South China Morning Post (2014) 'Occupy Central – Night Seven: Full Coverage of the Night's Events', 4 October, www.scmp.com/news/hong-kong/article/1609580/live-chinese-university-urges-students-leave-thousands-gather, accessed 25 May 2015.

'The Basic Law of the Hong Kong Special Administrative Region of People's Republic of China', www.basiclaw.gov.hk/en/basiclawtext/index.html, accessed 17 August 2015.

Veg, S. (2015) 'Hong Kong's Umbrella Movement: Legalistic and Utopian', *New Left Review*, 92: 55–73.

Wu, X.G. (2010) 'Hong Kong's Post-80s Generation: Profiles and Predicaments', The Hong Kong University of Science and Technology/The Central Policy Unit, The Government of the Hong Kong Administrative Region, www.cpu.gov.hk/doc/tc/research_reports/HK%27s%20Post%2080s%20Generation%20-%20Profiles%20and%20Predicaments.pdf, accessed 13 July 2017.

Yau, C. (2015) 'Official Use of English Being "Neglected" by Hong Kong Government', *South China Morning Post*, 8 June.

1 The institutional context

The main principles of 'One Country, Two Systems' and the National People's Congress Standing Committee decision[1]

Hong Kong officially became a British colony under the 1842 Nanking Treaty that ended the first Opium War. According to the Treaty, Hong Kong Island was ceded in perpetuity to the British. In 1860, the Kowloon Peninsula across Victoria Harbour was added (also 'in perpetuity') to the original possession by the first Convention of Peking and on 1 July 1898, the colony was greatly enlarged by the adjunction of the New Territories through the signing of the Second Convention of Peking. In contrast to the Hong Kong Island and Kowloon Peninsula, the New Territories (which covers an area 12 times larger than the first two territories combined) were not ceded in perpetuity, but leased for 99 years. By the end of the 1970s, as the expiry date of the lease (30 June 1997) drew closer, the British pondered the future of the colony and opened discussions with their Chinese counterparts on this issue. The result was the 1984 signing of the Sino-British Joint Declaration (formally known as the Joint Declaration of the Government of the United Kingdom of Great Britain and Northern Ireland and the Government of the People's Republic of China on the Question of Hong Kong), by which the two countries agreed that all the three parts of Hong Kong would return to Chinese sovereignty at the end of the lease.

The Joint Declaration framed the conditions by which Hong Kong would be administered after 30 June 1997. These conditions, which were later translated in legal terms into the Basic Law (Hong Kong's 'mini constitution'), promulgated in 1990, were supposed to follow the 'One Country, Two Systems' principle (to be discussed later in this chapter). Even though 'One Country, Two Systems' had been continuously discussed since 1984, a short recall may be useful because of its impact on Hong Kong's governance – whether political or economic (Section titled 'A short recall of the main principles of the Basic Law and their interpretation'). This would serve as an introductory framework to the section titled 'The effective power of the Chief Executive between theory and practice: a literature review and interpretation of the crisis of legitimacy of the government', in which the authors insist that a combination of the situation inherited from the colonial era and the design of the Basic Law did not allow the CE to gain sufficient legitimacy to exert all the powers he is granted by the Basic Law.

On the contrary, the authors will only show that the CE has, in fact, *lost* some of the legitimacy the governor had enjoyed in most of the colonial era. This will be done through the classic differentiation between the procedural legitimacy (based on democratic elections) and the legitimacy-by-performances. While the first type has remained basically unchanged from the last decade of British rule over Hong Kong (despite minor evolutions), on the contrary and for reasons that will be presented in the section titled 'The effective power of the Chief Executive between theory and practice: a literature review and interpretation of the crisis of legitimacy of the government', the two main elements of the procedural legitimacy (namely, economic performance and governance) since the handover have encountered drastic evolutions which further eroded the ability of the CE to fully utilize its constitutional powers. The design of the Basic Law has reinforced the traditional imbalance in favour of the economic élites – this very last point being the focus of ensuing chapters – while, at the same time, these élites are less supportive of the current government than of its predecessor. In such a situation, the constitutional package proposed by Beijing in August 2014, if effectively implemented, would be far from sufficient to provide the CE with the additional legitimacy he needs. In other words, the Hong Kong government has been unable (and unwilling) to implement substantial reforms due to the opposition of the business élites, its own ideological positions and pressure from China. This has led to a certain paralysis of the political system just as the demand for change has strengthened. As the next few chapters will show, the same phenomenon occurs in the economic sphere, which creates a contradiction between a system that does not evolve and the pressure from people who feel trapped and have become increasingly restless.

A short recall of the main principles of the Basic Law and their interpretation

The objectives of 'One Country, Two Systems' were to grant Hong Kong a 'high degree of autonomy' (except in foreign and defence matters),[2] to respect its economic and social systems,[3] to safeguard its legal system (including the independence of its judiciary),[4] to assure the fundamental rights and freedoms of its residents,[5] etc. It also stated that China's socialist system would not be implemented in Hong Kong for 50 years starting from 1 July 1997, while the Hong Kong government could keep control of its economic (including its currency, the Hong Kong Dollar (HK$), and its own public accounting and tax systems) and immigration policies.[6] Hong Kong would remain separated from China by a border and distinct customs. Finally, by virtue of the principle, 'Hong Kong people govern Hong Kong', it was also decided that the leader of the Territory, the CE, must be a Hong Kong permanent resident (s)elected locally (albeit through a complex and restrictive election system). These are, in fact, the main items regulating the 'Two Systems' component.

Other principles were captured in the 'One Country' element, such as a 'high degree of autonomy' not being equated to independence. This is clearly stated in the Basic Law's very first article (Article 1): 'The Hong Kong Special

Administrative Region is an inalienable part of the People's Republic of China.' China, therefore, keeps a certain level of control over Hong Kong. For example, the final decision to appoint the CE belongs to the Chinese government.[7] Equally important, in case of any ambiguity in the Basic Law, the NPCSC (the Standing Committee of the National People's Congress – China's Parliament) has the final say in its reinterpretation. The NPCSC can also propose modifications to the Law – but these modifications would have to be voted on by at least two-thirds of the members of Hong Kong's legislature (the Legislative Council or LegCo) and then ratified by the NPC before being incorporated into the Basic Law.[8] As one will see, all these conditions have played a fundamental role in the recent institutional crisis.

Thus, the 'One Country, Two Systems' principle has a unique institutional design that has never been tested elsewhere. Notwithstanding the risk of failure, it is patent that 'One Country, Two Systems' leaves room for interpretation and ambiguity, so controversies have occurred since the handover.[9] The Basic Law cannot always answer all situations and, most notably, fails to fully clarify the intricate relationship between Hong Kong and the Central government: the former often enjoys a high degree of autonomy (in accordance with the Basic Law) and sometimes this causes tension between the two.[10]

The effective power of the Chief Executive between theory and practice: a literature review and interpretation of the crisis of legitimacy of the government

In this section, the authors will expose how the Hong Kong government's crisis of legitimacy, which already existed during the colonial period, has deepened since the handover. It will be argued that while the crisis has been, and still is, a powerful engine for introducing some kind of democratic reforms for the (s)election of the CE, it is also a major cause of the current institutional stalemate. In fact, the failure to enact political reforms, due to resistance from local economic élites and China (such failure was epitomized by the results of Beijing's 31 August 2014 decision), has exacerbated the existing political, economic and social crisis.

One major reason for this is that the CE is unable to fully exert the large powers that have been bestowed on him by the Basic Law. Three rationales can be put forward to support this statement (which will be fully presented in this section). First, the governing coalition has weakened since the handover, while the economic élites have become less supportive of the government. Second, Hong Kong's political system is increasingly disarticulated – and this is well explained in a thesis introduced by Ian Scott (1989, 2000, 2007, 2010). Third, Hong Kong society has diversified. As a result, (conflicting) demands by Hong Kong's political parties and social movements have proliferated in recent years and their demands have become more difficult to satisfy. While Beijing has constantly mentioned 'restoring' or 'maintaining social harmony' in Hong Kong (as well as in China), the increasingly polarized society and disarticulated political system in Hong Kong have left the CE more isolated than ever, with the Central government as his main backer. The government's inability to engage in suitable reforms has led to some degree of paralysis in its governance system, which has combined with the recent paralysis of the economic system (which will be examined in the next chapters).

Making use of the concept of legitimacy, the same thesis can be presented from a different perspective. It can then be noted that the government has to face the quasi absence of two forms of legitimacy: procedural legitimacy and legitimacy-by-performances (see below for their respective definitions). A weak procedural legitimacy is hardly a new phenomenon in Hong Kong. It existed during the colonial era, but the colonial authorities were able to accommodate it with legitimacy-by-performance to a certain extent. What is interesting, however, is that the change of sovereignty did not bring about an added procedural legitimacy to the current government. In fact, the reverse has happened.

In addition, the Hong Kong government has had to face a shrinking legitimacy-by-performance. This phenomenon is not only linked to the economic crises that have appeared since 1997, but also to the government's inability to address existing economic and social imbalances, which have led to declining opportunities for Hong Kong's young people. As the authors will show in the next chapters, the government's failure to implement necessary economic reforms has been one of the reasons why these young people have transferred their demands from the economic arena into the political arena, which further fuels the legitimacy crisis. Through a literature review, this section will concentrate on these different issues, particularly on the evolution of the political system and its crisis since the handover.

Procedural legitimacy and legitimacy-by-performance: an assessment

Once again, the starting point for analysis is the Basic Law. The fact that China and Hong Kong's economic élites want to keep the political and economic systems as close as they were to their colonial predecessors is strongly encapsulated in the Basic Law. This may seem counterintuitive or even paradoxical, but the

> belief enshrined in the Basic Law is that there is much value in the colonial legacy, which includes clinging the social goal or stability and prosperity, administrative efficiency, political neutrality of civil servants, the rule of law, and gradual political reforms.
>
> (Lam 2012: 3)

Whether or not the drafters of the Basic Law truly aimed to promote 'gradual political reforms' is arguable, but it is true that the

> general framework of governance [is] (…) highly similar to the colonial government's: continuing elitist rule, executive-led government, laissez-faire economic policy, a capitalist way of life, the protection of individual freedoms, and limited democracy.
>
> (Ibid.)

In policymaking, however, the same recipe does not necessarily create the same dish, as history matters, too. On the one hand, Hong Kong's 'laissez-faire economic policy' has been more a motto (before and after the handover) than a reality – a topic that will be analysed at length in the next chapters. On the other hand, Hong Kong's political and economic situation has progressively evolved and required some adaptations that never came. In order to understand the reasons behind these phenomena and their consequences, the authors will examine Hong Kong's historical evolution from the colonial era to the present. Their emphasis will be on structural and systemic factors, even though they do not deny that successive (world) economic crises and some ill-fated decisions by the CE and the government have also influenced public opinion.[11]

In the meantime, it is worth starting with a definition of 'legitimacy' and linking it to the concept of governance. This has been done quite clearly by Ian Scott:

> Legitimacy relates to the moral authority which a government possesses, the right to govern and that right, in turn, rests on consent of those affected by its decisions (…). When a government takes action by seeking to introduce new policies, it relies on the conviction of its citizens that it is entitled to take such action, that it has been given the authority to do so, either implicitly or explicitly. In the absence of such authority, government action can only be based on relationships of power; under such circumstances, its legitimacy will be contested. (…) Consent may be derived from a number of sources: from the election of the government through a fair and open process; through the efficient governance of the government whether or not it is elected; through religious sanction; of through the personal charisma of the leader. *In the Hong Kong case, the government can only rely on its performance* (…).
>
> (Scott 2007: 31; emphasis added)

With reference to Huntington (1991), Lo Shiu-Hing also spotted two different types of legitimacy, which coincide with Scott's first two categories: 'procedural legitimacy', which is schematically based on democratic elections, and another form, which is related to government performance (Lo 2001: 28–29). Both definitions call upon the notion of 'governance', which is a weak concept that can be defined in many different ways. Following Scott, governance is simply defined in this book as the capacity of a government to implement policies (Scott 2007: 31).

With these definitions in mind, it becomes clear that the Hong Kong government has been always lacking procedural legitimacy, since the colonial governor and now the CE have never been chosen 'through a [truly] fair and open process'. Nevertheless, the important point is elsewhere: while it is clear that colonial rule was imposed on Hongkongers together with an 'executive-led government',[12] the fact that the post-1997 *political system* (not only the CE and its government) suffers from the same weaknesses requires further elaboration before the authors turn to 'legitimacy-by-performance'.

As an important objective of the Basic Law is to guarantee Hongkongers that their way of life and individual freedoms would remain intact until at least 2047, it seems, at a first glance, that the new institutional framework should bring about more procedural legitimacy than the colonial one. After all, freedoms are now constitutionally sanctified, which is a substantial post-1997 improvement. However, this has not been the case and a major reason for this is that Hongkongers were not involved in the elaboration, discussion, and implementation of the 'One Country, Two Systems' principles and its 'by-product', the Basic Law, at any stage. More specifically, the Basic Law was unilaterally granted by China to Hong Kong, which had no influence over its contents or the sovereignty issue. That was perfectly captured by Ian Scott:

> The Basic Law was never approved by the Hong Kong people. It was imposed after a drafting process, dominated by the Chinese government, which led to the entrenchment of many of the former authoritarian colonial provisions. It did, however, include two possibilities for progress towards more democratic elections. The first was that specific provisions for the election of the Chief Executive in 2007 and the Legislative Council in 2008 were to be reviewed, raising the prospect of introducing universal suffrage or, at least, a faster pace of democratic reform.
>
> (Scott 2010: 16)

The fact that most Hongkongers (besides a few prominent businessmen and professionals, as will be seen below) were not consulted during the drafting of the Basic Law created, from the beginning, the same *systemic* deficit of procedural legitimacy that the colonial government had to face. This could be seen from the way the CE is selected, despite the fact that they must be a Hong Kong citizen, in sharp contrast from the governors during the colonial era.

Thus, whether or not the government and, above it, the CE, have a higher degree of procedural legitimacy since the handover is merely a matter of opinion, since the differences between the pre- and post-handover situations are not blatant in this respect. However, to fully grasp the issue of legitimacy, it is necessary to analyse the crucial aspects of governance (Scott 2007, 2010) and legitimacy-by-performance (Lo 2001) and their evolution. As these themes have been analysed in depth by these scholars and others, the presentation below will only include their main arguments. A chronological perspective will be followed starting from the colonial period and proceeding to the current changes.

The legitimacy-by-performance during the colonial era – adaptability and evolution

The legitimacy gap during the colonial era was not only due to the absence of elections, but also to the existence of a communication gap between the rulers and the ruled (Lo 2001; Pepper 2008). The challenge for the government then was to fill this gap and various strategies were adopted and modified according to the circumstances.

From the beginning, the major strategy in Hong Kong, as in Britain's other colonies, was to seek the consent of the ruled through the 'co-optation of economic and traditional élites into the system, by putting in place policies which entrench the position of these élites and by ensuring that there is an ideological consensus on the direction which government will take' (Scott 1989: 323). In addition, as Hong Kong was acquired not for settlement, but for 'diplomatic, military, and commercial purposes', according to Lord Stanley, the Colonial Secretary in 1842, the reliance on economic élites and setting up of an executive-led government were perfectly justified from the British point of view.[13] The co-optation base was progressively enlarged after each crisis of legitimacy (in addition to the introduction of ad hoc policies that will be detailed below), but, despite this policy, the basis of colonial governance always remained narrow (Lui and Chiu 2012: 101; Ma 2012).[14] During the 1970s, Ambrose King theorized this co-optation strategy under the concept of 'administrative absorption of politics'.[15] However, a major drawback of the administrative absorption of politics is to create another gap between the élites (who are, to some extent, incorporated into the government apparatus) and the general population – a drawback which has taken centre stage after the handover (see below).

The administrative absorption of politics was supplemented by other courses of action. In practice, the government was also able to reduce its legitimacy deficit 'by using public policy outputs to their maximum advantage', in the elegant words of Ian Scott (2007: 32). During the first phase of British rule over Hong Kong, this strategy mainly included maintaining law and order and respecting Chinese customs. After World War II, however, this proved to be insufficient and more proactive policies were included. Most significantly, for example, in the aftermath of the 1966–1967 riots,[16] the government aimed to restore its legitimacy-by-performance by enhancing or implementing many social policies such as public housing, education, health and other forms of social welfare. This was particularly the case after 1971, when Sir Murray MacLehose took over as governor and Sir John Cowperthwaite, the then-financial secretary and architect of 'positive non-intervention', stepped down. His departure, however, should not be understood as the end of Hong Kong's liberal economic policies, as social services were implemented with a view to keeping costs at a reasonable level and to efficiency – which meant that taxes remained ostensibly low. These policies were presented to (and generally accepted by) the Hong Kong population as proof of good governance.[17]

Over time, these social services were taken for granted by Hongkongers who initially supported them, announcing another cycle of crises and reforms. The capital of legitimacy, which was garnered by the MacLehose reforms, was progressively loosened and had to be rebuilt again – on the contrary, people thought the existing social welfare safety net was insufficient and should be enhanced. At the same time, after the signing of the Joint Declaration (1984) and Tiananmen Square protests (1989), the demands from citizens took on a more political tone. With the handover in sight, the government finally agreed to introduce long-delayed (and limited) reforms. Differently stated, with the handover in sight and given the political turmoil in China, the introduction of new social welfare was perceived as insufficient to restore the colonial government's legitimacy and, despite the opposition of China, political reforms were seen necessary. The first-ever LegCo election was held in 1985 and in 1991, some lawmakers were finally elected by universal suffrage. For the 1995 election, the last governor, Chris Patten, carried out far-reaching reforms (Lo 2001: 28; Scott 2010: 10), but they were cancelled immediately after the handover.[18]

All in all, while lacking procedural legitimacy for most of its history, the colonial government were able to rely on 'legitimacy-by-performance'. It could boast of good governance, supplemented by sound economic performance, which included strong economic growth, full employment despite waves of inbound migration, and the provision of limited, but expanding, social services. The system was supported by an efficient bureaucracy that was portrayed as politically neutral in the sense that it could freely provide advice or even criticisms on policies. This result, however, was not produced at no cost, as the government had to face periodic crises of legitimacy, which, at times, devolved into open dissent and sometimes riots.

Most interestingly, however, this historical background shows that contrary to the postulates of the drafters of the Basic Law, this legitimacy-by-performance was not secured through an irremovable system, but through constant adaptation and evolution – from law and order to the introduction of social policies and, finally, a certain degree of democratization. As the situation after the handover dramatically evolved, further flexibility in the system was also expected to restore (or maintain) the legitimacy-by-performance, but that has yet to happen. The reasons for it are examined below.

Towards a crisis of the two-form legitimacy after the handover

The withdrawal of many of Patten's democratic reforms (including the far-reaching LegCo reforms) deprived the government of its newfound (but incomplete) procedural legitimacy, which could not be compensated for by the mode of election of the CE. In terms of governance, the current government has had to face uncooperative (economic) élites at the top, an uprising by disaffected elements of civil society from the bottom, and the fragmentation of Hong Kong's political system. All in all, the design of the Basic Law, while bestowing the CE with large powers (following the tradition of an executive-led government), does not give him sufficient leverage to exert them. These points will be briefly addressed below.

First, the Basic Law did not add significant procedural legitimacy to the CE and the post-handover government. The opaque way in which the Basic Law was drafted, with little involvement from ordinary Hongkongers, is a big reason for this, with another being its content, particularly that which covers the mode of the CE's selection. As stated in Annex 1 of the Law, 'the Chief Executive shall be elected by a broadly representative Election Committee in accordance with this Law and appointed by the Central People's Government'. However, the 'broadly representative' Election Committee only comprises 1,200 members who represent various professional and interest groups in Hong Kong.[19] Thus, in practice, an aspiring CE does not need to run a time-consuming and expensive campaign, but only has to lobby for and gain the support of the majority of the 1,200 members of the Committee.[20]

On the other hand, the CE lacks a political base to govern from because he cannot belong to any political party.[21] While governmental policies are usually supported by pro-China, pro-government parties, none of these parties makes up a governmental platform.[22] Differently stated, these parties are accountable only to their members and voters and are not the government's rubber stamp. To give a significant example, James Tien Pei-chun, the then-Chairman of the Liberal Party, resigned from the Executive Council (ExCo) in 2003 after half a million people protested a proposed security law.[23]

The CE, then, suffers to some extent from the same weaknesses as the colonial governors before him: the lack of networks between, on the one hand, himself and his team and, on the other, the 'grassroots'. In order to cope with this lack of legitimacy, the CEs adopted the same policy of co-optation as the colonial governors, in which some 'élites' were incorporated into the organs of the government and its advisory committees (Cheung and Wong 2004).[24] Cheung and Wong, who analysed the composition of these committees, noted that the

> SAR government (…) has largely extended the previous colonial pattern of advisory appointments. (…) The pattern has become even more skewed in favour of the 'business' sectors, whose members constituted 34.7 per cent of the total number of appointments made in 2000 in major advisory committees.
>
> (Ibid.: 882)

On the contrary, 'what is dismaying is that despite the end of the colonial rule, the labour sector continued to fare poorly in the government's pool of policy advisers' (ibid.: 883).[25]

It is interesting to note that this same system of co-optation was also extensively adopted by China in its Hong Kong policy. Since the beginning of the 1980s, when the return of Hong Kong to China was agreed upon, China looked to expand its reach beyond traditional leftist circles in Hong Kong. This was deemed necessary because these circles were marginalized or, at least, 'shunned out of public power and mainstream society' (Ma 2007: 35).[26] An alliance between Hong Kong's capitalists and the communist government in Beijing may first seem unnatural, but there were at least three strong reasons for it. The first is linked to the economic reforms in the Mainland, which made investments from Hong Kong particularly sought after by the central and local governments in China.[27] The second one was their mutual desire to preserve the executive-led government, which has always been dominated by the economic élites and frowned upon an implementation of democracy (Goodstadt 2000: 733; Ma 2012: 71). The economic élites have been opposed to democratization from an early stage, as they understood – quite correctly indeed – that more democracy would lead to more demand for social services from Hongkongers, leading to tax increases. But these first two reasons could only lead to this unlikely alliance if one last condition was fulfilled: a guarantee from Beijing that the economic system would not be changed after 1997.[28] The fact that British firms in Hong Kong have been progressively replaced by local Chinese conglomerates since the 1960s has fostered this system of co-optation, which favours (liberal) economic policies – a bias that was endorsed in the Basic Law (see Article 5), as will be seen below.

Before the authors move on to the causes of the loss of legitimacy-by-performances, a further specification of the nature of this alliance between the Hong Kong and Chinese governments and the business sector (before and after 1997) is necessary. The dominance of the business community in the workings of the government and its advisory committees, while it fosters the implementation of policies that favour the business sector (see below), does not guarantee that the economic élites have given their unconditional support to the government: 'like the SAR government, the colonial government was torn between the contradictory tasks of offering privileges to business in exchange for political support, assuming an arbiter role among competing business interests, and acting as a watchdog against rent seeking to prevent widespread discontent' (Ng 2002: 112, cited by Lui and Chiu 2012: 100). Nonetheless, even though there was no general consensus within this group during the colonial era, the cohesion between big businesses and the Hong Kong government was strong enough to allow policymaking to proceed (ibid.: 119).[29]

This cohesion has progressively unravelled since the 1980s. The reason for this lies on the shift of economic power from British (business) interests to local Chinese ones or, more precisely, to the interests of a limited number of local family-controlled conglomerates (Lui and Chiu 2007, 2012; Williams 2005, 2009). Unlike British companies, which were usually organized into networks (largely under the leadership of the Jardine Group and the Hong Kong and Shanghai Bank), the local Chinese conglomerates became increasingly independent of each other (Lui and Chiu 2007: 15–25).[30] Consequently, these families developed very intricate relationships: on the one hand, they competed intensely for a limited number of economic sectors; on the other hand, they also managed to build alliances among themselves. In any case, they agreed to share power and limit new entrants (see the example of international supermarket chain Carrefour, detailed in Chapter 3).

These powerful local Chinese families did not need to give unconditional support to the Special Administrative Region (SAR) government, but only to remain in the position to influence its economic policies.[31] In addition, as noticed by Fong, their cooperation, or alliance with the Chinese government, by providing a direct access to the central leadership, already allows them to modify, or even ban, some existing or planed policies which were against their interests:

> With Beijing, rather than the Chief Executive, as the de facto power centre of the state-business alliance since the handover, local capitalists can take their concern directly to Beijing or the Liaison Office and thereby exert pressure on the HKSAR government if they see their interests affected by government policies. From this perspective, the partnership between Beijing and Hong Kong's capitalists has effectively changed the balance of power.
>
> (Fong 2014: 210)

Thus, compared to the governors, the CEs gradually became more isolated within Hong Kong, as they could no longer rely on the *systematic* support of local Chinese business groups, while they failed to earn sufficient political capital with the majority of Hongkongers – Tien's resignation during the 2003 crisis is a case in point. During more recent periods of social unrest, such as the Umbrella Movement, the divide between the rulers and the economic élite on the one hand and ordinary people on the other only widened due to the CE's weak and detached leadership.

Thus, the government has seen its ruling coalition weakened, while it has not been able to build a new one. This is a sign of a weak governance capacity and constitutes an important part of the disarticulated post-handover administration. Other elements of this disarticulation, as analysed by Ian Scott, are that 'the relationships between the executive, the legislature, and the bureaucracy today are uncoordinated, poorly-developed, fractious, and sometimes dysfunctional' (Scott 2000: 29; see also Scott 2007: 39). The causes of it are numerous and include a more assertive LegCo, which has considerable capacity *of obstruction*, especially in financial matters (despite its overall declining power, its major successes have included the withdrawal of the proposed security law and the failure of the government to introduce a GST; see Littlewood 2010: 249);[32] a CE who makes decisions without informing ExCo as well as civil servants;[33] a civil service that is seen as less efficient after the handover and has lost some of its prerogatives;[34] etc.

In other words, each single organ of Hong Kong's political apparatus aimed to expand its zone of influence as much as the Basic Law would allow, while the coordination among them has diminished. Regarding the civil service's nominal political neutrality, for example, it has come under pressure (Scott 2010: 7). In practice, this means that it has lost some of its capacity to initiate policies. Also, it has been affected by the implementation of the New Public Management (NPM) model. The NPM was initiated by Patten with the aim of sticking to a 'small government policy'. But only after the Asian Financial Crisis reached Hong Kong in 1997 were its effects really felt with the reinforcement of the private-public partnership in the provision of social services and cutbacks in some welfare programmes – services that had provided enhanced legitimacy to the government since the 1970s (Goodstadt 2013; Wong 2012).

All in all, it becomes clear that the government has lost part of its 'legitimacy-by-performance', as illustrated by the following factors: a lack of cohesion among the governing élite, the disarticulation of the political system, the implementation of the NPM, along with the lower performances of the civil service and social service reductions (this last point will be developed further in Chapter 4 with the analysis of housing policies). In addition, policymaking has become more difficult with the increased and diversified demands from the people. On one hand, Hong Kong's civil society, which has emerged since the 1980s, is diverse and often split, which makes it difficult for the government to address demands that often conflict. On the other hand, new political parties have developed since the 1990s and are now well represented in bodies such as the LegCo. Even though LegCo has lost some of its powers since the 1990s, the fact that half of its members are elected by universal suffrage gives it and the parties they represent some kind of legitimacy, which they can use to exert some pressure on the government.[35]

All these factors have merged to create an unknown crisis of legitimacy for the government. Critically, its governance capacity has dropped at a time when some recent worldwide economic difficulties called for a strong governmental response. To be fair, the Hong Kong government had little or no responsibility for the spread of these (global) crises, which started with the 1997 financial crisis, continued through SARS in 2003, and culminated in the global recession of 2007–2009. But the rise in Hong Kong's unemployment rate from 6.4 per cent in 1998 to 8.4 per cent in 2003 (C&SD 2016, Table 6) impressed upon ordinary Hongkongers that the pre-1997 period was Hong Kong's golden age, while the post-handover administration has not been able to deliver good economic performance. Even strong economic growth in recent years – GDP per head increased by over 57 per cent from 2001 to 2015 in chained (2013) HK$ – did not restore public confidence, as Hongkongers have become increasingly aware that this growth has largely benefited the few at the top, some of whom have manipulated Hong Kong's economic policies for their own gain (this will be elaborated on in greater detail in the next chapters).

In this difficult context, it should come as no surprise that the tenures of the three CEs have all been tainted by scandals or social unrest. The Tung administration ended two years after a mass protest in response to the proposed security law, while the Leung administration ends some three years after the Umbrella Movement. In between, Donald Tsang's tenure was marred by controversy and corruption scandals. If Patten ended his governorship with an approval rate close to 60 per cent, neither Tung (48.4 per cent) nor Tsang (who started with an approval rate of 72.3 per cent but left office with a meagre 44.9 per cent) reached 50 per cent at the time of their departures, while Leung's was at 41.3 per cent in January 2017 (after a low of 35 per cent at the beginning of December 2016).[36] These data should not be taken as proxies for 'legitimacy ratings', but they indicate that Patten, despite his lack of procedural legitimacy, was approved by over half of all Hongkongers in 1997 – in sharp contrast to his three successors.[37]

As a conclusion: legitimacy, universal suffrage and the 31 August Decision

To summarize, despite the large powers granted to him in the Basic Law, the CE does not have sufficient leverage with the people to fully exert them and, therefore, lacks legitimacy in their eyes. In this sense, the election of the CE by universal suffrage, as stated in the Basic Law (Article 45),[38] is often presented as a means to reinforce this weak legitimacy. However, it remains doubtful if that would have been sufficient to fulfil this objective because the conditions that are stipulated in the same Article 45 are quite restrictive and still grant a large power to the elective committee: 'the ultimate aim is the selection of the Chief Executive by universal suffrage upon nomination by a broadly representative nominating committee (…)'. The Basic Law also makes it clear that any change of this sort would have to be ratified by the NPC (Article 159; see above).

Thus, in practice, the structure of the Basic Law lets Beijing have the final say in implementing (or not) universal suffrage (and the form it will assume). It was in this specific institutional context that the NPCSC Decision of 31 August 2014 regarding the election of the CE by universal suffrage was issued. In accordance with the Law, the Decision specified that a

> broadly representative nominating committee shall be formed. (…) The nominating committee shall nominate two to three candidates for the office of Chief Executive in accordance with democratic procedures. Each candidate must have the endorsement of more than half of all the members of the nominating committee.[39]

Thus, under the proposal, Hong Kong citizens would be able to vote, but only after the nominating committee had selected two to three suitable candidates.

If this scheme had been implemented, it remains to be seen if it would really give more legitimacy to the CE. On the contrary, it is likely that it would not have dramatically changed the existing balance of power. An indirect confirmation of this statement was provided a few weeks later (and just a few days before the class boycotts started at several Hong Kong universities) when Beijing believed it necessary to explain its 31 August Decision. To do this, it invited a delegation of Hongkongers to Beijing to expound, in detail, the proposal and collect the views of its members. The group, led by the former CE, Tung Chee-Hwa (currently the Vice Chairman of the National Committee of the Chinese People's Political Consultative Conference), uniquely comprised top businessmen such as Li Ka-shing (the richest man in Hong Kong) and Henderson Land Development Chairman Lee Shau-kee (Ng and Cheung 2014; Ng and Ng 2014). It is remarkable that even though the Basic Law stated that the Decision had to be voted on by at least two-thirds of LegCo members before it could take effect, Beijing chose to invite a tycoon-heavy delegation led by the patriarchs of local family-led conglomerates to hear its pitch rather than a group of lawmakers who were in charge of voting up or down the proposal. Not only did the invitation indicate a lack of consideration by the Chinese leadership for Hong Kong lawmakers, it was another indication of political bias in favour of economic élites: as already noted, Beijing, like the Hong Kong government, relies on a tiny economic community that has been co-opted (as well as an older group of 'loyalists', some of whom have being active since the Cultural Revolution – see Cheung 2009; Ma 2007) and this select group weighs heavily on the selection of the nominating committee.

Thus, for opponents of the proposal, the method of election put forward in the Decision does not provide the CE with the true legitimacy he needs (contrary to its stated objective). Rather, they contend that it reinforces the power structure of the previous system and does not provide Hong Kong citizens with what they called a 'genuine choice'. Participants of Occupy Central and the Umbrella Movement consequently asked for the withdrawal of the Decision, even before it was read by LegCo, but this was emphatically denied by both the Hong Kong and Mainland authorities – even though the chances of securing a vote by LegCo were very slim. Indeed, the forces in support of the Decision fell four ballots short of reaching the two-thirds quorum. The vote of June 2015 confirmed these predictions – the Decision was rejected by LegCo in a memorable fashion.[40]

This presentation introduces the institutional background of Hong Kong after the handover. It frames a 'strategic action field' in the sense of a

> meso-level social order where actors (who can be individual or collective) interact with knowledge of one another under a set of common understandings about the purposes of the field, the relationships in the field (including who has power and why) and the field's rules.
>
> (Fligstein and McAdam 2011: 3; see, also, Fligstein and McAdam 2012)

More precisely, the institutional environment designs an

> interpretative frame that individual and collective strategic actors bring to make sense of what others are doing. Here, we consider the fact that the degree to which all actors actually share the same perception of what any other actors' actions mean is an open question. We expect that actors will tend to see the moves of others from their own perspective in the field.
>
> (Ibid.: 4)

In short, in this chapter, the institutional framework is considered given (it is the product of historical evolution) and bends, to some extent, the decisions of its actors. These decisions, in turn, are influenced by the individual position each actor occupies in the field and by her/his own cognitive perception of the system. External and internal shocks (be they economic and/or political) also affect the decisions made within and stability of the system.

In this very broad framework, the CE has only little room for manoeuvre, as his moves are constrained by the local economic élites and the Chinese leadership. This chapter has shown the existence of a certain sclerosis of the system, which can only evolve with great difficulties – or with a CE with considerable ability and determination to negotiate. This sclerosis can be explained by the fact that both the Hong Kong government, the Chinese government at its back, and the economic élites, do not want to change a system that has benefited them for so many decades.

More precisely, since the 1980s, the economic élites perfectly understood that the introduction of democracy would inevitably lead to a change of the economic system, by means of the development of social services – and the increase of tax. Progressively, this created a gap between the aspiration of the ordinary people, who demanded more democracy, and the economic élites who resisted to it.

Thus, the genuine demand of Hong Kong's people for more democracy cannot be separated from economic factors, since these factors constituted one of the reasons to block the democratization process in the 1980s. In such a situation, it can be hypothesized that the demands of the (relatively educated) youth for what they called 'genuine democracy' were *also* motivated by other, especially economic, factors: not only did they believe that their personal situations were deteriorating, but they also understood that the economic system was biased in favour of certain groups. As the Umbrella Movement participants well expressed, the fight for democracy was, and still is, also the fight for a fairer economic and social system. Then, by demanding the implementation of 'genuine democracy', they challenged a system that they thought no longer suited their interests (often similar to the interests of the 'middle class') anymore and saw the Decision of the NPCSC as a reinforcement of the existing system. At the same time, these economic factors further reinforced the role of the political factors: it is clear that this call for democracy occurred in a context in which many Hongkongers felt their individual and civil liberties may be jeopardized. Thus, all in all, the NPCSC's Decision can be seen as the straw that broke the camel's back.[41]

Finally, the implementation of 'genuine democracy' (in which candidates standing for CE are not unnecessarily screened) is understood (rightly or not) as a means to empower younger people in Hong Kong's political and economic affairs. In other words, the fight for greater democracy may also be a manifestation of deeper social and economic contradictions, which did not disappear after the LegCo vote. The next three chapters aim to elaborate on this statement by showing how the evolution of Hong Kong's economy, in the context of globalization, has led to a deteriorating economic situation for its youth and middle class.

Notes

1 This chapter will not recall all the events and institutional principles that accompanied the handover. For a detailed account of the vicissitudes related to the painful negotiations between China and Great Britain, see Augustin-Jean and Padovani, 2007 among many others.

2 Basic Law, Art. 2: 'The National People's Congress authorizes the Hong Kong Special Administrative Region to exercise a high degree of autonomy and enjoy executive, legislative and independent judicial power (…).' All references to the Basic Law come from www.basiclaw.gov.hk/en/basiclawtext/index.html.

3 Basic Law, Art. 5: 'The socialist system and policies shall not be practised in the Hong Kong Special Administrative Region, and the previous capitalist system and way of life shall remain unchanged for 50 years.'

4 For example, Basic Law, Art. 6 states:

> The laws previously in force in Hong Kong, that is, the common law, rules of equity, ordinances, subordinate legislation and customary law shall be maintained, except for any that contravene this Law, and subject to any amendment by the legislature of the Hong Kong Special Administrative Region.

See also Art. 18:

> The laws in force in the Hong Kong Special Administrative Region shall be this Law, the laws previously in force in Hong Kong as provided for in Article 8 of this Law, and the laws enacted by the legislature of the Region.
>
> National laws shall not be applied in the Hong Kong Special Administrative Region except for those listed in Annex III to this Law (…).

5 Basic Law, Art. 11:

> In accordance with Article 31 of the Constitution of the People's Republic of China, the systems and policies practised in the Hong Kong Special Administrative Region, including the social and economic systems, the system for safeguarding the fundamental rights and freedoms of its residents, the executive, legislative and judicial systems, and the relevant policies, shall be based on the provisions of this Law.

6 Basic Law, Art. 154: 'The Government of the Hong Kong Special Administrative Region may apply immigration controls on entry into, stay in and departure from the Region by persons from foreign states and regions.' This applies to citizens of Mainland China.

7 Basic Law, Art. 45: 'The Chief Executive of the Hong Kong Special Administrative Region shall be selected by election or through consultations held locally and be appointed by the Central People's Government.'

8 Less important in the context of this book, foreign policy and national defence are also undertaken by Beijing. Hong Kong, however, has a full membership in various international institutions such as the World Trade Organization (WTO), but not the International Monetary Fund.

9 The title and headlines of a recent article from the *SCMP* suffice to show the validity of this statement: 'Beijing and Hong Kong 'must look at [the] Basic Law from each other's perspective' justice minister says…Rimsky Yuen warns failure to do so could have 'negative effects' on cross-border cooperation' (Cheung, 13 September 2015). See also note 14.

10 Schematically, some people emphasize the importance of 'Two Systems' and the 'high degree of autonomy', while others prefer to insist on 'One Country' and the subordination of Hong Kong (as a regional government) to Chinese rule. These divergences obviously played a certain role in the institutional and social crisis that led to the Umbrella Movement.

11 That was especially the case for Tung Chee-hwa, the first CE, who was often criticized for his 'failure (…) to carry out effective governance [and which] really united critical voices from different corners of the Hong Kong society' (Lui and Chiu 2012: 91). Despite the relevance of some of these personal criticisms, this book advances the idea that the current problem of legitimacy outstrips the issue of a weak governance of specific individuals and stems more from the design of the system.

12 However, Suzanne Pepper wondered why, unlike for many of its other colonies, Britain never introduced more democratic elections; she attributed this to the 'British aim of preserving its power in East Asia' (Pepper 2008: 24). She also noted that, 'Hong Kong's original status as an integral part of the Chinese empire could never be discounted (…), leaving uncertain the exact nature of its standing as a full-fledged

British possession' (ibid.: 27). In the authors' opinion, these factors have some degree of truth and supersede the traditional explanation that Hongkongers were not interested in democratic reforms.

13 Cited by Pepper 2008: 38.

14 In 1977, a legal scholar, Davies, noted 'there are some one hundred to two hundred people who can be found with a dominant voice in all parts of the policy process' (Davies 1977, cited by Lui and Chiu 2012: 101). These very same people also dominated the business groups and, thus, the 'commanding heights of the Hong Kong economy are controlled by remarkable few interests' (ibid.). This point will be developed below.

15 King defined the administrative absorption of politics as 'a process through which the British governing elites co-opt or assimilate the non-British socio-economic elites into the political-administrative decision-making bodies, thus attaining an elite integration on the one hand and a legitimacy of political authority on the other' (King 1975: 437).

16 The 1966–1967 riots, which stemmed from the Cultural Revolution in China, caused the death of 51 people. Afterwards, the government appointed a commission to investigate the riots, which found that there was a 'gap' between the government and the public, resentment towards the police, and the need for labour reform and improvement in social services (Scott 2010: 10).

17 More details on taxation in Hong Kong will be presented below. On this point, see Wong (2012) and Littlewood (2010).

18 It is beyond the scope of this book to detail Hong Kong's political system and its evolution. There was a progressive, but slow, democratization of the colonial system from the 1980s onward. The 1995 LegCo elections were the most democratic ever in terms of the total number of legislators elected directly or indirectly. But that version of LegCo was replaced by a Provisional Legislative Council on 1 July 1997 before new (and less democratic) elections were held in 1998. Since 2004, half of all LegCo members have been elected by universal suffrage (the 'geographical constituencies'), while the other half have been elected through a complicated system of 'functional constituencies', which mostly represent sectors of the Hong Kong economy.

19 The Committee was increased from 400 members to 800 and then 1,200, but this expansion remains too limited to really bring about fundamental changes. A candidate can run if he has the support of at least 150 members.

20 During the last campaign, which saw the selection of C.Y. Leung in 2012, the candidates still felt it necessary to present their programme to the citizens, even though most citizens had no power whatsoever in the (s)election process. This effort to introduce more transparency may be seen as a strategy to increase communication, leading to a better governance system. On communication, legitimacy, and governance in Hong Kong, see Lo, 2001.

21 See Section 31 of the Chief Executive Election Ordinance, www.legislation.gov.hk/blis_pdf.nsf/6799165D2FEE3FA94825755E0033E532/0B621C1E1F7C5B7A482575EF001BF072/$FILE/CAP_569_e_b5.pdf.

22 The two main two supporting parties are the DAB (the Democratic Alliance for the Betterment and Progress of Hong Kong) and the Liberal Party. The DAB supports the government on a series of broad principles and ad hoc policies voted on by LegCo. The Liberal Party is mainly a pro-business party, but it usually backs the government (see below for more on the alliance between the government and Hong Kong's economic élites).

23 Article 23 of the Basic Law makes it clear that Hong Kong must enact such a law, but the proposed draft was surrounded by controversy and was seen as threatening the freedom of speech and other civil liberties in Hong Kong. Tien's resignation

effectively led to the withdrawal of the proposed legislation. On the 2003 mass protest, see also note 41 below.

ExCo, according to Article 54 of the Basic Law, is defined as 'an organ for assisting the Chief Executive in policy-making'.

24 Without analysing the Hong Kong political system, these advisory bodies are an important part of the governance system of Hong Kong. There were 375 of these committees by 2000, some of which were major importance. See Cheung and Wong (2004: 874).

25 Unsurprisingly, the three CEs selected since 1997 come from a small group of people who were business leaders and/or government bureaucratic élite. They not only had strong ties with the colonial government before 1997, but were also co-opted by China as its relay in the Territory. The first CE, Tung Chee-Hwa, came from a family of businessmen who specialized in shipping, an important economic sector in Hong Kong. He was member of the governor's ExCo before the handover, but maintained an extensive network with politicians in his native Shanghai – including the then-Chinese President, Jiang Zemin. The second one, Donald Tsang Yam-kuen, was a career civil servant who was Financial Secretary in 1995. Finally, Leung Chun-ying was an executive in a real estate firm and real estate advisor for Zhu Rongji (who was, at that time, Mayor of Shanghai before he became Prime Minister) during the 1990s. Leung was co-opted by China to be a Member (1985) and then Secretary-General (1987) of the Hong Kong Basic Law Consultative Committee, which was a body established in 1985 to canvass views in Hong Kong on the drafts of the Hong Kong Basic Law.

26 Citing the Memoirs of Xu Jiatun, Ma estimated that there were about 6,000 members of the Communist Party in Hong Kong in 1983, which 'was still considerable' (ibid.).

27 At its height in 1988, 76 per cent of all FDI into China originated from Hong Kong. See Zhang (2005) and Chapter 2 below.

28 Goodstadt (2000) analysed the way in which China has courted these economic élites. Generally, it appointed them to committees in charge of preparing for the handover, as well as to Chinese institutions such as the National People's Congress or Chinese People's Political Consultative Conference (with 136 members from Hong Kong appointed in 1992). It is no surprise that of the 23 Hong Kong members of the Basic Law Committee (out of 59), '16 had business or professional backgrounds and another five were public figures' (Goodstadt 2000: 729).

29 For an example of a disagreement between the business community and the colonial government, Goodstadt mentioned the 'frustrations' of the economic élites, which developed from the 'administration's constant refusal to provide the low-cost capital (…) available in Singapore and other industrializing economies in Asia' until the end of the 1970s (Goodstadt 2010: 281). This request seemed exaggerated since industrialists did not lack funds to invest. But it did not damage the overall good relationship between the economic élites and the government, especially regarding the 'postponing [of] crucial social investments for several decades at the expense of the community's well-being' (ibid.: 284).

30 Lui and Chiu studied the evolution of the (cross) directorships of Hong Kong's top 250 listed companies in 1983, 1998 and 2004. See Lui and Chiu (2007).

31 Another evidence to support the fact that economic policies are influenced by business interests comes from the crony capitalism index, compiled by *The Economist* in 2014. In this index, Hong Kong occupied the top position in a list of 23 countries/economies. Even though this index, which aims at estimating the wealth extracted by rent seeking (usually generated by favourable economic policies), contains loopholes and limitations, it is still indicative of the role played by Chinese tycoons in the elaboration of policies. For more details on the methodology and the full ranking, see *The Economist* (2014) 'Our Crony-capitalism Index: Planet Plutocrat', www.economist.com/news/international/21599041-countries-where-politically-connected-businessmen-are-most-likely-prosper-planet.

32 The fact that half of the LegCo members are now elected by universal suffrage gives it added legitimacy. Its major power remains in financial matters and it can theoretically (at least) trigger a constitutional crisis by refusing to vote on the budget. However, the Basic Law has greatly reduced its effectiveness. For example, the way lawmakers can propose legislation has become much more restrictive. According to Article 74 of the Basic Law, legislators 'are only allowed to introduce bills that do not relate to public expenditure or the political structure of the operation of the government' (Lui 2012: 51). In addition, the bills proposed by lawmakers are voted through a complicated system that makes it highly unlikely for legislation that would not be approved by the government to pass (ibid.).

33 There are several examples of this. The most notorious may be the abandonment of the grand plan to provide 85,000 new flats:

> Despite its commitment to the formal consultative process, the Tung administration was also prone to making announcements from the top which arrived on the agenda without prior consultation or notice. In the decision to provide 85,000 flats a year, which was later abandoned, in its educational policies [etc.], the government simply laid out its proposals and ultimately bore the wrath of a highly critical public.
>
> (Scott 2010: 193)

34 One criticism of the way the civil service has handled some issues concerned the computer problems that affected the operations of Chek Lap Kok Airport when it opened in 1998, which created economic losses for an already-reeling Hong Kong economy. In addition to the government, the civil service was blamed for its decision to open it too early. In 1997, the civil service was also criticized for poorly handling the bird flu crisis, during which 1.3 million chickens were slaughtered and left to rot in the New Territories. More details on the civil service will be provided below.

35 However, it should also be noted that 30 legislators from the functional constituencies are elected by a tiny minority of voters who generally represent business interests. Among them, 12 seats were even returned uncontested in the 2016 LegCo election. This factor reinforces further the bias of the policy making towards economic interests.

36 All data came from the University of Hong Kong's Public Opinion Programme and could be found at www.hkupop.hku.hk/english/archive/poppolls/chris/overall/index.html.

37 Of course, these data are only informative, nothing more. The approval rating of political leaders can vary greatly depending on short-term conditions, economic situation, etc. In the case of Patten, the specific political context of the handover, its uncertain aftermath, and Hong Kong's booming economy at the time probably boosted his ratings.

38

> The Chief Executive of the Hong Kong Special Administrative Region shall be selected by election or through consultations held locally and be appointed by the Central People's Government.
>
> The method for selecting the Chief Executive shall be specified in the light of the actual situation in the Hong Kong Special Administrative Region and in accordance with the principle of gradual and orderly progress. The ultimate aim is the selection of the Chief Executive by universal suffrage upon nomination by a broadly representative nominating committee in accordance with democratic procedures.

39 See *SCMP* 'Full text: NPC Standing Committee decision on Hong Kong 2017 election framework', 31 August 2014.

40 The Pan-Democratic group (a loose coalition of forces that usually supports 'genuine democracy' and opposes the Hong Kong government) usually wins most of the 'geographical constituencies', but fails to obtain a majority in the LegCo, as business and pro-establishment groups have cornered the lion's share of the functional constituencies. But this coalition was still large enough to reject the NPCSC Decision. The authors will not present the epic story of that vote, but recall the final result: the proposal was defeated 28 to 8.

41 The Umbrella Movement was not the first mass protest in the history of post-handover Hong Kong. As we have seen, the most notable one occurred in 2003 to successfully oppose the implementation of an anti-subversion law in Hong Kong. Protesters, numbering some 500,000, marched on 1 July to criticize the proposal, which was seen as jeopardizing civil rights and eroding the freedom of speech (the purpose of the protest was not to object to the implementation of an anti-subversion law, which had already been imposed under the Basic Law's Article 23, but mostly to oppose the content of this specific proposal). Like the Umbrella Movement, the protest had some economic roots due to the economic crisis in Hong Kong following the SARS epidemic. The law was subsequently shelved and led to the resignation of the first CE, Tung Chee-Hwa, in 2005. It also created to a new tradition of mass protest every year on 1 July (Chan and Lee 2009; Ku 2009).

Another example was the 2013 dock strike, which started as a labour movement before assuming a more political stance. The striking dock workers were working for contractors who provided staff for Hongkong International Terminals, Ltd., which formed part of Li Ka-shing's business empire. They complained that their salaries had remained almost the same as in 1997 and demanded a pay rise of over 20 per cent. After a 40-day strike, they finally agreed on a 9.8 per cent salary increase and better working conditions. See below for more details related to salary developments in Hong Kong since 1997.

These examples are, of course, of a different nature, but they illustrate that mass protests have always been part of Hong Kong's social and political life since its early days. It should be noted that the separation between labour/economic strikes and political demands is somewhat artificial because some conflicts, which started as protests against austere economic or labour conditions, have sometimes evolved into full-fledged political protests. The best examples are the 1966 and 1967 riots (Cheung 2009).

Bibliography

Augustin-Jean, L. and F. Padovani (2007) *Hong Kong: Economie, Société, Culture*, Paris: L'Harmattan.

Census and Statistics Department, the HKSAR (2016) 'Statistics on Labour Force, Unemployment and Underemployment; Table 6', 18 October 2016, www.censtatd.gov.hk/hkstat/sub/sp200.jsp?tableID=006&ID=0&productType=8, accessed 6 April 2017.

Chan, J.M. and F.L.F. Lee (2009) 'Who Can Mobilize Hong Kong People to Protest? A Survey-Based Study of Three Large Rallies', in M. Sing (ed.) *Politics and Government in Hong Kong: Crisis under Chinese Sovereignty*, Abingdon: Routledge, pp. 14–37.

Cheung, A.B.L. and P.C.W. Wong (2004) 'Who Advised the Hong Kong Government? The Politics of Absorption before and after 1997', *Asian Survey*, 44(6): 874–894.

Cheung, G.K.W. (2009) *Hong Kong's Watershed: The 1967 Riots*, Hong Kong: Hong Kong University Press.

Cheung, T. (2015) 'Beijing and Hong Kong "Must Look at Basic Law from Each Other's Perspective" Justice Minister Says', *South China Morning Post*, 13 September.

Davies, S.N.G. (1997) 'One Brand of Politics Rekindled', *Hong Kong Law Journal*, 7: 44–80.

Fligstein, N. and D. McAdam (2011) 'Towards a General Theory of Strategic Action Fields', *Sociological Theory*, 29(1): 1–26.

Fligstein, N. and D. McAdam (2012) *A Theory of Fields*, New York: Oxford University Press.

Fong, B.C.H. (2014) 'The Partnership between the Chinese Government and Hong Kong's Capitalist Class: Implications for HKSAR Governance, 1997–2012', *The China Quarterly*, 217: 195–220.

Goodstadt, L.F. (2000) 'China and the Selection of Hong Kong's Post-Colonial Political Elite', *The China Quarterly*, 163: 721–741.

Goodstadt, L.F. (2010) 'Fiscal Freedom and the Making of Hong Kong's Capitalist Society', *China Information*, 24(3): 273–294.

Goodstadt, L.F. (2013) *Poverty in the Midst of Affluence. How Hong Kong Mismanaged its Prosperity*, Hong Kong: Hong Kong University Press.

Huntington, S.P. (1991) *The Third Wave: Democratization in the Late Twentieth Century*, Norman: University of Oklahoma Press.

King, A.Y.C. (1975) 'Absorption of Politics in Hong Kong: Emphasis on the Grass Roots Level', *Asian Survey*, 15(5): 422–439.

Ku, A.S.M. (2009) 'Civil Society's Dual Impetus – Mobilizations, Representations and Contestations over the July 1 March in 2003', in M. Sing (ed.) *Politics and Government in Hong Kong: Crisis under Chinese Sovereignty*, Abingdon: Routledge, pp. 38–57.

Lam, W.M. (2012) 'Political Context', in W.M. Lam, P.L.T. Lui and W. Wong (eds) *Contemporary Hong Kong Government and Politics*, expanded 2nd edition, Hong Kong: Hong Kong University Press, pp. 1–21.

Littlewood, M. (2010) *Taxation without Representation. The History of Hong Kong's Troublingly Successful Tax System*, Hong Kong: Hong Kong University Press.

Lo, S.H. (2001) *Governing Hong Kong: Legitimacy, Communication and Political Decay*, New York: Nova Science Publishers.

Lui, L.T.P. (2012) 'The Legislature', in W.M. Lam, P.L.T. Lui and W. Wong (eds) *Contemporary Hong Kong Government and Politics*, expanded 2nd edition, Hong Kong: Hong Kong University Press, pp. 45–66.

Lui, T.L. and K.W.S. Chiu (2007) 'Governance Crisis in Post-1997 Hong Kong: A Political Economy Perspective', *China Review*, 7(2): 1–34.

Lui, T.L. and K.W.S. Chiu (2012) 'Governance Crisis and Changing State-Business Relations. A Political Economy Perspective', in Chiu K.W.S. (ed.) *Repositioning the Hong Kong Government*, Hong Kong: Hong Kong University Press, pp. 91–122.

Ma, N. (2007) *Political Development in Hong Kong: State, Political Society, and Civil Society*, Hong Kong: Hong Kong University Press.

Ma, N. (2012) 'Eclectic Corporatism and State Interventions in Post-Colonial Hong Kong', in K.W.S. Chiu (ed.) *Repositioning the Hong Kong Government*, Hong Kong: Hong Kong University Press, pp. 63–90.

Ng, T.W. (2002) 'Money, Power and the Problem of Legitimacy in the Hong Kong Special Administrative Region', in F. Mengin and J.L. Rocca (eds), *Politics in China: Moving Frontiers*, New York: Palgrave.

Ng, J. and G. Cheung (2014) 'What Can You Do for Hong Kong? Tycoons to Sketch Future for Xi Jinping', *South China Morning Post*, 19 September, www.scmp.com/news/hong-kong/article/1595614/what-can-you-do-hong-kong-tycoons-sketch-future-xi-jinping, accessed 14 August 2015.

Ng, J. and K.C. Ng (2014) 'Beijing to Take a More Active Role in Hong Kong's Affairs, Hints Xi Jinping', *South China Morning Post*, 22 September, www.scmp.com/news/hong-kong/article/1597637/hong-kong-tycoons-urge-constructive-approach-political-reform-debate?page=all, accessed 14 August 2015.

Pepper, S. (2008) *Keeping Democracy at Bay. Hong Kong and the Challenge of Chinese Political Reforms*, Lanham: Rowan & Littlefield.

Public Opinion Programme, the University of Hong Kong, 'Popularity of Chief Executive', www.hkupop.hku.hk/english/popexpress/ce2005/, accessed 10 January 2017.

Scott, I. (1989) *Political Change and the Crisis of Legitimacy in Hong Kong*, Hong Kong: Oxford University Press.

Scott, I. (2000) 'The Disarticulation of Hong Kong's Post-Handover Political System', *The China Journal*, 43: 29–53.

Scott, I. (2007) 'Legitimacy, Governance and Public Policy in Post-Handover Hong Kong', *The Asia Pacific Journal of Public Administration*, 29(1): 29–49.

Scott, I. (2010) *The Public Sector in Hong Kong*, Hong Kong: Hong Kong University Press.

South China Morning Post (2014) 'Full Text: NPC Standing Committee Decision on Hong Kong 2017 Election Framework', 31 August, www.scmp.com/news/hong-kong/article/1582245/full-text-npc-standing-committee-decision-hong-kong-2017-election, accessed 3 June 2015.

The Economist (2014) 'Our Crony-capitalism Index: Planet Plutocrat', www.economist.com/news/international/21599041-countries-where-politically-connected-businessmen-are-most-likely-prosper-planet, accessed 24 July 2017.

'The Basic Law of the Hong Kong Special Administrative Region of People's Republic of China', www.basiclaw.gov.hk/en/basiclawtext/index.html, accessed 17 August 2015.

Williams, M. (2005) *Competition Policy and Law in China, Hong Kong and Taiwan*, Cambridge: Cambridge University Press.

Williams, M. (2009) 'The Lion City and the Fragrant Harbour: the political economy of competition in Singapore and Hong Kong compared', *Antitrust Bulletin*, 54(3): 517–577.

Wong, H. (2012) 'Changes in Social Policy in Hong Kong since 1997: Old Wines in New Bottles?' in W.M. Lam, P.L.T. Lui and W. Wong (eds) *Contemporary Hong Kong Government and Politics*, expanded 2nd edition, Hong Kong: Hong Kong University Press, pp. 277–296.

Zhang, K.H.L. (2005) 'Why Does So Much FDI from Hong Kong and Taiwan Go To Mainland China?' *China Economic Review*, 16(3): 293–307.

2 The bumpy road of Hong Kong economy between China and globalization, and the disenchantment of the youth

The emphasis on economic factors, which can be seen from the disproportionate and overwhelming participation of the business community in advisory bodies, has been one of Hong Kong's dominant characteristics in recent decades. The government's business-friendly policies led to economic growth, but in recent years, this growth is far from benefiting all Hongkongers. In order to show that a large portion of Hong Kong's population (including many young people) have been left behind and why, the authors will proceed in two steps. First, this chapter will demonstrate that if Hong Kong has always played the key role of middleman between China and the world economy – a role that was reinforced after China launched its 'open door policy' in 1978 – this unique function has subtly shifted in recent years (see section titled 'The changing position of Hong Kong as intermediary: globalization process and China's influence'). The increasing economic interdependency of Hong Kong and China is not as smooth as one may expect, and some key components of its role of intermediation between China and the world (e.g. foreign investments; logistics, especially the container port; finance; and tourism) have been affected, or even eroded, by the recent evolution of China's economy and its new leadership in the world economy. In short, if the role of Hong Kong as a global city cannot be separated from its economic relations with China, this role has changed as China has become more integrated in the world economy and Hong Kong, in China. This creates a situation of uncertainty for many Hongkongers and a certain disenchantment among the educated youth with the existing economic system (see section titled 'The disenchantment of the youth and the difficulties of the middle class').

Then, in the second step, the last two chapters of the book will illustrate that this disenchantment has been fuelled by increasing hardship for the educated youth and middle class, including stagnated incomes, difficulties in getting lodging at affordable prices, etc. These difficulties were due, in part, to the conjunction of globalization forces, the influence of China's economy in the Territory and governmental policies that were biased towards entrenched economic interests and favoured the creation of oligopolistic markets.

The changing position of Hong Kong as intermediary: globalization process and China's influence

Since the mid-nineteenth century and its creation as a free port, Hong Kong's *raison d'être* has been to serve as a middleman between China and the rest of the world – including during the Maoist era. The opening up of China during the late 1970s and the progress of globalization further enhanced this role and determined Hong Kong's position in the international division of labour (Augustin-Jean 2005; Zhao *et al.* 2012). However, in recent years, Hong Kong's function as a (business) hub has been subtly affected by China's changing position in the world economy. This can be seen in the evolution of four major elements of the Hong Kong economy, which have played a key role in its function as an intermediary between China and the world on one hand and as a global city on the other: (1) Foreign Direct Investments (FDI); (2) trade and logistics; (3) finance; and (4) tourism – the last three having been declared 'pillar industries' by the Hong Kong government during 2002–2003.[1] This section does not aim to present a comprehensive view of the Hong Kong economy or to deny the reality of its economic growth – GDP increased by over 46 per cent in real terms from 2004 to 2014 and by nearly 68 per cent from 2000 to 2014[2] – but it will introduce selected parameters showing how Hong Kong's position in the world and the Chinese economies has evolved in recent years.

A brief presentation of Hong Kong's foreign direct investments

Hong Kong attracts a large amount of FDI – in 2015 it was the second biggest recipient of FDI in the world behind China and ahead of the United States (Nylander 2015), as well as the second biggest provider of foreign investments behind the US (UNCTAD 2015) – but one should go beyond this quantitative aspect. To start with, it should be noted that since the launch of China's reforms during the late 1970s, the nature of Hong Kong FDIs has changed dramatically. During the first stage of China's reforms, a large number of Hong Kong factories were relocated to the Mainland and the Territory enhanced its command function by developing world class services in trading, finance, insurance, transports, etc. It sustained the development of China not only through its traditional role of middleman, but also through the large amount of FDI it supplied to China, which compensated for the lack of capital there.[3]

In more recent years, however, the importance of Hong Kong capital for China's economic growth has diminished (at least proportionally compared to other countries' investments) because most of its industries had already relocated across the border and because other countries or regions (e.g. Taiwan) have invested in China at increasing levels (not to mention the fact that most investments are now performed by domestic companies). Similarly, Hong Kong's function of channelling investments from other regions or countries to China has proportionally diminished after many companies began to invest directly in China.

This pattern can be observed from statistical tables, but up to 2005 only. After that year, the pattern shifted significantly and Hong Kong's FDIs in China started to increase again in absolute, as well as in relative, value, which is rather surprising. To elaborate, the share of Hong Kong in the flow of FDI to China progressively decreased from a historical high of 76 per cent in 1988 (Zhang 2005: 297) to an all-time low of 24.3 per cent in 2005. But, that year also marked the beginning of a spectacular recovery for Hong Kong investment in China, the flow of Hong Kong FDIs in China re-increasing to 58.7 per cent in 2012.[4]

The reasons for this reversal have yet to be fully understood, as a comprehensive analysis of this phenomenon is lacking. A possible explanation is to link this unexpected shift to the implementation of the Mainland and Hong Kong Closer Economic Partnership Arrangement (CEPA), which was first signed in 2003 in the aftermath of the severe acute respiratory syndrome (SARS) crisis and its negative effects on the Hong Kong economy.[5] According to Zhang Yang, 'Out of the 167 new foreign companies assisted by InvestHK in setting up business in Hong Kong, 20 per cent identified CEPA as one of the major reasons for their decision to invest in Hong Kong' (Zhang 2006: 13). However, if such data tended to highlight the importance of CEPA in the rejuvenation of Hong Kong FDI in China, it fell short of explaining the magnitude of this phenomenon. Similarly, the volume of FDI in and out of Hong Kong can certainly be explained by its close relationship to the Mainland (see below), but this is not a new factor and it does not explain the reversal of the trend since 2005.

A closer look at the statistical data shows two additional (though also not recent) characteristics. First, the outflow of Hong Kong FDI into China was coupled with an inflow of Chinese investments into Hong Kong. In 2011 and 2012, 42.3 and 47.8 per cent of Hong Kong's inbound direct investments (DIs), respectively, came from China.[6] Second, and more interestingly, there was an over-reliance on tax havens, especially the British Virgin Islands (BVIs), by both inward and outward investors. In 2002, the BVIs were already the largest investor in Hong Kong with a total of HK$779.4 billion (29.7 per cent of the total), which was much higher than China's (HK$594.6 billion, or 22.7 per cent of the total) investment in the Territory (LegCo Secretariat 2004). Moreover, from 2011 to 2013, the stock of investments from/to China and the BVIs remained relatively equivalent (C&SD 2014a: Tables 2 and 4).[7] A recent report by the C&SD explains this large share of tax havens in Hong Kong DIs in these words:

> the importance of offshore financial centres such as the BVI and Bermuda to Hong Kong's external DI was due to their popularity for some Hong Kong enterprises in setting up non-operating companies to channel DI funds back to Hong Kong or to other places, and also for some non-resident enterprises in re-directing funds to Hong Kong.
>
> (C&SD 2014a: 11)

In other words, there is a continuous flow of capital and investments linking the BVIs (and, to a lesser extent, Bermuda), Hong Kong and Mainland China. A certain part – difficult to quantify, but far from negligible – of these investments is therefore just circular (i.e. round-tripping investments), flowing from China to

Hong Kong and/or the BVIs or Bermuda before re-entering China with the status of FDIs. This type of hidden domestic investment is hardly a new phenomenon: in one of the most comprehensive articles on the topic, Xiao tried to estimate these circular flows, but could not come up with a definitive answer:

> [B]ased on the available FDI statistics from Hong Kong (…) and the PRC, the ratio of round-tripping FDI from Hong Kong (…) to the PRC during the period of 1998–2002 is likely to be in the range of 26.3% to 53.4% [of the total flow of direct investments from Hong Kong to China] with the middle estimate at 39.9%. It should be noted that this estimate of round-tripping FDI from Hong Kong (…) to the PRC includes only the type of round-tripping that is related to escaping regulations and does not include the type of round tripping that is related to capital market transactions such as listing PRC companies in Hong Kong, China's stock exchange.
>
> (Xiao 2004: 22)

The range of estimates is obviously too large to really help form an opinion on the extent of the illegal flow of money from China to Hong Kong (and back to China), but the study still showed that the flows were indubitably substantial. (It should also be noted that Xiao only aimed to estimate the circular flows that were related to escaping regulations, but not precise flows which were linked to tax evasion, illegal transactions and/or laundering money, which further increased quantitative uncertainty.) All in all, it is clear that the process involves a certain proportion – again, difficult to quantify, but also significant – of capital accumulated from corrupt practices to be laundered in Hong Kong and/or the BVI before re-entering China.

Finally, this highlights the role of Hong Kong as a tax haven, which is further enhanced by its connections to other tax havens. The Tax Justice Network, which operates a 'financial secrecy index', has ranked Hong Kong as the second most secretive financial centre in the world just behind Switzerland, while China and the BVIs were respectively ranked 20th and 21st (Tax Justice Network 2015a).[8] The 'narrative report', which is attached to this ranking, pinpoints that the 'top sources of inward direct investment into Hong Kong and destinations for funds out of Hong Kong contain a large number of jurisdictions with a high secrecy score' (Tax Justice Network 2015b: 7). The report also stressed that:

> Hong Kong's secrecy offerings have for years made Hong Kong into a major 'round tripping' turntable, particularly for China. Round-tripping involves Chinese investors shifting their money to Hong Kong, dressing it up in offshore secrecy, then returning it to China masquerading (illegally) as foreign investment, in order to obtain special privileges afforded to foreigners.
>
> (Ibid.: 6–7)

This quote takes on its full meaning after noting that a significant part of China's outward investments has been channelled through tax havens, most notably the

Cayman Islands and BVIs.[9] Finally, the importance of the tax havens has also been reinforced by the desire of some individuals and companies to escape the already low taxes in Hong Kong and/or to put their money in a secure place in the event the Chinese economy changes direction (see more on this point below).

In this respect, the sharp decline of Chinese investment in Hong Kong in 2013 may not be a coincidence.[10] On the one hand, since 2012, Hong Kong has made significant efforts, under pressure from the international community and G20 (see, for instance, OECD 2016), to reduce money laundering. In 2012, the enactment of the 'Anti-Money Laundering and Counter-Terrorist Financing (Financial Institutions) Ordinance' (AMLO) led to a 40 per cent increase in money laundering cases (Chan and Shih 2014). Also, the government will implement the 'automatic exchange of financial account information in tax matters' (AEOI), developed in 2014 by the OECD with an aim to prevent tax evasion (LegCo 2016; OECD 2016). On the other hand, purposely or not, such timing is similar to the anti-corruption campaign launched by Xi Jinping, so the decrease in China's investments in Hong Kong can be read as a sign of the campaign's partial success and/or that people have become more cautious about sending funds obtained from disreputable sources to Hong Kong or other tax havens.

It remains to be seen if these efforts will suffice to wipe out decades of fraudulent practices from the financial system. In line with the scandal of the 'Panama Papers' – a leak of 11.5 million files from the database of Mossack Fonseca, one of the world's biggest offshore law firms – it is, however, possible to raise a few doubts. Michael Bryane, a senior fellow at the HKU Law Faculty's Asian Institute of International Financial Law, has called for a series of measures so that 'companies should no longer be accepted as being from the British Virgin Islands without having a significant share of their revenue and assets actually produced there' (Bryane 2016). However, since he was, more or less, the only one to make such a claim publicly, this is unlikely to happen in the short term. The reasons for this are provided in the first lines of his article:

> Almost 25 per cent of the firm's clients [e.g. Mossack Fonseca's clients] originate from or through Hong Kong-based affiliates. HSBC alone has created more than 2,000 shell companies.
>
> The leaks unearthed the Panamanian firm's connections to tycoons Li Ka-shing and the Kwok brothers, and even to Polytechnic University.
>
> (Ibid.)[11]

To be clear, Bryane's proposition to end 'the automatic recognition of entities incorporated offshore, [so that] companies could no longer come from the British Virgin Islands without having a significant share of their revenues and assets actually produced there' (ibid.) has little chance of being adopted, since most members of the political and economic élite (and even universities) have set up entities in the BVIs.[12] This economic structure, with its ramifications in Caribbean tax havens, has consequences for other components of the political and economic organization – most notably for the domestic tax system. The authors will address this question in Chapter 4.

It would, however, be an exaggeration to restrict Hong Kong DIs to this circular flow and/or to corruption practices and tax evasion, as Hong Kong remains the headquarters of numerous foreign companies – including 97 from the Mainland (Zhao *et al.* 2012: 309). Nonetheless, the previous data pointed out that the importance of FDIs to Hong Kong's economy has been somewhat overrated and merit a re-evaluation of the recent role of FDIs and the financial sector in Hong Kong's globalization process, as the authors will explain below.

In any case, the movement of investments from/to China can be read in two different, but not necessarily compatible, ways: first, in terms of a deeper economic integration between the two entities and, second, as a sign of the strengthening of Hong Kong's bridging function between China and the rest of the world.[13] However, since it is difficult to interpret the reversed trend of Hong Kong investments in China since 2005, it is difficult to choose the more likely of these two alternatives.

'Integration' and 'bridging': two concepts with different implications for Hong Kong's role in the course of globalization and two themes that recur in other components of its economy. The balance between these two dimensions has also been affected by specific policies, such as the implementation of CEPA in 2003 (more on this below). While more and more enterprises have been investing directly in China, it still remains to be seen how Hong Kong's role in channelling FDI into the Mainland will evolve – which is partly linked to its intermediation function.

Trading and logistics at a crossroads

The review of the 'trading and logistic' sector offers similar alternatives between 'bridging' and 'integrating' on one hand and questioning on the other. The Hong Kong government defines 'Trading and logistics' as one of the four pillars of the local economy, as well as a sector that is expected to create employment and grow in size. However, recent economic evolutions did not seem to confirm the hopes the government placed on the growth of these industries. From 2002 to 2012, the share of the 'trading and logistic sector' in Hong Kong's GDP only managed to look relatively stable (24.9 per cent in 2002; 24.6 per cent in 2012). In more details, two periods can be identified: a sustained growth until 2005 (when the sector amounted to 28.5 per cent of GDP) followed by a slow decline ever since (LegCo Secretariat 2015: 3). 'The above developments were partly due to the export performance in recent years, amidst the waning trade intermediation of Hong Kong upon the continuing integration of Mainland with the global economy' (LegCo Secretariat 2015: 3). Beyond the eventual role of CEPA to support Hong Kong's economy (which needs to be re-evaluated, although this is beyond the scope of this book), the quote pinpointed that the integration of China with the world economy actually eroded the middleman function of the Hong Kong Special Administrative Region (HKSAR).

This was further confirmed by the slow decline of Hong Kong as a seaport – once the busiest in the world, but now number five. In 2013, it handled 22.35 million TEU (20-foot equivalent unit) containers, while 33.6 million TEUs transited through Shanghai that same year. Also in 2013, six of the ten busiest container ports (excluding Hong Kong) in the world were located in China.[14] In other words, for many observers, even though Hong Kong will continue to be an important seaport, it is no longer China's main gateway to the rest of the world. Instead, it is slowly becoming one of several Chinese ports with which it will have to compete.[15]

A recent research from the Department of Supply Chain of the Hang Seng Management School confirms this possibility, noting 'Hong Kong, as a container hub port, is (…) severely under threat' (Wong *et al.* 2016: 2). One of the problems, as noticed in the report, is that Chinese ports, such as Shanghai's, are closer to the country's factories. Hong Kong can still rely on transhipment, but as China has relaxed its rules on cabotage,[16] the port of Hong Kong may be further affected – by as much as 14 per cent of its current output (ibid.). Even though the situation may not be irreversible, some observers have expressed pessimism:

> '[Hong Kong's port] has lost its purpose and is looking for a role,' Stephen Davies, maritime historian and honorary University of Hong Kong professor said.
>
> 'As soon as China got its port act in gear, what Hong Kong had always traded on from 1841 and onwards, which was the fact that it wasn't China, simply disappeared. China can be its port a lot better than Hong Kong can be.'
>
> (Cited by Singh 2017)

The title of Singh's article in the *South China Morning Post* (*SCMP*) also expresses the opinion that the future has to be reinvented: 'Hong Kong's port seeks new role amid mainland China competition and decline in container throughput' (ibid.). Integration or bridging: in the case of logistics at least, the bridging function of Hong Kong has clearly declined.[17]

Some data on the recent evolution of the financial sector in Hong Kong's economy

Hong Kong's financial sector is another type of high-quality service industry that has helped bridge China's relationship with the rest of the world. It has an obvious role in channelling FDIs and in the creation of shell corporations in tax havens (see above).

More generally, its established position in international finance is attested to by being host to a number of regional headquarters of international and Mainland banks, which gives it a clear competitive advantage over its Mainland counterpart. However, a LegCo Secretariat report showed that after experiencing strong growth of 126 per cent (in real terms) from 2002 to 2007, the industry suffered from the effects of the global financial crisis of 2008 to 2009 and has yet to fully recover from it, recording a modest 7 per cent cumulative growth rate from 2008 to 2012 – much lower than Hong Kong's overall GDP growth (LegCo Secretariat 2015: 4–5). It was in this difficult context that the launch of the Shanghai-Hong Kong Stock Connect was decided upon in November 2014. This can be defined as

> a pilot programme that links the stock markets in Shanghai and Hong Kong. Under the programme, investors in Hong Kong and Mainland China can trade and settle shares listed on the other market via the exchange and clearing house in their home market.[18]

If this programme and its twin, the Shenzhen–Hong Kong Stock Connect (launched in December 2016, a year after it was originally planned – see Yiu and Hollingsworth 2016), helps integrate the financial systems of Hong Kong and the Mainland, it also poses the question of the future specificity of Hong Kong in the financial sector, as well as its autonomy and position in the Chinese and world economies – at a time when China's stock markets are seen as weak and volatile.

Thus, on the one hand, there is tremendous pressure from the international community (e.g. the G20 and the OECD) to introduce more transparency for tax havens. On the other hand, the integration of Hong Kong into China's financial system continues to proceed. This dual evolution calls for a full re-evaluation of the intermediation of the Hong Kong financial sectors – for the world and for China. Since Hong Kong is not just a tax haven, but has played a major role in China's industrialization and channelling investments from all over the world, its government, business community, media outlets and the general public should have made use of the opportunity offered by the 'Panama Papers scandal' to re-examine the role of its financial sector and its future after its attraction as a tax haven lessens. However, Bryane's article shows that this discussion has not occurred, at least not openly.

More generally, such a discussion on the future direction of Hong Kong's economy would be timely, as Hong Kong's regional and global position shifts, the evolution of FDIs, 'trading/logistics' and 'finance' sectors is attesting. An event, the economic crisis which was an unwelcome consequence to the 2003 SARS epidemic, accelerated this shift and signalled that Hong Kong's economy seems to undergo integration rather than continue to serve as a bridge to China. In order to help Hong Kong recover from the crisis, CEPA, under which Hong Kong companies and residents would enjoy preferential access to the Mainland market, was implemented that year. The signature of this agreement also signalled a complete reversal of the economic relationship between Hong Kong and China. Until CEPA, Hong Kong acted as a facilitator for China's international trade (bridging function), but from 2003 onwards, it had to accept some degree of interference from China in its economic affairs. Differently stated, if Hong

Kong is traditionally seen as supporting China's development through its FDIs or command functions, China could claim, for the first time and rightly or wrongly, to have rescued the Hong Kong economy. This reinforced the impression that Hong Kong's position in the world economy had evolved, but while its former role was perfectly defined and understood by local (economic) leaders and the general population, its new function has still to be reinvented (see more on that issue below).

Thus, CEPA, as well as the Shanghai–Hong Kong Stock Connect, Shenzhen-Hong Kong Stock Connect, and the construction of the Hong Kong–Zhuhai–Macau Bridge, have subtly modified the intricate economic relationship between China and Hong Kong. However, in no other industry has the introduction of new economic policies by Beijing been more visible and created more unease for Hongkongers than tourism. For that reason and, furthermore, because tourism is an activity that the Hong Kong government wants to develop on a large scale, the authors shall devote more attention to its recent evolution.

The tourism industry: a tool for growth or a nuisance?

Hong Kong's tourism industry has benefited since the introduction of the Individual Visit Scheme (IVS) in 2003 (the IVS is one of the measures under CEPA). Similarly to CEPA, its objective is to boost economic growth and 'rescue' Hong Kong's economy by increasing the number of Mainland tourists into Hong Kong. At a first glance, the policy has been largely successful. 'In 2002, before the launch of IVS, Hong Kong received 16.6 million visitors and 41.2 per cent of them came from the Mainland. In 2013, the number of visitors had soared to 54.3 million and 75.0 per cent came from the Mainland' (LegCo Research Office 2013). This figure further increased to over 60 million by 2014.

However, such a quantitative outcome should be mitigated by some negative qualitative consequences that have destabilized the retail sector. To understand why necessitates the inclusion of two monetary elements in the analysis. The first is the peg between the HK Dollar (HK$) and the US Dollar (US$) – since 1983, the HK$ has been linked to the US$ at about HK$7.75 to US$1;[19] and the second is the appreciation of the Renminbi (RMB) from 2005 to 2014. More precisely, from 1999 to 2005, the RMB traded at the rate of about ¥8.27 to US$1. After that date, it was progressively revaluated (partly under the U.S. pressure) to reach ¥6.2/US$1 by 2014.[20] An appreciation in the RMB of over 30 per cent to the US$ and, hence, HK$, does as much to explain the dramatic surge of tourists from the Mainland (who benefited from artificially lowered prices) as the introduction of the IVS.[21] It, along with the absence of taxes in Hong Kong (contrary to the situation in the Mainland), was largely responsible for the boost in the trade of luxury goods and beauty products.

The result has been a remarkable increase in the number of shops selling luxury goods and a substantial decrease in those selling daily necessities, which weighed negatively on Hongkongers' livelihoods. While most local residents can perceive this trend, not many can precisely assess the seriousness of the situation, in the absence of publicized data. Yet, according to a LegCo study, from 2004 to 2013, the number of outlets selling cosmetics and personal care products increased by a staggering 1,500 per cent. Those trading leather goods, jewellery and watches, and electronics (camera, audio equipment, etc.) jumped by 32.9, 30.5 and 21.6 per cent, respectively. However, at the same time, the number of shops selling daily necessities, and books and newspapers dropped by nearly 30 and over 25 per cent, respectively (LegCo Secretariat 2014: 8, and Figure 10).

Boosted by this inflow of tourists and their demand for luxury products, the rents for commercial properties exploded, which further strengthened the hand of retailers (usually chains) of luxury items. This allowed them to outbid retailers that sold daily necessities for prime street shop rentals in Causeway Bay and Tsim Sha Tsui, which increased 3.2 times and 3.7 times, respectively, between the first quarter of 2003 and the fourth quarter of 2013 (ibid.: 7, note 14). On average, shop rents surged by nearly 70 per cent during the same period (ibid.: 8). In 2013, for the second year in a row, 'Causeway Bay rank[ed] as the world's most expensive retail hub, outpacing New York's Fifth Avenue (…) according to data released by Cushman & Wakefield. Average prime rents in Causeway Bay jumped 14.7 per cent for the year to just above US$3,000 per square foot on an annual basis' (Oliver 2013).[22] On the positive side, the sustained growth of tourism generated over 100,000 jobs between 2002 and 2012, but mainly for lower-skilled, lower-paid workers (thus, at the same time, the tourism boost exacerbated inequality in Hong Kong – see below).[23]

In short, even though tourism contributes only a tiny portion to Hong Kong's GDP,[24] the influx of over 60 million tourists into a territory of just 7.24 million people and an area of 1,104 km^2 has had a profound influence on the daily lives of Hong Kong residents.[25] In 2013, their private consumption expenditures amounted to HK$1,401 billion in current prices (about 65 per cent of GDP). In the same year, the expenditure of non-residents reached HK$304 billion (or 21.7 per cent of residents' total consumption[26]) – the latter figure is counted as 'export' in Hong Kong's GDP. A first comment is that the growth of tourism in Hong Kong had less effect on its GDP increase than in many other tourist destinations (a fact that is seldom mentioned by commentators and scholars) because most goods consumed by tourists in Hong Kong are imported and not produced locally – unlike Japan, Italy or France. This is why, despite the large inflow of tourists in recent years, the contribution of tourism to Hong Kong's GDP remained quite modest and came with few spillover effects on the rest of its economy (beyond the creation of low-paid jobs).

Still, to some extent, the windfall from tourism impacted the growth of Hong Kong's GDP and compensated for the relative stagnation of salaries, albeit to a minor extent (see below on household incomes). However, and this is the second comment, with an influx of tourists that equalled about eight times its total population (and over four times higher than the total number of visitors to Japan), Hong Kong's capacity to accommodate a further increase seems limited, despite the common wish of the Hong Kong government, luxury retailers and commercial landlords (as the authors will detail in Chapter 4) for it to happen. Its transport network has been stretched to its limits. The development of the tourism industry, then, only led to mixed results. While the economic gains have been modest in terms of its contribution to the GDP and for the general population alike, luxury retailers and commercial landlords have profited greatly and the creation of jobs should not hide that these jobs are essentially low-paid ones.

To summarize the influence of tourism on Hong Kong's economy, market forces have not been the main engine for the development of tourism: the political element was a bigger driver of this growth – whether through the implementation of the IVS or the drastic change in the exchange rate. That includes the decision to maintain the peg between the HK$ and US$ and the decision of Beijing to appreciate the RMB. In recent months, however, the sharp drop of several Asian currencies confirmed the dominance of politics in the evolution of the regional tourism industry (even though tourism was not the primary target of the political manipulations). The large devaluation of the Japanese Yen (under 'Abenomics') and the Korean Won, along with the slight depreciation of the RMB, combined with the effect of China's anti-corruption campaign to depress Mainland tourist numbers into Hong Kong and curbed their consumption of luxury goods.[27] In light of this evolution over the last decade, this should only be seen as a market correction, but many fear that the 'tourist bubble' will burst. The closure of a handful of luxury shops and the lowering of commercial rents point to this scenario,[28] but that does not necessarily mean that Hong Kong has lost its edge in the luxury market, to paraphrase a recent alarmist title of a newspaper article.[29] However, total retail sales dipped 1.6 per cent in value during the first half of 2015 compared to a year earlier (Sit and Xu 2015). Even though the drop in sales has been sharper for luxury products than for mid-ranged ones, the situation in Hong Kong is far from a tourist defection.

In conclusion, recent developments in Hong Kong's economy confirmed that its traditional position of middleman is evolving, but its future role has yet to be redefined. To make use of the title of an article by Chiu and Lui (2009), it remains highly unclear if Hong Kong is really 'becoming a Chinese Global City' – an interrogation with which the authors of this book agree. The Hong Kong government's campaign (launched in 2001) to declare Hong Kong 'Asia's World City (...) where opportunity, creativity and entrepreneurship converge' has been more advertisement than reality.[30] More precisely, its traditional function of developing networks between China and the rest of the world (the function of 'bridge') has been altered by the impressive economic growth of Mainland China over the past two decades. The pressure to further integrate Hong Kong and China has resulted in tension because the two concepts of 'integration' and 'bridge' are not fully compatible, while Hong Kong's new role within China's economic sphere has yet to be clarified. The Hong Kong government's current discourse does not permit it to alleviate these tensions and the resulting ambiguities concerning the economic future of the Territory.[31]

Thus, there is a current sense of uncertainty for many Hong Kong citizens, which has also been fuelled by the economic decisions of many of its local tycoons. For example, Li Ka-shing, after his aborted attempt to sell ParknShop, which is one of Hong Kong's two major supermarket chains (*Reuters* 20 October 2013), decided to switch his 'base of incorporation to the Cayman Islands from Hong Kong (…) added fresh grist to rumours about his waning interest in Hong Kong as he unveiled a sweeping restructuring of his business empire' (Li and Sito 2015).[32]

This uncertainty over the future has contributed to a state of anomie among a significant proportion of Hongkongers and fuelled their disenchantment with the existing economic system. The next section presents stylized facts regarding this disenchantment, which is, nevertheless, not equivalent to calling into question the economic system or even challenging it. Then, in Chapter 3, some of the reasons for this disenchantment will be highlighted: neither the globalizing economy nor China's economic growth has benefited large segments of the Hong Kong population – some groups even perceive these factors as more a liability than an opportunity. The old policy of promoting a 'free economy' (or positive non-intervention, as famously stated by the former Financial Secretary John Cowperthwaite in 1971) and to increase the size of the pie (i.e. a continuous growth of the GDP) has become increasingly contentious among some groups of citizens – and with good reason. In particular, young people – including fresh graduates – have generally not benefited from these policies, at least as much as it is generally thought. As inequality gradually increases, it has reinforced the crisis of legitimacy for the government (already discussed in Chapter 1). The details of this disenchantment will be discussed in the next section, which will also show that Hong Kong's current difficulties have also been exacerbated by the global environment, including its relationship with China.

The disenchantment of the youth and the difficulties of the middle class

The previous section showed that the position of Hong Kong as a middleman between China and the world has shifted, but its new role has still to be defined. In this situation, its economic system has been perceived as no longer serving the interests of the great majority of its people. This is especially true for its better-educated middle class youth who, without generally challenging Hong Kong's capitalist system, now call for more government intervention in the economic and social affairs. The reasons for this situation will be analysed in the following chapters. This section only aims to present the extent of the phenomenon, which is another manifestation of the state of anomie and the lack of direction for the Hong Kong economy, which were presented earlier.

This apparently contradictory picture is neither new nor limited to Hong Kong, but it has become a more visible phenomenon in recent years, which has been confirmed by all existing studies. Based on a 1999 survey, Lau Siu-kai, a Hong Kong sociologist who became, in 2002, the head of the Central Policy Unit (the major government think tank), already noted this contradiction:

> At the abstract level, there is overwhelming support for a minimal role of the government in the economy. Conversely, Hongkongers expect the

> government to be very interventionist in specific economic areas for the sake of achieving non-economic goals or alleviating social or economic pain. The simultaneous attachment to economic liberalism and support for economic intervention is not peculiar to Hongkongers, for the Western public is also susceptible to ideological inconsistencies.
>
> (Lau 2003: 378–379)

More specifically, he acknowledged that:

> People older in age are more supportive of the capitalist system than those younger in age. Secondly, the better educated, in comparison with the less educated, are less supportive of the capitalist system. Thirdly, people employed in managerial and professional jobs are less enamored of Hong Kong's capitalism than those who hold the less prestigious white-collar and manual jobs.
>
> (Ibid.: 378)

These sentiments are even more valid today than they were in 1999. There are signs that recent economic downturns have affected Hongkongers' perceptions of the economy. The unofficial title of the 'freest economy in the world', which was awarded by the ultraconservative Heritage Foundation[33] and which the Hong Kong government has promoted with pride since the mid-1990s, is now being criticized and even mocked by some, including the mainstream media. George Chen, for example, titled one of his regular columns on the *SCMP*, 'Hong Kong's top ranking for economic freedom feels a good laugh. Doubts are growing over the city's competitive edge as a business hub (…)' (Chen 2014). In the same column, Chen noted that a 'few days after the Heritage Foundation released its global ranking, *The Economist* group's advisory service unit for senior corporate executives issued a warning on the outlook for Hong Kong's business, saying that the city was "at serious risk of losing its position as a pivotal business centre in Asia"' (ibid.).

More generally, during the mid-1990s, there was a shared belief that a freer economy was the key to entrepreneurship and providing people with opportunities to climb the social ladder,[34] and the ranking of the Heritage Foundation was seen positively. Even in 1999, during the recovery from the Asian Financial Crisis, Hong Kong was still seen as a land of opportunity. In the words of Lau Siu-kai:

> A (…) large majority (83%) was found in 1997 agreeing with the portrayal of Hong Kong as a land of bountiful opportunities where everyone could succeed through hard work. Even in the aftermath of the economic crisis, still 71% of the respondents in 1999 agreed with the statement that 'Hong Kong is a land of abundant opportunities, everyone can succeed through hard work.'
>
> (Lau 2003: 384)

However, signs of changing perception of the above notion slowly began to turn up throughout the 1990s. In 1993, 'more than half (53%) believed that it was personal factors that made people poor'. By 1999, however, 'less than half of the respondents (32%) attributed poverty to personal factors, whereas 21% alluded to unfair treatment by society, and 35% to both personal and social factors' (ibid.: 382). Clearly, a growing proportion of the population, in the aftermath of the 1997 economic crisis, started to express doubts over the ability of the present economic system to provide fair and equal opportunities to everyone.[35] Differently stated, capitalism and economic liberalism continue to be viewed as bringing opportunities to people, but have also been accused of causing increased inequality and poverty (see below).[36] It is interesting that even the most prominent supporters of economic liberalism, like former CE Donald Tsang, have now come around to accepting this view, which, in Tsang's case, somewhat contradicts his 1995 stance. In 2006, 'Tsang Yam-kuen appealed for the public to realise that the gap between rich and poor was one of the "inevitable phenomena" of capitalist societies, something that cannot be avoided except "in a socialist state in which everyone receives the same wages"' (Goodstadt 2013: 74).[37] So, according to policymakers such as Tsang, capitalism generates inequality and even poverty, but these evils must be accepted by the people. This is quite a new type of thinking for society's élites, but it is now typical for them.

However, most ordinary people (and most notably the youth) do not share this perspective and are increasingly favouring equal opportunities and fairness. A survey conducted by the Hong Kong Transition Project of the Baptist University of Hong Kong just before C.Y. Leung was selected CE indicated that

> nearly 8 in 10 respondents want Chief Executive candidates to address what they consider the most urgent issues of the wealth gap, affordable housing, socio-economic stress, and systemic reforms to healthcare, education, policy-making, and pollution. These are all matters in which the rich and powerful exercise considerable advantage and influences beyond those available to most others.
>
> (Hong Kong Transition Project 2012: 2)

In an earlier study held in 2009, the Project also emphasized 'the most persistent area of dissatisfaction with the Chief Executive since 2005 has been his handling of the poor and unemployed. While Tsang has partially implemented Hong Kong's first minimum wage, and done a fair amount for older citizens (who are the least dissatisfied but show fully 3 in 4 dissatisfied), *he is strongly hit by the youth on this issue*' (Hong Kong Transition Project 2010: 37; emphasis added).[38]

These data were confirmed by another study from the Project conducted in 2014, just a few months before the Umbrella Movement erupted. It indicated 'three out of four [Hong Kong residents were] dissatisfied or very dissatisfied with government's performance in dealing with their greatest personal concern' (Hong Kong Transition Project 2014: 2). More generally,

> [t]he level of dissatisfaction with the performance of the SAR government, 63%, is (…) near that of the dissatisfaction found during the 2003–04 period of massive demonstrations. 90% of student respondents are dissatisfied, with one third very dissatisfied. *90% of those in their 20s are dissatisfied, while 85% of those under 40 are dissatisfied.*
>
> (Ibid., emphasis added)[39]

A last survey, conducted by the Faculty of Liberal Arts and Sciences and the Centre for Greater China Studies at the Hong Kong Institute of Education (HKIEd) and the Round Table Community and Powersoft Consultancy Limited (HKIEd 2013) before being analysed by Mok (2015), gave further details on the reasons for this dissatisfaction among the younger generation and linked it to perceptions of social mobility and inequality held by younger adults.[40] The survey confirmed that the dissatisfaction of the younger generation was linked to the performance of the Hong Kong government, especially with regards to the increasing lack of youth social mobility (32.6 per cent of interviewees were dissatisfied) and access to higher education (36.2 per cent of the respondents 'thought that the government has not made enough efforts in helping poor students to gain fair access to education and the opportunity for upward movement'; ibid.: 128, and Table 1, pp. 130–131).[41] Still more revealing, maybe, the survey also showed that younger people believed that their career prospects were directly correlated to the career achievements of their parents:

> For instance, 67.2% of the respondents agreed that 'family background and wealth is vital for long-term prospect,' while 54% agreed that 'family background and relationships are significant for university graduates in getting jobs'.
>
> (Ibid.: 127, see also Table 1, pp. 130–131)

And a great majority of them (82 per cent!) also believed that 'as compared with the 1970s or 1980s, university graduates nowadays are finding it increasingly difficult to climb into the middle class'.[42] *In fine*, the survey confirmed that 'the perception of the gap between rich and poor had deteriorated since the 1997 handover'. The respondents tended to believe that social inequality was prevalent in Hong Kong, with younger respondents holding more negative perceptions (Mok 2015: 127).

Of course, perceptions do not necessarily equal reality and these data need to be reconciled with reality (but Chapter 3 will show that the facts corroborate most of these beliefs). However, they confirmed that the younger generation has been much less supportive not only of the current political system, but also of capitalism, especially in the context of globalization. Beyond the question of the implementation of more democratic elections, the social contract between the government and its citizens is experiencing tensions, which has added to the crisis of legitimacy that was presented in Chapter 1. In more technical terms, it could be hypothesized that the mode of accumulation of capital creates distortions that finally poses a threat in social cohesion, and, in return, may call for an evolution of this mode of accumulation itself (Aglietta 1998; Smart and Lee 2003). The reinforcement of capitalist forces – both externally (e.g. the contradictions generated by the spreading of globalization) and internally (e.g. the concentration of capital in the hands of a few and the creation of oligopolies) – are prone to generate social conflicts as Polanyi emphasized long ago (Polanyi 1944/1957).[43] More specifically, the system of 'positive non-intervention', coined by the then-Financial Secretary, John Cowperthwaite, in 1971 and used as a broad *conceptual* framework for economic policy ever since, no longer appealed to many Hongkongers, especially the youth, who want the government to be more interventionist on their behalf. The general public has even raised doubts over Hong Kong's status as a free market and it may not be completely wrong, as will be analysed in the last two chapters.[44]

However, the authors insist that a diminishing support for the capitalist system and the political structure which is backing it does not equate to an outright rejection of it: even though many Hongkongers, especially the young, have expressed distrust of the government, Hong Kong's economic system, and the élites that partly write its rules, they know too well that the (communist) alternative across the border may be no better and the launch of the Umbrella Movement tended to demonstrate this point. In this sense, the conceptual contradiction that was noted at the beginning of this section finds an easy answer: the great majority of young Hongkongers are not 'revolutionary', but only expect the government to intervene more in the market, extend the welfare system and create a fairer economy that would provide more opportunities for them. The next chapters will stress this point and show why the economic system (like the political one) is biased in favour of the élites.

In this context, the government announced its intention to revise its 'positive non-intervention' dogma. This could have been perceived as a positive sign, but the opportunity may have been wasted because the government's main focus remains business interests rather than social welfare, and the announcement may not suffice to satisfy people.[45] In addition, since the details regarding these possible changes were not clearly specified, the possible policy shift may just add to current uncertainties and worries over the future of Hong Kong's economy. The title, 'A Slow Drift towards Economic Intervention?' and its headlines, 'Chief Executive's Call for Greater Government Involvement in the Economy Raises Questions about Where Hong Kong Should Now Be Heading' of a recent newspaper article give grounds to this analysis (Cheung and Lee 2015).[46]

The disenchantment of Hongkongers confirms that the gap between the economic élites and the government on one hand and the so-called grassroots on the other has widened in recent years. The government has lost, in alarming proportion, the support of Hong Kong's youth and better-educated middle class. As will be examined in Chapter 3, these phenomena are related to the deteriorating conditions and prospects for these two groups. These factors are not unique to Hong Kong and are present in most developed economies (Chavagneux's interview with Stiglitz 2015; Petit 2010), but they have been exacerbated in the Territory due to its role as a financial centre, the proximity of China and the specificity of 'One Country, Two Systems'. In relation to its changing role in the global and Chinese economies, Hong Kong's economic system has generated poverty, inequality, and, above all, a lack of opportunity for fresh university graduates and a growing percentage of the middle class. This will be analysed in the last two chapters of this book. More specifically, Chapter 3 will document the rise of inequality and link it to the globalization process before showing that the polarization effect generated by globalization has pushed many of Hong Kong's young to study longer and obtain more higher education qualifications, but perhaps for naught. Chapter 4 will close the loop in showing that Hong Kong's inequality and related problems can also be linked to the extreme concentration of capital in the hands of a few families. Again, this was made possible by globalization and, more importantly, by policies promulgated by the Hong Kong government since at least the 1960s and this was reinforced by the latest wave of investments from Mainland China in the Territory in the last few years.

Notes

1 The four pillar industries are tourism, professional and producer services, financial services, and trading and logistics. Professional and producer services include architecture and engineering; legal, accounting, and auditing services; information technology and advertising; and others. See Research Office, LegCo Secretariat (2015).

2 See C&SD (2015), 'Gross Domestic Product (GDP); Table 30, implicit price deflator of GDP and per capita GDP', www.censtatd.gov.hk/hkstat/sub/sp250.jsp?tableID=030&ID=0&productType=8.

3 For a short account of Hong Kong's economic development since the end of World War II, see Augustin-Jean (2004, 2005), among others.

4 See http://unctad.org/Sections/dite_fdistat/docs/webdiaeia2014d3_CHN.pdf.

5 The Mainland and Hong Kong Closer Economic Partnership Arrangement (CEPA) is the first free trade agreement ever concluded by China and Hong Kong. Its main text was signed on 29 June 2003. CEPA opened up huge markets for Hong Kong goods and services in China and greatly enhanced the already-close economic cooperation and integration between the two.

(See Trade and Industry Department (2014), www.tid.gov.hk/english/cepa/cepa_overview.html)

6 C&SD, 2014a, Table 2, p. 16. The amount for 2013 is unusually low (about 8 per cent) and will be discussed below.

7 For example, in 2011, 2012 and 2013, the inflow of FDIs from the BVIs was, respectively, HK$151.5 billion, HK$191.0 billion and HK$341.9 billion. The total amount was higher than China's (HK$597.4 billion) (ibid.).

8 It should be noted that Hong Kong is also part of the 30 world tax havens blacklist dressed by the European Union. See EU business (2015) www.eubusiness.com/news-eu/economy-politics.120n; *SCMP* (2015) www.scmp.com/news/world/article/1823567/blacklist-worlds-30-worst-offending-tax-havens-published-hong-kong. However, for this book, the authors privileged the report of the Tax Justice Network (rather than the European Union blacklist) because it is not only more detailed, but also more objective: the list of the European Union has been criticized for avoiding to include Luxembourg (ranked sixth by the Tax Justice Network), as well as Jersey and Switzerland. Finally, the OECD and G20 have also jointly established a list of tax havens since 2009, but it

lacks readability. Countries and territories are classified into four categories (Compliant, Largely Compliant, Partially Compliant and Non-Compliant). Hong Kong (like the United States, UK and BVIs) was classified under the second category (Largely Compliant), while China was considered Compliant. Only five entities (including Panama) were in the last group (OECD 2016: 16).

9 This is not the purpose of developing this theme further, but in 2006, the combined share of the Cayman Islands and BVIs for China's total outward investments reached 47.5 per cent (see Mork *et al.* 2008, Table 2: p. 340). In 2013, this share somewhat dropped, but remained significant and exceeded 30 per cent of China's outward investments – this time, excluding Hong Kong in its total investments (see Casanova *et al.* 2015: 6). However, as the authors will show, more than a real shift in the destination of Chinese FDIs, this change might have been triggered by two sets of events: the campaign against corruption launched by Xi Jinping in China and the international efforts to curb tax evasion and increase financial transparency worldwide (see, also, note 8, Chapter 2 on the tax havens' blacklists).

10 The flow of investments from China to Hong Kong dropped from HK$318.1 billion in 2011 to HK$232.7 billion in 2012 and then to a meagre HK$46.6 billion in 2013 (or less than 15 per cent of 2011's amount).

11 See, also, Stuart Lau:

> Four more Hong Kong lawmakers, all from the pro-establishment camp, have joined the list of prominent politicians and business leaders revealed to have stakes in offshore companies set up in world-famous tax havens, according to the latest batch of Panama Papers examined by the *South China Morning Post*.
>
> (Lau 2016)

12 Of course, the Panama Papers scandal also hit politicians and businessmen in China – so much that the family of the Prime Minister, Wen Jiabao, had to deny investing in offshore companies with American hedge fund billionaires (Mimi Lau 2016).

13 Our purpose, in this section, is to show that there was a lack of a perceived direction in the economy, which, in return, created an anomie for the Hong Kong population. Thus, this perspective diverges from the existing debate over Hong Kong's 'structural integration' with the Chinese economy. Similarly, the two related debates – first, whether or not this possible economic integration conforms to the Basic Law and, second, if it may lead to a 'dissolution' (i.e. if Hong Kong loses its advantages and becomes just another Chinese city) – are not the purpose of this book. For a more detailed discussion of these two points (and a review of the different arguments over them), see Tsang Shu-ki (2007). The author suggested that the alternative to the 'structural integration' for the Hong Kong economy is to 'maintain some 'coherence' of its own and keep a 'healthy distance' from the Mainland' (Tsang 2007: 39). In other words, Hong Kong should continue to serve as a 'bridge' between China and the rest of the world, but this role has diminished in recent years, as will be shown later.

14 World Shipping Council: www.worldshipping.org/about-the-industry/global-trade/top-50-world-container-ports. In defence of Hong Kong, it should be noted that in 2013, its port was affected by a 40-day dock strike (see above), which skewed its 2013 and 2014 results. These data can also be read in two different ways. The first is to consider that Hong Kong has lost ground compared to China's main ports, especially Shanghai. The second is to note that Shanghai (as well as other ports in the Pearl River Delta) is, for a large part, controlled by Hong Kong capital (notably Hutchison Whampoa, one of the companies of Hong Kong magnate, Li Ka-shing). Accordingly, some people consider that what is more important is not where the containers transit, but who controls the financial flows and networks of the logistics industry (Martin 2007: 95–122). This second approach nevertheless has to be taken cautiously, especially after Li Ka-shing relocated his headquarters to the Cayman

Islands and has slowly divested from the Chinese property market. In short, the strike probably affected Hong Kong's economy more than it affected Li.

15 It has been noted that a reason for the decline of Hong Kong as a seaport is its high operation costs. But some scholars suggested that these high costs might not be due to the difference in salary between Hong Kong and Mainland workers, but to a '"non-poaching" cartel agreement' between the main port operators, for whom the containers' transit port matters little because they profit either way. For a discussion of the oligopoly situation in the Hong Kong port, see Williams (2005: 288–291). For a discussion of the implementation of the Competition Ordinance, see Chapter 4 of this book.

16 Briefly stated, only vessels hoisting Chinese flags are allowed to conduct coastal shipping between Chinese ports; but under the 'One Country, Two Systems' principle, Hong Kong is not considered a Mainland port (Wong *et al.* 2016: 8).

17 The decision to build the Hong Kong–Zhuhai–Macau Bridge is more ambiguous in this respect. The bridge is designed to integrate Hong Kong (and Macau) with the Pearl River Delta and Guangdong. However, the consequences of the bridge on Hong Kong's intermediation function are not clear. The same applies to the Hong Kong Express Rail Link, which will connect Hong Kong to China by high-speed rail. However, the timing of the final decision to build the bridge, in August 2003, can be seen as one of the 'Mainland economic gifts' to first defuse the political crisis by economic means (see Chapter 1) and, second, to boost growth in the aftermath of SARS (see more on that point below).

18 See Hong Kong Exchanges and Clearing Limited: www.hkex.com.hk/eng/market/sec_tradinfra/chinaconnect/videos.html.

19 The peg has also influenced Hong Kong's property market (see below).

20 See the data of the Federal Reserve: www.federalreserve.gov/datadownload/Preview.aspx?pi=400&rel=H10&preview=H10/H10/RXI_N.A.CH.

21 The price differential also encouraged cross-border trading (so-called 'parallel trading'), even though other parameters (such as a lack of trust in the quality of Chinese goods) also played a part.

22 The Champs-Elysées, in Paris, was a distant third, with an average of US$1,601 per square foot (ibid.).

23 The disappearance of shops that catered mainly to locals due to the jump in commercial rents also destroyed a number of jobs. The net effect of the boost in tourism in terms of job creation was, therefore, not as positive as the data indicated (see more on this below).

24 The share of tourism in the GDP was only 4.7 per cent in 2012, up from 2.9 per cent in 2002 (see LegCo Secretariat 2015, and below). This was its direct contribution to Hong Kong's GDP. In 2013, its indirect contribution was an estimated 21.8 per cent, according to the World Travel and Tourism Council (2014), but this percentage encompassed a broad category of services, such as travel (including by Hong Kong residents), marketing campaigns in Hong Kong and abroad by the Tourism Board and the government, etc.

25 Of this total area of 1,104 km^2, less than 25 per cent have been developed and some districts recorded some of the highest population densities in the world – the record being Kwun Tong, with 57,250 persons per square kilometre (Informational Services Department 2015).

26 This was an underestimate because overnight visitors and same-day in-town visitors (the numbers of which were significant) were excluded. See C&SD (2014b).

27 There have also been a number of protests against Mainland tourists in recent months, most of which were directed against parallel traders, but others were organized in popular shopping districts selling luxury products (e.g. in Tsim Sha Tsui). Newspapers regularly reported such confrontations. See, for example, Lai and Lam (2015).

28 This point will be elaborated on in Chapter 3.

29 See the alarmist titles from the international media: 'Hong Kong Loses Edge in the World of Luxury' ('Dans l'univers du luxe, Hong Kong perd de son attrait', Vulser 2015), or 'Tag Heuer Intends to Shut Down a Flagship Store in Hong Kong' ('Tag Heuer compte fermer une boutique phare à Hong Kong'), *Reuters*, 4 August 2015. See also, in more detail, Sit and Xu in *The Standard*:

> In June, visitor arrivals from the Mainland were down 1.8 percent year-on-year. Adding to the woes of luxury goods vendors are the changing spending patterns of Mainland visitors, who are now looking for more mid-priced products.
>
> Meanwhile, Midland IC&I (0459) chief executive Daniel Wong Hon-shing said retail rents have plummeted in the past six months, tumbling 20 percent from a year earlier. Rents in areas where Mainland visitors are concentrated, such as Causeway Bay, Tsim Sha Tsui, and Yuen Long, were hit hardest. Wong expects a further drop of 10–15 percent in retail rents by year end.
>
> (Sit and Xu, 6 August 2015)

30 'Asia's World City': www.info.gov.hk/info/sar5/easia.htm. This book is not the place to examine this issue in depth, but Hong Kong has experienced a dramatic drop in entrepreneurship in recent years. See Augustin-Jean, 2010.

31 See the recent speech of C.Y. Leung to commemorate Saudi Arabia's National Day:

> Hong Kong is the world's China financial centre, and China's international financial capital. We are the 'super-connector' between the rest of China and the rest of the world. That means helping Mainland enterprises 'go global' with their services, products, and their capital, while enabling overseas companies (…) to find Mainland markets. (…) Those everyday strengths, and our ever-deepening economic integration with Mainland China, help power Hong Kong's global success.
>
> (C.Y. Leung (2015) 'Hong Kong World's China Financial Centre', 29 September, Hong Kong's Information News Department, www.news.gov.hk/en/record/html/2015/09/20150929_191641.shtml)

32 See also his reply, which nevertheless did not ease the worries of some:

> Li, however, rejected suggestions that the proposed reorganisation is a sign of his withdrawal from the city. 'More than 75 percent of companies that have listed in Hong Kong in the past 10 years or so are incorporated in Cayman Islands, including state-owned enterprises. Have they also lost confidence in Hong Kong?' said Li, adding that the company was just 'following the trend'.
>
> (Li and Sito, 9 January 2015)

Cayman Islands or the BVIs, as developed earlier…

33 For a critical analysis of the meaning of this ranking for Hong Kong, see Augustin-Jean (2004).

34 The government's opinion that a free economy can bring opportunities to everyone is reflected by the following statement by Donald Tsang, the then-financial secretary (and later CE), commenting on the ranking of the Heritage Foundation, which placed Hong Kong as the freest economy in the world in 1995: 'We firmly believe in private enterprise and small government so that business will have the freedom and the opportunity to generate the wealth our economy needs' (cited by Yim (1995), *SCMP*).

35 Another series of surveys shows that the 'perception of the seriousness of income disparities has increased from 58.5% of the respondents who thought the situation was serious or very serious [in 1995] to over 75% in 2006 (with a peak of 80.4% in 2001)'. The authors of the survey also asked respondents if they think this income disparity is 'just' or not, but they only provide data from 1990 to 2001, so it is of little usefulness to analyse the more contemporary period. See Wong *et al.* (2011).

36 From the WiseNews database, Chan *et al.* counted the number of times expressions such as 'profiteers', 'hatred towards the business sector', or 'hatred towards the rich' occurred from 2001 to 2010. They documented an impressive upward trend in the usage of these terms, especially between 2009 and 2010. The word 'profiteers' increased from 252 times in 2001 to 620 in 2008, 420 in 2009, and 564 in 2010; 'hatred towards the business sector' appeared up to 33 times between 2001 to 2009, but 638 times in 2010 alone; 'hatred towards the rich' increased irregularly from 0 in 2001 to 100 in 2009, but totalled 1,257 in 2010 (See Chan *et al.* 2014: 77 and Table 5, p. 77). For a similar tally regarding 'income inequality', see Tang and Wong (2011) and below.

37 This remark was made by Donald Tsang in front of LegCo to justify the growing level of inequality in Hong Kong (see Chapter 3 on the rising inequality in Hong Kong) and it represents an interesting attitude shift. Such comments echoed similar ones made by Hong Kong's tycoons as early as 2000 (Goodstadt 2013: 68).

38 Of interviewees aged 18–29, 86 per cent were very dissatisfied or dissatisfied of the performance of Donald Tsang on the issue, while the level of dissatisfaction 'only' reached 74 per cent of the people from 60 to 85 years old (Hong Kong Transition Project 2010: 37, Table 47).

39 Interestingly, but not surprisingly, the poor and lower middle classes were more supportive of the government and its economic policy – even though they have benefited little from them.

40 From December 2012 to January 2013, 500 people aged from 18 to 34 were randomly interviewed by phone (see Mok 2015).

41 At the same time, only 32.8 per cent of the interviewees found these measures very adequate or adequate.

42 This last data has been retrieved from the press release of the HKIEd 'Hong Kong Youth Envision Tougher Road in Moving Upward, Survey Finds', which provides other details of the same survey. See HKIEd (2013) www.ied.edu.hk/media/news.php?id=20130430.

43 The demonstration of these hypotheses will constitute the core of Chapters 3 and 4.

44 The 'positive non-intervention' was more an ideology than a real practice; it has been shown long ago that the Hong Kong government has regularly and heavily intervened in economic affairs, before and after the handover. For more on this issue, see Schiffer (1985), Augustin-Jean (2005) and Goodstadt (2006).

45 In the words of Goodstadt: 'In 1998, Tung announced that the government had redefined the traditional economic policy of 'noninterventionism'. In future, it would identify growth industries and create new profit opportunities for the private sector' (Goodstadt 2013: 61). The 'growth industries' became the 'four pillar industries' that were analysed earlier. More recently, on 10 August 2015, C.Y. Leung stated that the 'laissez-faire economic policy is outdated'. It remains to be seen what he really meant by that, but since he emphasized that the 'role [of the government] should be one of a proactive leader and coordinator with the business sector', we should not expect a radical turn in the economic policy (Lam 2015).

46 The article did not mention anything about social policies; it indicated that the government may 'pick up winners' in the future and distort policies in favour of some industries.

Bibliography

Aglietta, M. (1998) 'Capitalism at the Turn of the Century: Regulation Theory and the Challenge of Social Change', *New Left Review*, 232: 41–90.

'Asia's World City', www.info.gov.hk/info/sar5/easia.htm, accessed 21 September 2015.

Augustin-Jean, L. (2004) 'Intervention publique et dévelopment à Hong Kong: un libéralisme en trompe-l'œil?' *Espaces et Sociétés*, 116–117(1–2): 209–233.

Augustin-Jean, L. (2005) 'Urban Planning in Hong Kong and Integration with the Pearl River Delta: An Historical Account of the Local Development?' *GeoJournal*, 62(1–2): 1–13.

Augustin-Jean, L. (2010) 'Entrepreneurship as a Contributor of Growth in Asia: an Analysis of Hong Kong's Case', *Canadian Journal of Development Studies*, 31(3–4), 314–340.

Bryane, M. (2016) 'Hong Kong Must Work towards a "Panama Papers Ordinance" to End Automatic Recognition of Offshore Firms', *South China Morning Post*, 16 May, www.scmp.com/news/hong-kong/politics/article/1945700/hong-kong-must-work-towards-panama-papers-ordinance-end, accessed 16 November 2016.

Casanova, C., A. Garcia-Herrero and L. Xia (2015) 'Chinese Outbound Foreign Direct Investments: How Much Goes Where after Round Tripping and Offshoring?', BBVA (Banco Bilbao Vizcaya Argentaria) Working Paper 15/17, June.

Census and Statistics Department, the HKSAR (2014a) 'External Direct Investment Statistics of Hong Kong 2013', www.statistics.gov.hk/pub/B10400032013AN13B0100.pdf, accessed 4 July 2015.

Census and Statistics Department, the HKSAR (2014b) '2013 Gross Domestic Product', www.statistics.gov.hk/pub/B10300022013AN13E0100.pdf, accessed 20 September 2015.

Census and Statistics Department, the HKSAR (2015) 'Gross Domestic Product (GDP); Table 30 Implicit Price Deflator of GDP and Per Capita GDP', 14 August, www.censtatd.gov.hk/hkstat/sub/sp250.jsp?tableID=030&ID=0&productType=8, accessed 25 August 2015.

Chan, C.M.A., Y.L.S. Cheung and C.K.L. Lai (2014) 'Widening of a Poverty Gap: A Condition of Governance Crisis in Hong Kong', *Advances in Applied Sociology*, 4(3): 69–84.

Chan, S. and T.H. Shih (2014) 'Money Laundering Investigations in Hong Kong up Sharply Following 2012 Law', *South China Morning Post*, 14 April, www.scmp.com/news/hong-kong/article/1481405/money-laundering-investigations-hong-kong-sharply-following-2012-law, accessed 16 November 2016.

Chavagneux, C. (2015) '"Le 1% les plus riches met tout en œuvre pour maintenir des sociétés inégalitaires" – Interview with Joseph Stiglitz', *Alternatives Economiques*, 350 (October), www.alternatives-economiques.fr/le-1-nbsp-25-les-plus-riches-met-to_fr_art_1391_73617.html, accessed 5 October 2015.

Chen, G. (2014) 'Hong Kong's Top Ranking for Economic Freedom Feels a Good Laugh', *South China Morning Post*, 19 January, www.scmp.com/business/article/1409190/hong-kongs-top-ranking-economic-freedom-feels-good-laugh, accessed 2 June 2015.

Cheung, T. and E. Lee (2015) 'A Slow Drift towards Economic Intervention?' *South China Morning Post*, 24 August.

Chiu, S. and T.L. Lui (2009) *Hong Kong: Becoming a Chinese Global City*. New York: Routledge.

EU business (2015) 'EU Releases World Tax Havens Blacklist', 18 June, www.eubusiness.com/news-eu/economy-politics.120n, accessed 16 November 2016.

Federal Reserve System, 'G.5/H.10 – Foreign Exchange Rates', www.federalreserve.gov/datadownload/Preview.aspx?pi=400&rel=H10&preview=H10/H10/RXI_N.A.CH, accessed 3 August 2015.

Goodstadt, L.F. (2006) 'Government without Statistics: Policy-making in Hong Kong 1925–85, with Special Reference to Economic and Financial Management', *HKIMR Working Paper No. 6/2006* (April), Hong Kong Institute for Monetary Research.

Goodstadt, L.F. (2013) *Poverty in the Midst of Affluence: How Hong Kong Mismanaged its Prosperity*, Hong Kong: Hong Kong University Press.

Hong Kong Exchanges and Clearing Limited, www.hkex.com.hk/eng/market/sec_trad infra/chinaconnect/videos.html, accessed 1 August 2015.

Hong Kong Institute of Education (2013) 'Hong Kong Youth Envision Tougher Road in Moving Upwards, Survey Finds', 30 April, www.ied.edu.hk/cgcs/en/pub_details_title.php?id=4&pid=6, accessed 21 December 2015.

Hong Kong Transition Project (2010) 'Protest and Post-80s Youth. Sources of Social Instability in Hong Kong', the Baptist University, February, http://hktp.org/list/protest_and_post_80s_youths.pdf, accessed 12 July 2017.

Hong Kong Transition Project (2012) 'Where is the Love? Hong Kong's Search for a New Direction under the Next Chief Executive', the Baptist University, 13 February, http://hktp.org/list/where-is-the-love-small.pdf, accessed 10 August 2015.

Hong Kong Transition Project (2014) 'Confrontation Looms as Hong Kong Consults', the Baptist University, April, http://hktp.org/list/constitutional-reform.pdf, accessed 10 August 2015.

Informational Services Department, Hong Kong Special Administrative Region Government (2015) 'Hong Kong: The Facts – Population', April www.gov.hk/en/about/abouthk/factsheets/docs/population.pdf, accessed 21 December 2015.

Lai, Y.K. and J. Lam (2015) '"Stop Attacking Chinese Tourists": Hong Kong Leader Says Protests are Threatening City's "Hospitable" Image as Visitor Numbers Drop', *South China Morning Post*, 2 September, www.scmp.com/news/hong-kong/economy/article/1854349/hong-kong-localists-are-driving-mainland-chinese-tourists?page=all, accessed 13 October 2015.

Lam, J. (2015) 'Hong Kong's Laissez-faire Economic Policy is "Outdated", Says CY Leung', *South China Morning Post*, 10 August.

Lau, M. (2016) 'Family of Ex-Chinese Premier Wen Jiabao Denies Investing in Offshore Company with US Hedge Fund Billionaire', *South China Morning Post*, 16 May, www.scmp.com/news/china/policies-politics/article/1945584/family-ex-chinese-premier-wen-jiabao-denies-investing, accessed 17 November 2016.

Lau, S. (2016) 'Prominent Hong Kong Politicians and Businessmen Named in New Round of Panama Papers Leaks', *South China Morning Post*, 21 April, www.scmp.com/news/hong-kong/politics/article/1937250/prominent-hong-kong-politicians-and-businessmen-named-new, accessed 16 November 2016.

Lau, S.K. (2003) 'Confidence in Hong Kong's Capitalist Society in the Aftermath of the Asian Financial Turmoil', *Journal of Contemporary China*, 12(35): 373–386.

Legislative Council (2016) 'Bills Committee on Inland Revenue (Amendment) Bill 2016. Background Brief', LC Paper No. CB(1)518/15–16(03), www.legco.gov.hk/yr15-16/english/bc/bc07/papers/bc0720160202cb1-518-3-e.pdf, accessed 16 November 2016.

Legislative Council Secretariat (2004) 'Information Note: Foreign Direct Investment in Hong Kong', Hong Kong Legislative Council www.legco.gov.hk/yr04-05/english/sec/library/0405in03e.pdf, accessed 31 July 2015.

Legislative Council Secretariat – Research Office (2013) 'Individual Visit Scheme', *Research Brief* No. 6.

Legislative Council Secretariat – Research Office (2014) 'Individual Visit Scheme', *Research Brief* No. 6.

Legislative Council Secretariat – Research Office (2015) 'Four Pillars and Six Industries in Hong Kong: Review and Outlook', *Research Brief* No. 3.

Leung, C.Y. (2015) 'Hong Kong World's China Financial Centre', 29 September, Hong Kong's Information News Department, www.news.gov.hk/en/record/html/2015/09/20150929_191641.shtml, accessed 19 February 2016.

Li, S. and P. Sito (2015) 'Li Ka-shing Business Empire Shifts Base from Hong Kong to Cayman Islands', *South China Morning Post*, 9 January.

Martin, M. (2007) 'Le développement de l'économie de Hong Kong', in L. Augustin-Jean and F. Padovani (eds) *Hong Kong: Economie, Société, Culture*, Paris: L'Harmattan, pp. 95–121.

Mok, K.H. (2015) 'Enhancing Global Competitiveness and Human Capital Management: Does Education Help Reduce Inequality and Poverty in Hong Kong?' in M. Lau (ed.) *Special Issue: Poverty in a Rich Society – The Case of Hong Kong, The China Review*, 15(2): 119–146.

Mork, R., B. Yeung and M.Y. Zhao (2008) 'Perspectives on China's Outward Foreign Direct Investments', *Journal of International Business Studies*, 39(3): 337–350.

Nylander, J. (2015) 'Hong Kong overtakes The US in FDI', *Forbes*, 25 June.

OECD (2016) *Tax Transparency 2016: Report on Progress*, www.oecd.org/tax/transparency/GF-annual-report-2016.pdf, accessed 11 January 2017.

Oliver, C. (2013) 'Causeway Bay Rents Continue to Outpace New York's Fifth Avenue', *South China Morning Post*, 19 November.

Petit, P. (2010) 'The Systemic Nature of the Rise in Inequality in Developed Economies', in W. Milberg and P. Petit (eds) *Special Issue: Inequality as a Source of Economic Vulnerability: Post-crisis Varieties of Capitalism, International Review of Applied Economics*, 24(3): 251–267.

Polanyi, K. (1944/1957) *The Great Transformation: The Political and Economic Origins of Our Time*, Boston: Beacon Press.

'RPT-Hutchison Drops Plan to Sell ParknShop Supermarkets Business' (2013), *Reuters*, 20 October, www.reuters.com/article/2013/10/20/hutchison-idUSL3N0IA08A20131020, accessed 3 August 2015.

Schiffer, J.R. (1985) 'Anatomy of a Laissez-faire Government: The Hong Kong Growth Model Reconsidered', in P. Hills (ed.) *State Policy and the Development Process*, Proceedings of a Symposium on Social and Environmental Development, Centre of Urban Studies and Urban Planning, The University of Hong Kong, pp. 1–29.

Singh H. (2017) 'Hong Kong's Port Seeks New Role amid Mainland China Competition and Decline in Container Throughput', *South China Morning Post*, 25 February, www.scmp.com/news/hong-kong/economy/article/2024633/hong-kongs-port-seeks-new-role-amid-mainland-chinas-rise-and, accessed 25 July 2017.

Sit, F. and A. Xu (2015) 'High End Pain Puts Pressure on Rents', *The Standard*, 6 August, www.thestandard.com.hk/news_print.asp?art_id=159827&sid=, accessed 21 September 2015.

Smart, A. and J. Lee (2003) 'Financialization and the Role of Real Estate in Hong Kong's Regime of Accumulation', *Economic Geography*, 79(2): 153–171.

South China Morning Post (2015) 'Blacklist of World's 30 Worst-offending Tax Havens Published … Hong Kong Features but Luxembourg Is Nowhere to be Seen', 19 June, www.scmp.com/news/world/article/1823567/blacklist-worlds-30-worst-offending-tax-havens-published-hong-kong, accessed 16 November 2016.

Tang, H.W. and H.W.S. Wong (2011) 'The Impact of New Immigration on Native Wages: A Cross-Occupation Analysis of a Small Open Economy', *Centro Studi Luca d'Agliano Development Studies Papers* 308.

Tax Justice Network (2015a) 'Financial Secrecy Index – 2015 Results', www.financialsecrecyindex.com/introduction/fsi-2015-results, accessed 15 November 2016.

Tax Justice Network (2015b) 'Narrative Report on Hong Kong', www.financialsecrecyindex.com/PDF/HongKong.pdf, accessed 15 November 2016.

'The Basic Law of the Hong Kong Special Administrative Region of People's Republic of China', www.basiclaw.gov.hk/en/basiclawtext/index.html, accessed 17 August 2015.

Trade and Industry Department, the HKSAR (2014) 'Mainland and Hong Kong Closer Economic Partnership Arrangement (CEPA)', www.tid.gov.hk/english/cepa/cepa_overview.html, accessed 29 July 2015.

Tsang, S.K. (2007) 'The Hong Kong Economy under Asymmetric Integration: Structural Transformation of Dissolution?' *The China Review*, 7(2): 35–63.

UNCTAD (2015) *World Investment Report 2015: Reforming International Investment Governance*, Geneva, UNCTAD, http://unctad.org/en/pages/newsdetails.aspx?OriginalVersionID=1023&Sitemap_x0020_Taxonomy=World%20Investment%20Report;#6;#Investment and Enterprise; #20; #UNCTAD Home, accessed 29 July 2015.

Vulser, N. (2015) 'Dans l'univers du luxe, Hong Kong perd de son attrait', *Le Monde*, 29 July.

Williams, M. (2005) *Competition Policy and Law in China, Hong Kong and Taiwan*, Cambridge: Cambridge University Press.

Wong, K.Y.T., P.S. Wan and W.K. Law (2011) 'Public Perception of Income Inequality; Trend and Implications', in Chiu S.K.W. and Wong S.L. (eds), *Hong Kong Divided? Structures of Social Inequality in the Twenty-First Century*, Hong Kong Institute of Asia-Pacific Studies, The Chinese University of Hong Kong, pp. 243–276.

Wong, W.H., E. Wong, Y. Wang, D. Mo and L. Leung (2016) 'Impact of Cabotage Relaxation and PRD Competition to Hong Kong Maritime Logistic Industry', *Report*, Department of Supply Chain and Information Management, Hang Seng Management College.

World Travel and Tourism Council (2014) 'Travel & Tourism. Economic Impact: Hong Kong', *World Travel and Tourism Council*, www.wttc.org/-/media/files/reports/economic%20impact%20research/country%20reports/hong_kong2014.pdf, accessed 20 September 2015.

Xiao, G. (2004) 'Round-Tripping Foreign Direct Investment and the People's Republic of China', *Asian Development Bank Institute*, Research Paper Series 58, www.adb.org/sites/default/files/publication/157240/adbi-rp58.pdf, accessed 15 November 2016.

Yim, S. (1995) 'Business Warns of High Costs Dangers', *South China Morning Post*, 28 November.

Yiu, E. and J. Hollingsworth (2016) 'Shenzhen-Hong Kong Stock Connect Strengthens City's "Super-connector" Role Says Chief Executive C.Y. Leung', *South China Morning Post*, 5 December, www.scmp.com/business/companies/article/2051733/were-underway-shenzhen-hong-kong-stock-connect-becomes-second, accessed 12 January 2017.

Zhang, K.H.L. (2005) 'Why Does So Much FDI from Hong Kong and Taiwan Go To Mainland China?' *China Economic Review*, 16: 293–307.

Zhang, Y. (2006) 'Hong Kong's Closer Economic Partnership with China', Briefing Series, 12, China Policy Institute, The University of Nottingham, www.nottingham.ac.uk/cpi/documents/briefings/briefing-12-hk-china-cepa.pdf, accessed 4 July 2015.

Zhao, S.X.B., Y.M. Chan and C.B Ramon-Berjano (2012) 'Industrial Structural Changes in Hong Kong, China under One Country, Two Systems Framework', *Chinese Geographical Science*, 22(3): 302–318.

3 China and globalization forces in the rise of inequality and the prospects for the educated youth

The first two chapters demonstrated that Hong Kong's role in the world and China's economy has been shifting, but in a way that is imperfectly reflected in how it defined itself: Asia's World City. In any case, the shift has brought a sense of uncertainty to many Hongkongers. The 'four pillars' of the economy are and will remain the largest share of Hong Kong's GDP, but, for various reasons, they have exhibited a certain fragility in recent years. The alignment of the HK$ with the US$ has also generated unexpected distortions in Hong Kong's tourism industry (and housing market, as will be seen below). In reaction, Hongkongers' support for its capitalist system (which is engraved in the Basic Law, see Chapter 1) has weakened, especially among the youth and/or better-educated people (as described in Chapter 2).

However, it is unlikely that Hong Kong's changing position in the world and China's economies and the fluctuations of the four pillars' share in its GDP *alone* suffice to explain these changes. They are more the signs of other imbalances generated by both globalization and governmental policies than the culprits of existing problems. After all, from 2000 to 2014, the GDP grew in real terms (2013 value) by a staggering 67.9 per cent, despite repeated economic crises;[1] and the unemployment rate has decreased from 8.4 per cent in 2003 to 3.2 per cent in 2015 (with another 1.4 per cent representing people who were underemployed).[2] Thus, the 'spleen' of the youth comes, for a part, from the fact that the fruits of this growth have not been shared equally, while opportunities have declined for them, especially in terms of employment and lodging; the educated youth also understand quite well that social mobility has greatly reduced in recent years, and their chance to get a high salary or a top job is much lower than the one of their elders. These factors are common knowledge (especially with regard to access to private property) for Hongkongers, even if they are not always substantiated by hard data. But they need to be examined in the context of globalization since Hong Kong is not the only metropolis in the world to experience factors such as growing inequality and declining opportunities.

This chapter will document these features. It will show that factors such as inequality, declining opportunities and salary stagnation for the (better-educated) youth and middle class were, in part, generated by globalization forces and, in another part, reinforced by migrations from Mainland China as well as by the 'non-intervention' bias of Hong Kong's pro-business government. Despite the premium granted to degree holders, salaries for fresh graduates have stagnated over most of the last 20 years and, in any case, have not kept pace with GDP growth or property price increases. Thus, while the better-educated members of the previous generation could expect to climb the social ladder, the younger generation today often feels trapped with few solutions: a degree is more than ever required to access most good jobs, but it is no longer a guarantee. Education by itself cannot significantly curb inequality in Hong Kong, which is rising to an unbearable level. This imbalance has been reinforced by housing costs, which have increased much faster than salaries and are out of reach for most of the middle class. While there are multiple reasons for the high cost of housing in Hong Kong, the oligopolistic nature of its property market and the effect of property speculation have certainly pushed prices up – and encouraged the creation of oligopolies in other markets. The peg and the international economic environment have also factored into this situation. These last issues – namely, the housing market and, more generally, Hong Kong's domestic economy – will be analysed in the next chapter of this book.

Documenting Hong Kong's inequality

The rise of inequality in Hong Kong in recent decades has become a hotly debated topic in academia, the media and the civil society. A sign of this new public interest in inequality is the number of times the expression, 'income inequality', was recorded in major Hong Kong newspapers: from 3,937 times during 1999 to 2003 to 9,789 times during 2004 to 2008.[3] Hong Kong's rising Gini coefficient (based on household incomes) provides a good explanation for this: at 0.537 in 2011 (the latest available data), it is one of the highest in the world[4] and has steadily increased from 0.420 in 1976 and 0.525 in 2001. The consequences of this trend in terms of policymaking remain unclear, as the whole debate over the income gap has been tainted with ideology. This section presents some of the main characteristics of inequality in Hong Kong and the next one will show what roles globalization and China have played in this increase.[5]

Table 3.1 complements the Gini coefficient index by providing data on the share of aggregate monthly income by decile. (As the focus of this chapter is to understand the economic reasons why Hong Kong's (better-educated) youth have taken to the streets, its 320,000 foreign domestic helpers (FDHs) have been excluded. This decision was also based on the fact that in addition to their salaries, domestic helpers are entitled to some advantages such as complimentary lodging, food, air tickets, etc., which make their economic situation harder to evaluate. However, if this section of Hong Kong's population were integrated into the analysis, it would make its measured inequality look even worse – and make the authors' argument stronger.[6])

It can be inferred from Table 3.1 that from 2001 to 2011 (the latest available data), the share of the median monthly household incomes of the lowest quintile

Table 3.1 Share of aggregate original monthly household income (excluding foreign domestic helpers) (%)

	2001	*2006*	*2011*
1st (lowest decile)	0.9	0.8	0.6
2nd	2.3	2.1	2.0
3rd	3.4	3.2	3.1
4th	4.5	4.3	4.3
5th	5.7	5.6	5.6
6th	7.0	7.0	7.0
7th	8.8	8.8	8.9
8th	11.1	11.3	11.5
9th	15.3	15.6	16.1
10th (highest)	41.1	41.4	41.0

Source: elaborated from the data published by the C&SD (2012a: 8), *Thematic Report. Household Distribution Income*.

and decile decreased from 3.2 per cent to 2.6 per cent and from 0.9 per cent to 0.6 per cent, respectively.[7] At the same time, the top 20 per cent of households saw their share of incomes increase from 56.4 to 57.1 per cent. The relative contraction of the percentage earned by the highest decile was probably due to the negative effect of the economic downturns of 2003 (SARS) and 2008 (world financial crisis) on non-salaried incomes (e.g. dividends, capital gains, etc.), which are usually higher for the wealthiest deciles. This hypothesis was partly confirmed by the data on monthly incomes from main employment. At constant (2011) prices, median monthly incomes from main employment *dropped* by about 10 per cent from 2001 to 2011 for the lowest decile (HK$3,940 in 2001, HK$3,480 in 2006 and HK$3,580 in 2011), but *jumped* by nearly 10 per cent for the highest one (HK$50,630 in 2001, HK$52,160 in 2006, and HK$55,000 in 2011).[8] In addition, it is likely that the incomes of the upper deciles were further biased downward, because part of them might not have been recorded in Hong Kong's statistics – an indication of which is the FDIs from and headed for tax havens such as the BVIs.[9] A 2014 study by Credit Suisse confirmed the escalating wealth of the upper decile and stated that the richest 10 per cent of Hong Kong's population owned as much as the 77.5 per cent of the poorest in 2013, which represent a sharp increase from 69.3 per cent in 2007 (Noble 2014).[10]

This trend is further confirmed by anecdotal evidence. *Forbes* indicated that the top 1 per cent is 'getting richer and richer'. To support its statement, the magazine noted that the number of US$ billionaires had mushroomed in recent years, reaching 45 in 2014 versus 25 in 2010 and 26 in 2008, just before the crisis (Chen 2014). Even though this comparison is not scientifically valid, *Forbes* also indicated that the cumulated wealth of these 45 billionaires is equivalent to 80 per cent of Hong Kong's GDP. In short, the official statistics probably underestimated the income of the highest decile(s).[11] In comparison, the 'middle class', loosely defined in this section as the fourth to seventh deciles in Table 3.1,[12] saw its share decline slightly from 17.2 per cent in 2001 to 16.9 per cent in both 2006 and 2011 – the two lower deciles being more affected than the upper ones.

Thus, these data clearly confirmed Hong Kong's rising inequality. To be more precise, however, the authors acknowledge that part of this measured increase in inequality was due to a statistical illusion because of the changing composition of households in recent years – for example, more low-income people (e.g. elderly and young adults) are living alone, which impacts any measurement of inequality.[13] Nevertheless, Hong Kong's growing inequality is an indisputable fact: when the 'monthly income from [one's] main employment' *alone* is taken into account (which eliminates households' size effect, but also poor and single elderly households without work *and* non-employment incomes), the Gini coefficient still rose significantly from 0.488 in 2001 to 0.50 in 2006 and again to 0.509 in 2011.

Finally, it should be noted that governmental transfers have moderately alleviated Hong Kong's inequality and the Gini coefficient was 'only' 0.47 in 2001 and 0.475 in 2006 and 2011 after taxes and social transfers are taken into account. However, governmental transfers are only an *ex post* correction that merely address the symptoms of inequality, but not its causes. An 'educational kit' on inequality written for high school students by the Education Bureau acknowledged this role of redistribution in smoothing over, *ex post*, the negative effects of inequality and easing social relations. Thus, they may mitigate social protests, but would not alter the systemic imbalance:

> Redistribution helps to lift poverty and inequality and thereby promotes harmony and stability. *It also works well for the rich, because it mitigates economic inefficiencies* that often come with a large income gap.
>
> (Education Bureau 2015: 33; emphasis added)

In this way, the authors can only agree with Richard Wong Yue-chim, who argued that 'redistribution will not halt the underlying forces that are driving the income distribution to become more unequal over time' (Wong 2015a), even though it provides relief to families in need.[14] The next section will elaborate on some of these forces.

Inequality, globalization and the China factor – an interpretation

The rise of inequality is not exclusive to Hong Kong; it has been recorded in all developed countries (Piketty 2013) and, when data are available, even more in the so-called 'global cities' (Mok 2015: 122). For some specialists on this issue, it is part of a more global phenomenon that they term 'social polarization' (Castells 2000; Sassen 2000; for a discussion on Hong Kong, see Chiu and Lui 2004; Lee, Wong and Law 2007; and below). For these scholars, the new economy is articulated around global informational networks, in which global cities play the role of coordinators. The effect has been the concentration of wealth and power in these cities, but also social polarization. The latter is also seen as a major cause of the mass protests and 'occupy movements' that erupted in many of these global cities – most notably 'Occupy Wall Street' in New York – and were directed against social and economic inequality. This link between inequality and mass protests in global cities is even acknowledged in the tool kit of the Education Bureau:

> Protests such as Occupy Wall Street in 2011 were triggered by income inequality. The popular slogan 'We are the 99%' referred to the disparity between the richest 1% and the other 99%.
>
> (Education Bureau 2015, note 20)

The question, then, is to explain why similar events pushed by similar situations appeared simultaneously in several global cities and if (and eventually how) globalization has exacerbated inequality.

Since it was first formulated, the pertinence of the polarization thesis, whether it is expressed in terms of income or occupational polarization (the two are strongly related) has been highly debated in Hong Kong and beyond. However, the purpose of this section is not to verify the overall validity of the theory (as will be seen, whether or not Hong Kong conforms to the polarization theory is a question of interpretation),[15] but to see which of its elements can explain the link between globalization, the increase in inequality, and, in a second step, the plight of Hong Kong's younger generation. The statistics showed not only a growing gap between the higher and lower income groups, but also a modification of the labour market with the rapid growth of middle-range incomes and occupations – a phenomenon that even the tenet of the polarization theory now acknowledges. A document from the 'Commission on Strategic Development Committee on Social Development and Quality of Life' (2006) clearly linked the two dimensions of inequality and the evolution of the labour market in the context of globalization and helped launch the discussion:

> International researches suggest that world cities such as London and New York are experiencing a widening income inequality. As Hong Kong is progressively moving away from an industrial production-based economy towards a producer service-driven world city (…), the experience of other world cities would be relevant (…).
>
> The emergence of world cities entails a major cluster of high level business services (…). In performing such transnational function, those world cities employ a large number of professionals and transnational elites supported by ancillary staff. (…) The employment tends to cluster at the bottom ends of the occupational and income distribution at the expense of the middle-ranking workers. (…)
>
> The income disparity and inequality experienced in other world cities also happen in Hong Kong.
>
> (Commission on Strategic Development 2006: 2–4)

The provocative headings of an article by Pascal Petit perfectly summarized the issue: 'Are Your Wages Set in Beijing? Downward Pressure on Wages of Low-Skilled Workers' and 'Are Your Wages Set in New York? Upward Pressure on Wage Formation of High-skilled, White-collar Workers' (Petit 2010: 256). Building on Freeman (1995), Petit explained that in the context of globalization, low incomes in developing countries (such as China) squeeze the wages of lower-skilled workers located in more developed regions such as Hong Kong. This effect is amplified by the development of information technology, which 'plays a role in facilitating both a new segmentation between high-skill[ed] and low-skill[ed] tasks, as well as a relocation of jobs' (Petit 2010: 256). On the other hand, Petit rightly pointed out that governance based on shareholder value among larger international firms has pushed the incomes of executives and, by diffusion, other top managers upward. The result is greater inequality, which, according to some authors, can become unbearable under certain conditions (Piketty 2013; Stiglitz 2015).

In Hong Kong, the strong presence of multi-national corporate regional headquarters (1,389 in 2014[16]) and regional offices (2,395 in 2014[17]) certainly favours this upward trend with a growing demand for high-level managers and well-qualified staff. Besides the direct import of specialists and highly qualified people (usually 'expats'), this demand has been fulfilled by expanding the size of university enrolments, so the 'Hong Kong education system has been transformed from an elite-oriented system to a mass-oriented one' (Zhao and Zhang 2005: 94). But, as will be shown below, the 'massification' of higher education has led to some unexpected consequences – notably the development of an intermediate category of workers ('associate professionals') who may not be able to become managers due to possible crowding.

At the other end of the spectrum, there are also reasons for the incomes of unskilled workers to be under downward pressure. The first is the existence of higher unemployment rates for lower-skilled workers (in comparison to skilled labour), especially during economic downturns. In February–April 2016, 'the unemployment rate of clerical workers, service and ship sale workers and craft workers [reached] (…) 3.3 percent, 4.9 percent and 5.0 percent respectively, while that for managers and professionals edged up to only 1.5–1.7 percent' (LegCo Research Office 2016: 3).

Another reason for this may be due to expanded trade between China and Hong Kong (part of the globalization process), as well as migration patterns. Despite diverging estimates, econometric studies tend to confirm this statement. In their 2003 study, Ho, Wei and Wong showed that by the end of the 1990s, there was 'a significant positive association between the volume of outward processing trade and the wage premium of university graduate over primary school graduates, and university graduates over secondary school graduates'. In addition, their 'econometric analysis show[ed] that it is the increased outward processing trade that cause[d] the widening of [the] skill wage gap, not vice versa' (Ho *et al.* 2003). However, their study did not continue into the twenty-first century, so it is difficult to know if this trend has been sustained in a similar fashion during this period (when most industrial activities had already been relocated to the Mainland). It is likely that, in recent years, the re-localization of some services to China has had some effect on the salaries of lower-skilled workers in Hong Kong (like elsewhere), but it is difficult to confirm this notion because of an absence of data. In other words, this study only confirms the widening gap between university graduates and other workers with less formal education before 2000, but not that the salaries of unskilled staff have been on a downward trend.[18] To gain more insight into this issue, one should examine Hong Kong's immigration policies and their effects.

A relaxation of Hong Kong's immigration policy in 1993 allowed Mainland Chinese with close family ties in Hong Kong to settle in the SAR (the 'one-way permit' policy). The quota amounted to 105 people a day – later increased to 150. These immigrants are, on average, less educated and possess fewer skills than the general Hong Kong population, so they directly compete with locals with similar credentials for low-income jobs. If they were not from neighbouring Guangdong, their lack of Cantonese language could also hurt their job prospects (Lee *et al.* 2007: 12), never mind their salaries (Law and Lee 2006; Tang and Wong 2011). In 2011, the median income for a new migrant from the Mainland was HK$7,500, while it was HK$12,000 for the whole population. Even though the situation slightly improved in recent years – the proportion of Mainlanders who settled in Hong Kong through the 'one-way permit' and owned a university or post-secondary school education has increased from 5 per cent in 1995 to 21.6 per cent in 2016[19] –, the gap between the two groups remains significant.[20] This finding perfectly matches the analyses of Pascal Petit, but in Hong Kong, the effects of globalization have been more obvious due to the geographical proximity between the Territory and China and because the two economies are increasingly intertwined: as stated earlier, in Hong Kong, it is difficult to strictly separate the effects of globalization from those generated by the Chinese economy.

In addition, even the recent introduction of a minimum wage does not seem to affect deeply this evolution of salaries at both ends of the ladder. The Minimum Wage Ordinance, which was voted by the LegCo in 2010 after lengthy debates and the opposition of liberal economists and many business people (Matthew Wong 2014), became finally effective in 2011. The floor rate was set at HK$28 per hour, and was to be revised every two years. Consequently, it increased progressively to HK$32.5 per hour (and it should reach HK$34.5 on 1 May 2017). If, at the beginning, the introduction of a statutory minimum salary had boosted lower revenues, the medium or long-term impact of this policy remains questionable, because the regular nominal increases have been eaten up by inflation, as shown in a recent OXFAM report:

> Under the current biannual review system, the increase in minimum wage has continued to lag behind the rate of inflation. When the Minimum Wage Commission suggested the first minimum wage level of $28/hour in October 2010, the Composite CPI [Consumer Price Index] was 82.9 (using 2014/15

as the base year); in August 2016, the Composite CPI rose 24% to 102.8. With this inflation rate, the actual purchasing power of the current minimum wage level ($32.5/hour) is only equivalent to $26 in October 2010, which is even lower than the original minimum wage level.

(OXFAM 2016: 13)

However, if the abovementioned studies confirmed the role of globalization and China in widening the income gap (as well as inequality), they did not fully demonstrate the validity of the polarization theory in its narrowest definition because globalization did not preclude the development of an intermediate category of workers. As stated by Lee *et al.* (2007), the creation of high-quality services not only requires well-trained managers and highly specialized people, but also supporting staff – the so-called 'associate professionals' in the official statistics. From 2001 to 2011, the number of 'associate professionals' increased by nearly 40 per cent from about 500,000 to 695,000, while their share of the total number of employed workers rose from 15.4 per cent to 19.6 per cent – an even higher share than 'elementary occupations' (19.5 per cent[21]) and 'services and sales' (16.2 per cent – down from 17.4 per cent in 2006, despite the rise in tourism).[22]

In terms of salary, 'associate professionals' perfectly fill this intermediate category: their median monthly income (HK$18,000 in 2011) was exactly half that of 'managers and administrators',[23] 50 per cent higher than the overall median monthly income (HK$12,000), and double that of 'services and sales' staff. In other words, Hong Kong is assisting with the rapid transformation of its 'middle class',[24] which has become better educated, with many having a tertiary level education (degree or sub-degree[25] – see below), and this is true whether it is in terms of relative income or job category. Thus, the polarization theory can be understood in different ways, depending on how the statistical categories are constructed. For Chiu and Lui (2004), the theory still holds because they grouped 'professionals' and 'associate professionals' in the same category. But for Lee, Wong and Law (2007), this operation was dubious because of the income gap between the two groups. On the contrary, they argued that a 'new middle class' had been created:

> Chui and Lui (2004) note that 'social polarisation is clearly observable in Hong Kong through the changes in occupational structure'. (…) There is a dramatic growth of elementary occupations in terms of absolute numbers. The number of managers, professionals, and associate professionals are also increasing substantially. (…) Despite their findings, we contend whether associate professionals can be classified into the same rank as top professionals and administrators. According to the Hong Kong Census and Statistics Department, the associate professional level comprises a wide range of occupation categories including technicians, supervisors, survey interviewers (…), Chinese medicine practitioners, nurses, and the like.
>
> (Lee *et al.* 2007: 5–6)

This question is clearly related to the definition of the middle class and to the construction of statistical categories (see note 12, this chapter): the element of subjectivity, which is involved in building classes, affects a comprehension of the polarization phenomenon. Beyond the two diametrically divergent opinions that were introduced above, the authors propose a middle ground perspective based on two observations. First, the evolution of the occupation pattern draws a new line between, on one hand, people with low education levels (including many new Mainland migrants to Hong Kong) and, on the other hand, those in the population with university qualifications. At the same time (and this is the second observation), it draws another line between the managerial/professional category and the growing number of 'associate professionals': education is only part of their story and the likelihood of the theory of polarization to be accepted, in its strictest sense, ultimately depends on the amount of social mobility between 'associate professionals' and 'professionals'. This book cannot answer this question, but some of its elements that will be explored further in the section titled 'The push for higher education and the evolution of incomes' (when the evolution of tertiary graduates' incomes will be presented), inclined the authors to answer negatively.

Even before that step, it can already be hypothesized that, boosted by the expansion of tertiary education, Hong Kong may well witness the creation of a 'new middle class', as Lee, Wong and Law claimed. Nonetheless, even if one conforms with the newest version of the polarization theory and reject its original idea of the decline of the middle class, it must be noted that statistics still show a growing gap between the lower and upper ends of the spectrum (see Table 3.1): on the one hand, the lower deciles generally have lower qualifications and are, hence, trapped with low prospects of social mobility; on the other hand, it has become indispensable, if not always sufficient (and, as will be seen, increasingly insufficient), to gain a university degree to reach the 'professional' ranks (see the section titled ''The push for higher education and the evolution of incomes'). The authors propose that this situation be termed a 'truncated social polarization', in which the development of higher education has played a pivotal role.

In summary, if the increased demand for 'managers and administrators', 'professionals' and 'associate professionals' in the context of globalization has boosted the demand for higher education, the category of workers that has increased the most has been 'associate professionals'. However, the higher demand for 'associate professionals' in itself does not guarantee that they have benefited in terms of salary and social mobility – they may be better off than people with lower levels of qualification, but have still experienced stagnated compensation. This needs to be assessed precisely, especially since a university education entails significant costs for the average student and his/her family, who expect rewards in the form of a good income and living standards (consumption, housing, etc.) – in the short and middle run. To address this concern, economists often calculate the income premium between university and high school graduates, but most students generally rely on cruder tools such as comparing the salaries they could obtain after graduation to those they could get without attending university. In the absence of official published statistics for fresh graduates' incomes, they resort to their personal experiences or information they could gather in the media to answer this question.

Thus, the next section aims to address two issues. First, it analyses the income evolution for fresh graduates based on the available data. The conclusion is that fresh graduates' incomes have not progressed since the end of the 1990s while their prospects of social mobility are reduced. Second, it tries to provide some explanations for this evolution – possible answers being that the increase in the number of graduates led to a decline in their overall quality and/or has generated a crowding effect (i.e. the presence of too many graduates on the job market). Differently stated, the next section will try to show what was emphasized above: it is becoming increasingly necessary to have a university degree, but this is far from sufficient to secure a better life.

The push for higher education and the evolution of incomes

The development of higher education is currently a hot topic and seen by some as the miracle remedy to cure inequality. As stated earlier, Richard Wong noted that 'rising inequality can only be prevented by expanding education opportunities (...)'[26] (Wong 2015a; see also, Wong 2013, Chapter 16). This section will examine the evolution of fresh graduates' income as well as their perspectives for social mobility.

In dealing with the graduates' incomes, economists have usually resorted to measuring the income premium between workers with a university qualification and other categories of staff. This indicator is certainly important for formulating policies and should not be discarded. However, such a measurement suffers from two weaknesses. On the one hand, there are several ways to calculate the 'premium' and the results are divergent and highly dependent on the method of calculation. On the other hand, there are also ambiguities regarding the interpretations of the findings, which leads to different policy prescriptions: even a premium increase over time can signify two different things with opposed consequences. First, it may correspond to a relative scarcity of highly qualified people, which would boost salaries for degree holders; but it could also correspond to a reduced demand for poorly qualified staff. Under this second scenario, the premium may be higher, even if the incomes of degree holders stagnate, which eventually signifies the advent of a 'crowding effect'. In short, a university degree is then required to get a job, but perhaps not sufficient to get one that pays well. As it can be inferred from the above, these two interpretations have different consequences in terms of policymaking. The works of Richard Wong (2006, 2013) and Lui Hong-Kwong (2013) are representative of these two diverging interpretations; both scholars acknowledged that the premium for degree holders has grown significantly since 2006, but they drew different conclusions from this fact.[27]

To start with, Wong suggested 'expand[ing] education to meet demand for skilled workers' (Wong 2013: 161). To support this conclusion, he indicated that the net annual percentage increase in Hongkongers with a degree was at its lowest from 2006 to 2011 (+3.1 per cent, compared to +4.1 per cent from 2001 to 2006; Wong, 2014: 162, Table 16.3), which showed a 'slowdown in the scale of tertiary education' (ibid.: 163). However, this slowed growth in the number of graduates is insufficient, in itself, to prove that Hong Kong needs to train more graduates. Therefore, the link between the statistical evidence and the stated conclusion is rather weak.

Similarly, other scholars like Liu Pak-Wai and his colleagues (who, like Wong, are close to the Hong Kong government), advocated to boost human capital and thus to resort to immigration policies to attract qualified individuals and students from the Mainland. However, while they base their analysis on medium to long-term demographic perspective (in particular, the aging population), they fail to take into account the current situation of the job market, and especially to the current demand of qualified people (see below).[28]

In fact, it is not obvious that Hong Kong has, or will have, a shortage of qualified personnel. This can be seen from two factors. The first is the number of graduates in Hong Kong in comparison to other developed economies, while the second is provided by the situation of supply and demand in the job market. The first factor can be estimated through a widely used comparison between the percentage of the population with a tertiary level education in different places and at different times. The proportion of Hong Kong's population with a university degree has increased steadily since the beginning of the 1990s from 11.3 per cent in 1991 to 23 per cent in 2006 and 27.3 per cent in 2011. This includes 18 per cent and 7.3 per cent of degree (Bachelor's degree) and sub-degree or higher diploma holders, respectively (LegCo Research Office 2015b: 4; Lui 2013: 55). Furthermore, the share of Hong Kong's 25–34 age group that held a degree in 2011 was 48.4 per cent (C&SD 2012b: 89–93), which was higher than the corresponding OECD rate of 38.09 per cent in 2011 and 40.53 per cent in 2013 (OECD 2015). The only Asian countries with a greater percentage of their populations in the same age group with degrees during that time were Japan and Korea (58.72 and 63.82 per cent, respectively). In short, these statistics do not show that Hong Kong has too few people with university training – a statement that is confirmed by the situation in the labour market.

This last point is assessed by Lui, who approached the problem not from the supply side, as Wong did, but from the demand side. For Lui, the

> question (…) is whether the market is able to provide enough vacancies to accommodate the supply of workers with higher education. (…) Comparatively speaking, the financing, insurance, real estate and business services tend to recruit more university graduates than other industries. (…) The magnitude of increase [in qualified employment] is much lower than that of the increase in the supply of workers with tertiary education. It is doubtful that this is enough to absorb all the graduate workers.
>
> (Lui 2013: 55)

Even though the arguments elaborated in the citation are not fully conclusive, they are still a sign that the number of degree holders has outpaced the demand for their qualifications. This was further confirmed by a recent study by LegCo's Research Office, which indicated that from 1994 to 2015, the number of additional workers with degrees – '*excluding* sub-degree and non-degree qualifications in post-secondary education' – increased by 854,000, while at the same time, the number of higher-skilled jobs – *including* Associate Professionals – had only increased by 666,000 (LegCo Research Office 2016: 8; emphases added). In other words, the market was unable to provide jobs that suited the qualifications of nearly 200,000 people.[29] As the authors will demonstrate below, the slow rise of salaries for fresh graduates in recent years suggests, in accordance with the above data and Lui's interpretation (and against Richard Wong's analysis), may indicate an oversupply of qualified staff, as well as other imbalances in the job market.

The inconclusiveness regarding the consequences of the premium increase justifies analysing the question from a different angle. For students (and their parents), the issue of the premium is of marginal interest – they don't need to know by how much the premium has fluctuated to realize that they have to invest in higher education. What they are more interested in are their (expected) incomes after graduation, their possible trajectories, and the pay gap between a job with and without a degree or a sub-degree. This method of calculation is cruder, but also more straightforward and closer to an observation made by Richard Wong:

> One factor cited as evidence of rising inequality is the survey finding that fresh university graduates are not paid much more than HK$10,000. Since a person working 48 hours a week and paid the minimum wage of HK$32.50 an hour can make more than HK$6,760 a month, this would suggest that the investment in schooling and a university education might not substantially improve earnings.
>
> (Wong 2015a)[30]

The values used by most students, however, are probably different. It is unlikely that potential or current students used the minimum wage as their benchmark. Instead, they may look at incomes in the service and sales sector or even at clerical positions. In 2011, the median monthly income in the sales and services sector was around HK$9,000 and for clerical support workers HK$10,000 (C&SD 2012a: Table 2.10).[31] But, at the same time, the expected monthly salary for fresh university graduates was slightly higher than the data provided by Wong. According to unpublished official data from the C&SD, the 'median monthly employment earnings of people aged 20–24 who attained post-secondary education' were HK$10,800 in current value in 2014 (see Table 3.2).

The important point, however, is that students *cannot* base their reasoning on these latest data because they have *not* been publicly disclosed.[32] Therefore, students and their parents had to rely on estimates released by the media, which were often significantly higher than the official data. A good example came from a recent article in one of Hong Kong's most popular newspapers, the *Oriental Daily*. The newspaper, basing its story on an analysis carried out by the New Youth Forum and New Century Forum (which, by their own accounts, relied on data collected by the C&SD), stated that monthly salary starting point for local fresh graduates from top-level universities in 2013 was, on average, around HK$18,000 – about 20 per cent lower than in 1993. When the inflation is taken into account, this amount equates to only HK$10,860 (1993 chained prices), which is 17 per cent lower than what it was then (HK$13,158). The newspaper also reported that an increasing number of university graduates were working in low-skilled positions – which is confirmed by official data, as the author will show below. In 1993, over 18,000 graduates (about 9 per cent of that year's total) were in such a situation, whereas this figure climbed to over 130,000 by 2013 (about 14 per cent). Finally, the salary increases (if applicable) for these graduates were seen as unsatisfactory even after five years of work experience. The Class of 2008, for example, only enjoyed a 25 per cent rise by 2013, while their forebears from 1993 enjoyed a 45 per cent boost to their incomes by 1998 (*Oriental Daily* 2015).[33]

It is difficult to really know the accuracy of these data, which greatly varied in comparison to the official unpublished tables of the C&SD reproduced in Table 3.2. However, their legitimacy does not come from their accuracy, but from their publication in a major local newspaper. The fact that the government does not publish data on fresh graduates' incomes further enhances this legitimacy. But, at the same time, it also causes confusion, since other media publish their own data with sometimes lack consistency with one another, as the two following examples illustrate.

First, another element of this puzzle, the jobsDB website (a well-known online job listing and recruitment platform in Hong Kong and other Asian countries) conducted a survey of 124 Hong Kong corporations in 2013 and found an average monthly salary of HK$12,125 for fresh graduates and HK$9,204 for 'non-degree tertiary graduates or below' (jobsDB 2014). More interestingly, perhaps, the survey also indicated that for 62 per cent of newly hired staff, the proposed salary matched their original expectations, but it was lower for 31 per cent, while a lucky 7 per cent were offered more than they expected (ibid.). However, the results contradicted those from another survey conducted in Hong Kong and Singapore with a much larger sample of over 13,000 students. This one stated that in 2014, the expected monthly salary for a fresh graduate in Hong Kong was HK$17,314 for his/her first job (*Hong Kong Business* 2014). If the results of these two surveys could be confirmed, the mismatch between offered and expected salaries would have caused discontent among fresh graduates. In any case, the important point here is not the accuracy of the data, but, again, the self-reinforcing beliefs of the people whose opinions are both reflected in the media through the results of the surveys and then strengthened by them – even if the results diverge.

Negative feelings, however, are more likely to come from the slow salary increases over long periods of time than from this mismatch. Even though they likely do not have evidence, students and their families still have a clear picture of the slow salary growth. If people cannot always confirm their perceptions with hard data, in this case they were quite right: unpublished figures from the C&SD confirmed that fresh graduates' monthly salaries (or, more precisely, the salaries of people 'aged 20–24 with a post-secondary education') did not progress since 1997 (see Table 3.2).

Before discussing this table, the authors would like to complement it with the set of data they compiled from the 'Graduate Employment Survey' (hereafter, 'the Survey') that is carried out every year by the Hong Kong Polytechnic University (PolyU).[34] The Survey, despite its loopholes, is useful for several reasons. First, it directly provides figures of fresh graduates' incomes for up to six months after graduation. Second, it supplies 'thinner' information (e.g. it differentiates between degree and sub-degree holders, as well as between different specializations).[35] On the negative side, however, the available data did not cover the whole period since 1997, but only from 2004 to 2014. Second, they only provided the average, not median, incomes, which makes a direct comparison with the official data reported in Table 3.2 difficult.[36] Third, the figures were based on a 'self-completed questionnaire sent to each graduate',[37] which may indicate another bias: from punctual observation and discussions, it can be safely hypothesized that there is a tendency for students who find low-paid work to declare higher incomes and for those who are still without jobs to declare that they hold down well-paid ones, but it is obviously difficult to assess the extent of these embellishments. Despite these phenomena, it is likely that the trend recorded in these data should reflect reality and that the level of misreporting was quite similar from one year to another.[38] Finally, despite PolyU's middle rank among Hong Kong's seven publicly funded universities, fresh graduates' salaries are significantly higher than average – possibly due to its emphasis on technical fields and professional qualifications.[39] In 2014, the average monthly income

Table 3.2 Median monthly employment earnings of people aged 20–24 who attained post-secondary education, 1997–2014 (in HK$)

Year	*Median earnings*	*Year*	*Median earnings*
1997	11,000	2006	8,000
1998	11,000	2007	8,500
1999	10,000	2008	9,000
2000	10,000	2009	8,500
2001	10,000	2010	8,700
2002	8,500	2011	9,100
2003	8,000	2012	10,000
2004	7,500	2013	10,000
2005	8,000	2014	10,800

Source: unpublished data from the C&SD.

Note
Figures are rounded to the nearest hundred.

reached HK$16,434 for degree holders with lows of HK$12,960 and HK$12,980 for the Institute of Textile and the Department of Chinese and Bilingual Studies respectively and highs for the School of Optometry (HK$28,164) and the School of Nursing (HK$26,867).[40] With these caveats in mind, Table 3.3 provides the evolution of the average monthly income for fresh graduates (degree and sub-degree holders) from 2004 to 2014 and offers interesting complementary information with the official data of Table 3.2.

Despite their limitations, Tables 3.2 and 3.3 offered some interesting insights. On the positive side, Table 3.3 showed that, from 2003 to 2014 the average monthly income of fresh graduates increased slightly quicker than inflation. It also progressed more than the median monthly income of the overall workforce – which actually experienced a relative drop from HK$12,380 in 2001 to HK$11,590 in 2006 before increasing slightly to HK$12,000 in 2011 (in 2011 prices). On the negative side, however, Table 3.2 showed that in 2014, the median monthly income for fresh graduates remained basically unchanged since 1997 – while Hong Kong's GDP grew by over 74 per cent and the GDP per capita by about 53.5 per cent over the same period (in 2013 chained dollars). Similarly, from 2003 to 2013, GDP grew by 59.3 per cent and the GDP per capita by 45.6 per cent (C&SD, 2014b and c), but the incomes of degree holders only rose by 26.8 per cent and those for sub-degree holders by 23.2 per cent (Tables 3.2 and 3.3 give comparable results). Thus, even though the two series of data had slightly different periodicities, most of the income growth from 2003 to 2008 rather than being a real increase, simply made up for the income drops that happened during the economic crises of 1997 and 2003.[41] After 2008, salaries again experienced a sharp drop before another recovery allowed them to reach 2008 levels in 2013/2014 (adjusted for inflation, as shown in Table 3.3). The crisis also affected degree and sub-degree holders differently – the drop was immediate for the former, but delayed until 2011 for the latter (see Table 3.3).

It may, therefore, be useful to detail degree and sub-degree holders separately. For degree holders, the bulk of their income growth occurred between 2003 and 2008 (+31.9). After that, their incomes mostly stagnated. In real terms, their 2008 income levels have yet to be reached and even decreased again in 2014 (see Table 3.3). At the same time, Hong Kong's GDP increased by 35 per cent from 2003 to 2008 (slightly outpacing graduates' incomes) and by another 17 per cent from 2008 to 2014.

For sub-degree holders, the situation was different. Their incomes increased steadily until 2010 before dropping by 10 per cent in 2011 and recovering rather slowly since then.[42] However, the reasons for their recovery lag compared to degree holders are difficult to determine – in part because the sample was small, as many sub-degree graduates decided to further their studies to obtain Bachelor's degrees. The different evolutions of sub-degree and degree holders may well indicate a segmentation of the labour market with separated dynamics for sub-degree holders (mainly 'programmed' to become technical and support staff – part of the so-called 'associate professionals') and for Bachelor's degree holder who are supposedly destined to be future managers. The evolution of the wage

Table 3.3 Average income for fresh graduates from the Hong Kong Polytechnic University, 2004–2014

Year	*Average monthly salary (current price)*		*Increase (%)*		*Inflation rate (%)*	*Average monthly salary (in 2013 prices)*		*Annual increase (2013 prices)*	
	Bachelor's degree	*Sub-degree*[1]	*Bachelor's degree*	*Sub-degree*		*Bachelor's degree*	*Sub-degree*	*Bachelor's degree (%)*	*Sub-degree*
2003	9,644	10,421	–	–	–0.6	12,387	13,385	–	–
2004	10,108	10,278	4.81	–1.37	–0.4	13,035	13,254	5.2	–1.0
2005	11,133	10,712	10.14	4.22	1	14,214	13,677	9.0	3.2
2006	11,826	11,467	6.22	7.05	2	14,803	14,354	4.1	4.9
2007	12,881	12,152	8.92	5.97	2	15,808	14,913	6.8	3.9
2008	13,891	12,938	7.84	6.47	4.3	16,344	15,223	3.4	2.1
2009	12,791	13,587	–7.92	5.02	0.5	14,975	15,907	–8.4	4.5
2010	13,279	14,308	3.82	5.31	2.4	15,182	16,358	1.4	2.8
2011	14,498	13,437	9.18	-6.09	5.3	15,741	14,589	3.7	–10.8
2012	15,219	15,338	4.97	14.15	4.1	15,873	15,998	0.8	9.7
2013	16,148	16,487	6.10	7.49	4.3	16,148	16,487	1.7	3.1
2014	16,434	(12,643)[2]	1.77	NA[3]	4.4	15,711	NA[3]	–2.7	NA[3]

Sources: CAPS, 'Graduate Employment Survey', various years; C&SD, *Annual Report on Consumer Price Index*, various years, C&SD 2015a.

Notes

1 Although over 1,000 students graduate from a sub-degree programme every year, only 200 to 400 (depending on the year) started working full-time after graduation; a large proportion of them (over 70 per cent) decide to further their studies.

2 'The significant drop of the average salary of sub-degree graduates resulted from the phased-out HD [Higher Diploma] Nursing programme as their graduates were usually able to secure offers from medical/hospital sectors with relatively higher salary level' (CAPS 2015). Indeed, the average monthly salary in healthcare for sub-degree holders reached HK$27,062 in 2013. For example, if 'health services' were discarded for 2013, the average monthly salary for the remaining sub-degree holders would be around HK$13,150 (a decrease of over 25 per cent). In short, the average income for sub-degree holders would be 20 to 25 per cent lower (depending on the year), if health services were not included.

3 Health services was excluded for 2014.

difference between degree and sub-degree holders, nearly inexistent at the start of their careers, but figures to become progressively larger as time goes by, supports this perspective and denotes better career prospects for degree holders – which, in turn, also explains why many sub-degree holders choose to further their studies.[43]

Overall, these data confirmed the general perception that fresh graduates' salaries stagnated and, when they increased, it was at a much slower pace than GDP growth. This trend remained even after factoring in population growth: from 2003 to 2014, Hong Kong's GDP per capita grew by over 50 per cent in real terms – much faster than fresh graduates' incomes and the median monthly incomes of workers in general.[44] Therefore, these data showed that while the expansion of tertiary level education is certainly a means to reduce polarization and even necessary to curb inequality, it is not sufficient in itself to fulfil this objective.

The stagnation of incomes, when it accompanies rising inequality, points back to a similar issue of the existence of a premium for university graduates, but from a different perspective. The premium unambiguously suggested that education is becoming increasingly indispensable. But the fact that degree holders' incomes have progressed much more slowly than GDP and fresh graduates' salaries have stagnated since 1997 indicates that having a tertiary level education does not automatically allow one to take advantage of Hong Kong's economic growth. What remains to be seen, however, are the reasons why this is the case. There are obvious parameters related to globalization forces and the influence of China's economy, as examined above, and to the (oligopolistic) nature of the local economy (see Chapter 4), but other factors can be traced to the situation of the labour market.

If one sticks to the latest data only, the divergences between the relative stagnation of graduates' income and the growth of the GDP can be analysed from two different perspectives: an excess of demand (too many graduates for too few suitable jobs) or a decrease in quality (the two dimensions being not exclusive of each other) – what Lui Hon-Kwong and Suen Wing called a quantity or a quality effect (Lui and Suen 2005). 'If the crowding effect is the major cause [for the declining college premium], this means that the demand for college workers is rather inelastic so that the labour market cannot accommodate a large increase in supply of college workers without reducing their wage' (Lui and Suen 2005: 253). Then, it would mean that the policy advocated by Wong to increase the number of graduates should be taken with caution by the government (which it did, as the authors will show below). On the contrary, 'if declining quality is the major cause, then, the policy focus falls on how to improve the quality of higher education' (ibid.). The results of econometric study performed by Lui and Suen in 2005 are not definitive, but they suggested that 'the declining university earning premium is *probably* more the result of declining quality of university graduates than of a labour market crowding effect' (ibid.; authors' emphasis). However, as mentioned above, Lui's opinion seemed to have shifted since the publication of his article, as he later doubted that the labour market can 'absorb all the graduate workers' (Lui 2013: 55; also see above) – an opinion that was confirmed by the sound data of the LegCo Research Brief, which estimated a gap of 200,000 people between the increase in the number of higher-skilled jobs and that of degree holders from 1994 to 2015 (LegCo Research Office 2016: 8; see above).

Such evidence, which aligns with the thesis of the crowding effect, also explains why a significant number of graduates accepted jobs whose requirements and compensation were not commensurate with their qualifications. In more detail, as reported by another LegCo Research Brief,

> the percentage share of youths aged 15–29 with degree education taking up clerical jobs increased from 11.0% to 18.2% during 2000–2011. The corresponding share for service and sales jobs also exhibited an increasing trend from 5.1% in 2000 to 6.8% in 2011.[45]

In more recent years, the number further increased because 'during 2008–2015, as much as 26% of the additional workforce with degree education worked as clerks, service workers, or shop sales workers, more than twice the respective figure of 12% during 1994–2001' (LegCo Research Office 2016: 9). In parallel, 'during 2008–2015, managerial, administrative and professional occupations could absorb only 38% of additional workers with degree education, noticeably down from 47% during 1994–2001' (ibid.). But, even more worryingly, degree holders have found it increasingly difficult to find jobs as associate professionals: the 'rate of absorption' decreased from 38 per cent for 1994–2001 to only 33 per cent for 2008–2015 (ibid.).

This crowding effect may partly explain why 'the expansion of post-secondary education since the 2000s has been almost exclusively in the two-year sub-degree programmes provided by the self-financed sector'[46] (LegCo Research Office 2015b: 5) and not in the university-funded degree programmes. From the 2000–2001 to the 2009–2010 academic years, the number of full-time degree places increased by 3,580, while the corresponding number for full-time sub-degree places grew by 26,388 during the same period – including 24,084 self-financed places (ibid., Figure 4, p. 5). In other words, the development of tertiary level education was largely financed by the private sector (i.e. by students and their families), with little contribution by the government. But, as the authors showed earlier, sub-degree holders can *at best* expect to fill 'associate professional' positions, which usually do not offer good career prospects (which may explain why most sub-degree graduates look to further their education). They may even be clustered in technical occupations with little chance of climbing the social ladder. Thus, such a policy may somewhat limit the crowding effect, but it would also displace the burden of developing cultural capital in Hong Kong from the government to families, most of which are from the middle and working classes, as explained below.

Therefore, the crowding effect and the increase in the number of sub-degree places in Hong Kong's tertiary level institutions have added to the relative lack of social mobility. In recent years, the labour market has been characterized by an upsurge (which is about to end) in the number of 'associate professionals', as well as a stabilization of the number of managers and professionals in relative terms. Thus, the new entrants (will) have more difficulties reaching the managerial and professional ranks, which signals declining social mobility (LegCo Research Office 2015b: 6). Such a lack of opportunity hits the younger generations the hardest, but it is also a diffuse phenomenon in Hong Kong society:

> A study conducted by the University of Hong Kong ('the HKU study') also underscores the trend of limited opportunities for people moving up the earnings ladder in recent years. The HKU study first ranked local workers in accordance with the level of their earnings in 2003 and grouped them into five quintiles. They were then re-ranked and regrouped based on their updated earnings level five years later in 2008. According to the study,[47] a high percentage share of workers stayed in the same quintile of earnings ladder over the five-year period of 2003–2008 and the 10-year period of 1998–2008 (…). It also unveiled the phenomenon of 'being trapped at the bottom,' i.e. 54.1% of the workers in the lowest income quintile experienced no mobility along the earnings ladder after 10 years of work.
>
> (LegCo Research Office 2015b)

The above data pinpointed the risk of the poverty trap for those in the lowest quintile. In 2011, 'the university enrollment rate of youths living in rich families was 3.7 times higher than those living in poverty', while the probability of a male getting a degree was as high as 73.6 per cent if his father already had one (ibid.: 8). Similarly, according to the findings of a survey conducted by the Hong Kong Institute of Education, the difference between students who could access tertiary level education in 1991 was, more or less, the same for households under the poverty line and those in the top 10 per cent – 8 and 9.3 per cent, respectively, for degree programmes (Mok 2015: 129 and Table 2, p. 132). In 2011, however, the proportion changed to 13 per cent and 48.2 per cent, respectively. These figures clearly indicate that students from less affluent families are gradually losing out on access to degree programmes in Hong Kong. Even when they can access them, the programmes tend to be self-funded associate degrees:

> there is a steady trend indicating that these young people have to enrol in self-funded undergraduate programmes or sub-degree programmes. Hence, this group of young people from families with a lower socio-economic status has to pay more for private higher education, generating more debts (…) but not necessarily guaranteeing good job prospects.
>
> (Mok 2015: 129)

These data are hardly surprising and should be linked to the evolution of Hong Kong's economy and society: after waves of migrations into the city during the 1950s and 1960s, Hong Kong's population has now stabilized and become more educated, thus reducing the opportunity for social mobility. Finally, the Research

Brief confirmed what was stated earlier, that 'the above development may not commensurate with the aspirations of today's young generation, particularly better-off environment and higher education attainment have heightened their expectations for career and life' (LegCo Research Office 2015a: 7).

In conclusion, Hong Kong experiences the same difficulties as other global metropolises: growing inequality and (truncated) polarization effects that cannot be eliminated by new education policies alone. Opportunities have been reduced for its youth, especially when they come from poorer families, and this has been aggravated by competition from Mainland students, who have won some of the highly coveted university slots (notwithstanding a drop in applications from China for the 2015/2016 academic year[48]). This has added to local students' worries about their future. Also, the growth in the number of degree holders in Hong Kong, which was in response to the demands of globalization forces, seems to have generated a crowding effect in the city. Therefore, Hong Kong's youth, especially its better-educated ones, feel trapped in an environment they cannot control. Younger degree holders may still have more opportunities than their peers who have less formal education, but they have not benefited sufficiently from Hong Kong's substantial economic growth over the years. In other words, their salaries have not increased very much and in any case, have fallen behind the growth Hong Kong's GDP per capita – a clear indication that the gains from such growth have not been shared equally. Moreover, the younger generations face rising costs in housing, groceries, etc., but have few or no assets of their own with which to face the uncertainty.

The last chapter of this book will detail this perspective by examining Hong Kong's housing market. Despite the rhetoric that Hong Kong is a free market, the reality is that it is characterized by an uncompetitive environment dominated by oligopolies that generate rents. In Hong Kong, more than anywhere else, there is a contradiction between the logic of capitalism, with centripetal forces that favour concentration, and the rationale of the 'free market', which implies a plurality of buyers and sellers. Unlike other developed economies, Hong Kong's paradox cannot be eased by a competition law, which was only implemented in December 2015 after over 20 years of intense discussion.

Notes

1 See C&SD, 'National Income', The Hong Kong SAR Government, www.censtatd.gov.hk/hkstat/sub/sp250.jsp?tableID=036&ID=0&productType=8 (accessed on 9 June 2015).

2 See C&SD, 'Labour', www.censtatd.gov.hk/hkstat/sub/so30.jsp, and 'Hong Kong Annual Digest of Statistics', The Hong Kong SAR Government, www.statistics.gov.hk/pub/B10100032014AN14B0100.pdf, both accessed on 14 August 2015.

3 Data calculated from the WiseNews database by Tang and Wong (2011: 5).

4 International comparisons provided by the C&SD showed that the Gini coefficient based on original household income was higher in Hong Kong than in other developed economies such as Great Britain (0.52), Singapore (0.482) and the United States (0.469). Furthermore, it remains very high (0.475) after taxes and social transfer payments are factored in. See C&SD (2012a: 137, 139), and below.

5 The authors will not discuss the (theoretical) links between economic growth and inequality in-depth here, as any discussion has been beset by numerous controversies since the original work of Simon Kuznets. For recent works regarding this issue, see Piketty (2013) and Stiglitz (2015). For how such controversies have affected Hong Kong, see Zhao and Zhang (2005); Richard Wong (2013, Chapter 16); Tang and Wong (2011); Lui (2013), among others.

6 Most specialists include Foreign Domestic Helpers (FDHs) in their analyses to document, in particular, the 'polarization thesis' (see below). However, since they generally take into account basic incomes, as they reported in the statistical tables, their calculations are slightly biased (without modifying the main conclusions): by law, households that hire FDHs have to provide decent lodging, which also means FDHs cannot rent their own places.

7 This discounts redistribution, which, if taken into account, would show that the lowest quintile's share decreased slightly from 4.6 per cent (2001) to 4.5 per cent (2011).

8 See C&SD (2012b) www.census2011.gov.hk/en/main-table/C129.html.

9 Following the Panama Paper scandal, three economists have shown that tax evasion is usually higher for upper revenues than from lower ones. This also applies to countries in which tax compliance is considered high (like Hong Kong). Furthermore, for the three authors, 'taking tax evasion into account increases the rise in inequality seen in the tax data since the 1970s markedly' (Alstadsaeter *et al.* 2017: 1). They also noted that 'the probability to hide wealth offshore rises very steeply for within the top one percent' (ibid.: 25). Even though the study only concerns three Nordic countries, the result remains suggestive for Hong Kong, where financial flows from/into other tax havens are so high.

10 Data on income and wealth should be seen as complementary, but distinctive of each other. Wealth can vary independently of income, following, for example, fluctuations in the stock market.

11 The C&SD did not provide data on wealth, which is difficult to establish, but it is likely that the Gini coefficient would be even larger if wealth, instead of income, were taken into account.

12 This quantitative definition gives a general idea in this section only, as it would be quite subjective to define the 'middle class' by only taking into account the income factor. In addition, if this definition were adopted more generally, it would then be impossible, by construction, to determine if the middle class is really shrinking, which is an important element, although contested, of the polarization theory, as the authors will detail below. In other words, this definition has the inconvenience of invariably and artificially fixing the size of the middle class at 40 per cent of the population (although this inconvenience can be partly compensated for by analysing the evolution of the composition and dynamics of this 40 per cent), but this categorization has the advantage of providing a quantitative benchmark that facilitates temporal comparisons and is easy to comprehend – and this is why it has been also been adopted by Piketty, in his recent book on inequality (Piketty 2013).

While defining the middle class is not the focus of this chapter, it should be noted that any definition is controversial. For example, the one provided by Lui Tai-Lok, a specialist in Hong Kong's middle class (2014a, 2014b, 2011), also suffers from inherent weaknesses because he regarded the middle class as the total of the 'upper service class' and the 'lower service class' (i.e. for the most part, the sum of managers, administrators, professionals, and associate professionals). In 2006, this represented 20.9 per cent of Hong Kong's working population. The remaining 79.1 per cent were classified as the 'intermediate class' (which included 'routine non-manual employees', 'small employers' 'petty bourgeoisie' and 'technicians and supervisors') or 'working class' (i.e. manual workers') (Lui 2014a: 39–42 and Table 3.3, p. 41). This typology can be challenged on the grounds that it grouped together people with very different positions in the social hierarchy (such as nurses and surgeons), while the lower classes (nearly four out of five Hong Kong residents) were disproportionately represented in this classification. In addition, according to Lui himself, his typology borrowed from British studies such as those conducted by Goldthorpe, who derived 'class positions from social relations in economic life or, more specifically, from employment relations' (Goldthorpe and McKnight 2004). Goldthorpe's analysis, therefore, was restrictive and better suited for analysing labour relations, even if it also ignored individuals who were not salaried workers. More significantly, Goldthorpe *did not use the expression, 'middle class'* – at least in the most recent representations of his 'social classes schema' (see Goldthorpe and McKnight 2004).

In short, Lui's classification was not more objective than ours and can equally be challenged. Thus, the definition that should be adopted depends on the type of analysis to be performed and any definition of the middle class is *always* subjective. The differentiation established by this author between 'a subjective [class] identification' (done by the people themselves) and 'an objective class position' elaborated on by researchers (which signifies that Lui (2014b: 97) denied that everyone should have 'a correct understanding of one's class position') seems highly artificial. It should also be added that most scholars who rely on this kind of 'subjective categorization' prefer to use the expression 'social status' rather than social class. See for example, the 'McArthur Scale of Social Status' of the University of California, San Francisco (Adler and Stewart 2007).

To this 'mechanical' mode of classification based on a typology of employment positions, another tradition relies more on class conflict and social relations. If one sticks to Bourdieu's framework (1984, 1994), in which researchers can construct social classes more or less 'objectively', then these classes exist only *on paper*. Their real existence only starts with social action (or, at least, with class consciousness), which greatly erases Lui's theoretical difference between a 'subjective identification' and an 'objective class position'. More generally, it was shown long ago that the measurement of categories depends on the elaboration of classes of equivalence (the definition of classes in the statistical sense of the term) and encoding. Thus, the measurement depends on conventions, but, at the same time, needs to reflect reality. This antinomy is resolved, according to Desrosières, by 'replacing the question of objectivity with that of objectification' (Desrosières 1998: 12).

13 At the same time, sky-high housing prices on the private market and the long waiting list for public housing have forced some young adults to live with their parents for much longer than they like (for more on this point, see Chapter 4).

14 But the authors cannot agree with Wong's proposed solution: 'Rising inequality can only be prevented by expanding education opportunities and encouraging couples to stay together' (ibid.). Richard Wong is Professor of Economics at the University of Hong Kong and was a doctoral student of Gary Becker at the University of Chicago. His words swing some weight (especially when they are published in major local newspapers) because he is also a close advisor to the Hong Kong Government and a member of numerous advisory boards. A proponent of neo-classical economics, he is famous for opposing the introduction of a minimum wage, as the title of his article in his blog unmistakably stated: 'Why the Minimum Wage Harms the Economy' (Wong 2006).

15 For contradictory arguments regarding the pertinence of the theory to Hong Kong, please refer to Chiu and Lui (2004) and Lee *et al.* (2007).

16 See the C&SD (2015b), www.censtatd.gov.hk/hkstat/sub/sp360.jsp?tableID=133&ID=0&productType= 8.

17 See the C&SD (2015c), www.censtatd.gov.hk/hkstat/sub/sp360.jsp?tableID=134&ID=0&productType=8.

18 On the issue of university graduates' salaries, see below.

19 And 14.3 per cent in 2012 and 20.1 per cent in 2014 (Home Affairs Department, 2017). Since 2014, the rate fluctuated but oscillated around 20 per cent. This is significantly

lower than the overall Hong Kong population (27.3 per cent of the population had a university qualification in 2011), and much less than the share of the Hong Kong's 25–35 age group (48.4 per cent had a university degree in 2011). The sources and details regarding these data will be provided in Section 3.3.

20 The new migrants are officially defined in the statistics as 'persons from the mainland having resided in Hong Kong for less than 7 years (PMRs)' (C&SD 2012a: 2). The median monthly income of a PMR was HK$6,000 in 2001 and 2006, while it was HK$11,000 and HK$10,000, respectively, for the whole population (C&SD 2012c: 14). See more on this point below.

21 This includes domestic helpers. If domestic helpers are excluded, elementary occupation workers comprised only 12.3 per cent. From 2001 to 2011, the expansion of their ranks by over 55,000 was only due to an increase in the number of domestic helpers, who, when subtracted, would result in this category *losing* about 18,000 people. This is another way – very straightforward – to link globalization and inequality.

22 C&SD (2012a), op. cit.: 35 and Table 2.10. At the same time, the percentage of 'managers and administrators' slightly decreased from 10.7 to 10.1 per cent, while 'professionals' increased from 5.5 per cent to 6.5 per cent. If one considers a longer timeframe, the statistics are even more telling: in 1991, the percentage of 'associate professionals', 'professionals', and 'managers and administrators' was only 10.3 per cent, 3.7 per cent and 9.2 per cent, respectively. See Chiu and Lui op. cit., Table 8, p. 1879, citing statistics from the C&SD.

23 Ibid.: 36, Table 2.10. 'Managers and administrators' had a median monthly income of HK$36,250 and 'professionals' HK$32,160.

24 Interestingly, the median monthly income of 'associate professionals' (HK$18,000) was on the upper range of the 7th decile (HK$16,500) or the lower range of the 8th decile (HK$20,000). Keep in mind that the previous 'quantitative' definition of the middle class classified the 7th and 8th deciles as the upper middle class. In any case, the important point to note is that despite the growing gap between higher and lower incomes, 'associate professionals' occupy an intermediate position. The authors will elaborate on this point below.

25 A 'degree' refers to a Bachelor's degree or equivalent. Until recently, most Bachelor's degree programmes generally comprised three years of university education, but have now changed to four-year programmes. Sub-degrees are non-degree qualifications, such as higher certificates, diplomas, higher diplomas and associate degrees, which consist of one to three years of post-secondary education.

26 The complete sentence is: 'rising inequality can only be prevented by expanding education opportunities and encouraging couples to stay together'. As this section focuses on education and salaries, the end of the sentence will not be discussed here.

27 However, only Lui provided calculations for this premium: 'In 1981, a graduate worker would receive a monthly income that was 233.2 per cent (…), higher than that of an uneducated worker. By 2011, the estimated earning premium for degree education increased to 377.6 percent' (Lui 2013: 59).

28 For example, Liu Pak-Wai, Emeritus Professor at the Chinese University of Hong Kong, and one of the authors of the report issued by Our Hong Kong Foundation, 'Riding on Mainland's Economic Development in a New Era', 2016, www.ourhkfoundation.org.hk/sites/default/files/media/pdf/ChinaHK_Report_English_28.10.16.pdf.

'Our Hong Kong Foundation' is a think tank created and directed by the former CE Tung Chee-Hwa.

29 According to a survey conducted by two groups, the New Forum and New Youth Forum, 'the number of jobs in the city requiring skilled workers had risen by only 66,500 between 1993 and 2013. But the number of university graduates that could fill these positions increased by 699,600 over that period' (Siu 2015, *SCMP*). These data seem exaggerated – the LegCo study's data were probably closer to reality – but since they were published in the newspapers, they gained more credibility among the

general population (see below on the role of the media in shaping public opinion). In any case, they confirmed a worldwide phenomenon: many graduates are unable to find jobs that are commensurate with their qualifications.

30 Wong continued: 'But this conclusion is misleading. Rates of return to schooling for those with secondary education rose from 12.5 percent in 1981 to 15.8 percent in 2011' (Wong 2015a).

31 According to the LegCo Research Office (2015a), the median hourly wage in Hong Kong's retail sector in 2013 was HK$40.9. During the same period, the median monthly income for service and sales workers was HK$9,880 (LegCo Research Office 2015a and 2015b), which suggested even longer work hours than in Wong's calculations.

32 Strictly speaking, the 'median monthly employment earnings of employed persons aged 20–24 who attained a post-secondary education' was not fully equivalent to the median fresh graduate income, but it constituted an acceptable proxy for our purpose. The authors would like to thank Ms Christy Leung, journalist at the *SCMP*, for sharing this data (and those included in Table 3.2) with us.

33 See also Phila Siu (2015), reporting on the same survey on the *SCMP*: 'Salaries of Hong Kong's university graduates dropped 20% in last 20 years, study finds.'

34 Other local universities have also compiled similar data, but it was not always possible to access them. Their aggregation, in any case, would lead to methodological difficulties. The authors will, however, refer to some of them punctually.

35 Since the authors did not intend to analyse tertiary level education in depth, this last type of information will only be used intermittently.

36 From the incomplete available set of data, one can safely assume that the average income was higher than the median income by over HK$1,000 in 2014.

37 The rate of return was quite high because the 'questionnaires [were] collected from graduates when they return[ed] to the PolyU campus to collect their graduation gowns' (CAPS 2014: 1). The Survey is conducted yearly between August and the end of the year (for example, for people who graduated in 2014, from 1 August to 31 December 2014). Reminders are issued from October to December to non-respondents and to those who reported to be seeking employment. In 2014, 4,516 valid responses were received out of a total of 5,345 graduates (a response rate of 84.5 per cent).

38 Another interpretation could be that misreporting is higher during economic downturns. In that case, the effect in the data of the impact of an economic crisis on the incomes of fresh graduates would be lower than it is in reality.

39 Partial data from similar surveys conducted at various local universities showed higher starting monthly salaries for the University of Hong Kong (HK$21,265 in 2014) and the Chinese University of Hong Kong (HK$18,220 in 2014) – generally regarded as the two top Hong Kong universities – but lower for Baptist University (HK$13,312 in 2013). See Centre of Development and Resources for Students, the University of Hong Kong, 'Graduate Employment Survey 2014', www.cedars.hku.hk/sections/careersplacement/GraduateEmploymentSurvey/report/GES/GES2014.pdf; Office of Student Affairs, The Chinese University of Hong Kong, 'The Chinese University of Hong Kong A Profile of 2014 Graduates in Statistics', www.cuhk.edu.hk/osa/doc/Survey2015/Profile_2014.pdf; and Office of the Student Affairs, The Baptist University of Hong Kong, http://sa.hkbu.edu.hk/career/wp-includes/survey/ges2014.pdf.

40 This actually would call for a differentiated approach of education (and a differentiated analysis of the labour market). The above data tend to indicate that the demand for health professionals (nurses, medical doctors, as well as physiotherapists, psychologists, etc.) is high and will further increase with population aging. More generally, in the job market, the equilibrium between supply and demand can only occur if a careful planning of the university training (e.g. number of degrees delivered in each academic field) has taken place *ex ante*. Therefore, a delicate balance between the

future conditions in the labour market and the desire of the students to enrol in a specific degree has to be found. In addition, as many tomorrow's jobs do not exist yet, this type of planning is difficult to achieve. Although this issue has important policy-making and theoretical implications (e.g. the interaction of market forces with social and political dynamics) and deserves deeper investigation, it falls outside the purpose of this chapter and will not be developed further in this book.

41 According to unpublished data cited by Lui Hon-Kwong, the mean monthly main employment income for degree holders decreased from HK$29,675 in 1996 to HK$27,943 in 2006 before rising again to HK$33,955 in 2011. At the same time, the overall mean monthly income for sub-degree holders rose from HK$13,834 in 1996 to HK$15,902 in 2001, HK$15,140 in 2006, and 17,793 in 2011 (see Lui 2013: Table 4.2, p. 57). Since these amounts were in *current* prices, they were only indicative – but Hong Kong experienced deflation from 1999 to 2004. Lui's data are also compatible with those in Table 3.2.

42 Unfortunately, the full data set is not available. The picture could be very different if the situation could be analysed since 1997 instead of 2003, as salaries dropped sharply between those 2 years. Again, citing unpublished data from the C&SD, researchers from the New Century Forum indicated that incomes for sub-degree holders decreased by nearly 20 per cent (adjusted for inflation) from 1995 to 2015 (from HK$20,463 to HK$16,898). While it is difficult to confirm the accuracy of the first data set, the second one is in line with the information in Table 3.3. See Shirley Zhao (2015).

43 On the other hand, it is clear that a significant proportion of degree holders have been unable to reach the managerial or administrators' ranks (more on this point below).

44 Income stagnation in Hong Kong has been widely reported in the media and commented on by politicians. See, for example, 'Hongkongers' median incomes grew only 10pc in the last decade' (Siu 2013). This increase, which occurred from 2001 to 2011, was measured in current prices. The author of the article added that the relatively high inflation during the period cancelled out a large part of this increase. For example, food prices increased even more rapidly: 'The average retail price for one kg of top-grade chicken was HK$35.82 in 2001, but had shot up to HK$83.4 in 2011. The price for one kg of *hung sam yu*, or golden thread, a common type of fish, also soared from HK$40.35 to HK$74.39 (…)'. This type of article reinforced many Hongkongers' belief that they no longer benefited from their city's economic growth (see above).

45 LegCo Research Office (2015a), note 13, p. 7, citing Chiu Stephen Wing-kai and Ip Chung Yan, 'Does 'Downward Movement' Become a Real Problem to the Youth?' 青年「下流」問題的虛與實, *Ming Pao*, 5 December 2014. See also Lui (2014a: 51):

> On the supply side, the expansion of higher education may shrink the earnings premium for university graduates. As the supply of university graduates becomes widely available, degree holders are forced to take jobs that previously did not require a university degree. For example, bank clerks were typical entry-level jobs for secondary school leavers in the past, but these vacancies have been taken up by graduate workers in recent years in Hong Kong.

46 Basically, these programmes can be provided by publicly funded universities, but their financing mainly comes from the tuition students and/or their families pay. The 'self-financed programmes' were created by the Tung Chee-Hwa government in 2000.

47 See Vere (2010).

48 For example, at Hong Kong Baptist University, the number of Mainland students in undergraduate programmes is 11 per cent. Nevertheless, Baptist received only 2,319 applications for the 2015–2016 school year – down 40 per cent from last year. PolyU,

which has the largest student body among Hong Kong's public universities, said it received about 2,300 applications from the Mainland this year compared to some 3,500 last year (Steger and Hu 2015). The reasons for the drop are unclear, but they might be related to improvements in the reputations of Mainland universities and the consequences of the Umbrella Movement (ibid.).

Bibliography

Adler, N. and J. Stewart (2007) 'McArthur Scale of Social Status', www.macses.ucsf.edu/research/psychosocial/subjective.php, accessed 25 March 2016.

Alstadsaeter, A., N. Johannesen and G. Zucman (2017) 'Tax Evasion and Inequality', working paper, https://gabriel-zucman.eu/files/AJZ2017.pdf, accessed 26 June 2017.

Bourdieu, P. (1984) *Distinction: A Social Critique of the Judgement of Taste*, Cambridge, MA: Harvard University Press.

Bourdieu P. (1994) *Practical Reason: On the Theory of Action*, Stanford: Stanford University Press.

Castells, M. (2000) *The Rise of the Network Society*, Oxford: Blackwell.

Census and Statistics Department, the HKSAR (2012a) 'Thematic Report. Household Distribution Income', www.statistics.gov.hk/pub/B11200572012XXXXB0100.pdf, accessed 18 August 2015.

Census and Statistics Department, the HKSAR (2012b) 'Population Census. Main Report', Volume 1, www.census2011.gov.hk/pdf/main-report-volume-I.pdf, accessed 18 August 2015.

Census and Statistics Department, the HKSAR (2012c) 'Population Census. Thematic Report. Thematic Report: Persons from the Mainland Having Resided in Hong Kong for Less Than 7 Years', www.statistics.gov.hk/pub/B11200612012XXXXB0100.pdf, accessed 3 December 2015.

Census and Statistics Department, the HKSAR (2014a) 'External Direct Investment Statistics of Hong Kong 2013', www.statistics.gov.hk/pub/B10400032013AN13B0100.pdf, accessed 4 July 2015.

Census and Statistics Department, the HKSAR (2014b) *Hong Kong Annual Digest of Statistics*, www.statistics.gov.hk/pub/B10100032014AN14B0100.pdf, accessed 14 August 2015.

Census and Statistics Department, the HKSAR (2014c) '2013 Gross Domestic Product', www.statistics.gov.hk/pub/B10300022013AN13E0100.pdf, accessed 20 September 2015.

Census and Statistics Department, the HKSAR (2014–2015) 'Annual Report on Consumer Price Index', www.censtatd.gov.hk/hkstat/sub/sp270.jsp?productCode=B1060002, accessed 2 September 2015.

Census and Statistics Department, the HKSAR (2015a) 'Gross Domestic Product (GDP); Table 30 Implicit Price Deflator of GDP and Per Capita GDP', 14 August, www.censtatd.gov.hk/hkstat/sub/sp250.jsp?tableID=030&ID=0&productType=8, accessed 25 August 2015.

Census and Statistics Department, the HKSAR (2015b) 'Table 133: Number of Regional Headquarters in Hong Kong by Country/Territory Where the Parent Company Was Located', www.censtatd.gov.hk/hkstat/sub/sp360.jsp?tableID=133&ID=0&productType=8, accessed 11 August 2015.

Census and Statistics Department, the HKSAR (2015c) 'Table 134: Number of Regional Offices in Hong Kong by Country/Territory Where the Parent Company Was Located', www.censtatd.gov.hk/hkstat/sub/sp360.jsp?tableID=134&ID=0&productType=8, accessed 11 August 2015.

Census and Statistics Department, the HKSAR 'Labour', www.censtatd.gov.hk/hkstat/sub/so30.jsp, accessed 14 August 2015.

Census and Statistics Department, the HKSAR 'National Income', www.censtatd.gov.hk/hkstat/sub/sp250.jsp?tableID=036&ID=0&productType=8, accessed 9 June 2015.

Chen, G. (2014) 'Hong Kong's Top Ranking for Economic Freedom Feels a Good Laugh', *South China Morning Post*, 19 January, www.scmp.com/business/article/1409190/hong-kongs-top-ranking-economic-freedom-feels-good-laugh, accessed 2 June 2015.

Chiu, S.W.K. and C.Y. Ip (2014) 'Does 'Downward Movement' Become a Real Problem to the Youth?' 青年「下流」問題的虛與實, *Ming Pao*, 5 December.

Chiu, S. and T.L. Lui (2004) 'Testing the Global City-Social Polarisation Thesis: Hong Kong since the 1990s', *Urban Studies*, 41(10): 1863–1888.

Commission on Strategic Committee on Social Development and Quality of Life (2006) 'Income Inequality and Social Mobility', www.cpu.gov.hk/doc/en/commission_strategic_development/csd_sc_7_2006.pdf, accessed 15 August 2015.

Desrosières, A. (1998) *The Politics of Large Numbers: A History of Statistical Reasoning*, Cambridge, MA: Harvard University Press.

Education Bureau, Personal, Social and Humanities Education Section, Curriculum Development Institute (2015) 'Income Inequality', www.edb.gov.hk/attachment/en/curriculum-development/kla/pshe/references-and-resources/economics/income_eng.pdf, accessed 25 October 2016.

Freeman, R. (1995) 'Are Your Wages Set in Beijing?' *Journal of Economic Perspectives*, 9(3): 15–32.

Goldthorpe, J.H. and A. McKnight (2004) 'The Economic Basis of Social Class', CASE-paper 80, Centre for Analysis of Social Exclusion, London School of Economics http://eprints.lse.ac.uk/6312/1/The_Economic_Basis_of_Social_Class.pdf, accessed 13 August 2017.

Ho, L.S., X.D. Wei and G.W.C. Wong (2003) 'The Effect of Trade on Wage Inequality: The Hong Kong', *Working Paper Series No. 139 (6/03)*, Centre for Public Policy Studies, Lingnan University of Hong Kong.

Home Affairs Department, the HKSAR (2017) 'Home Affairs Department and Immigration Department Statistics on New Arrivals from the Mainland (First Quarter of 2017)', www.had.gov.hk/file_manager/tc/documents/public_services/services_for_new_arrivals_from_the_mainland/report_2017q1.pdf, accessed 30 May 2017.

Hong Kong Business (2014) 'Salary Expectations of Hong Kong's Fresh Grads Hit $17,314 Per Month', *Hong Kong Business*, 30 April, http://hongkongbusiness.hk/hr-education/news/salary-expectations-hong-kongs-fresh-grads-hit-17314-month#sthash.IGevuyHS.dpuf, accessed 26 September 2015.

jobsDB (2014) 'Fresh Graduate Employment', jobsDB Q2 2013 Hiring Index/, http://hk.jobsdb.com/hk/en/staticcontent/hiring-survey/2013/Q2-hiring-index/fresh-graduate-employment.htm, accessed 1 September 2015.

Law, K.Y. and K.M. Lee (2006) 'Citizenship, Economy and Social Exclusion of Mainland Immigrants in Hong Kong', *Journal of Contemporary Asia*, 36(2): 217–242.

Lee, K.M., H. Wong and K.Y. Law (2007) 'Social Polarisation and Poverty in the Global City: The Case of Hong Kong', *China Report*, 43(1): 1–30.

Legislative Council (2016) 'Bills Committee on Inland Revenue (Amendment) Bill 2016. Background Brief', LC Paper No. CB(1)518/15–16(03), www.legco.gov.hk/yr15-16/english/bc/bc07/papers/bc0720160202cb1-518-3-e.pdf, accessed 16 November 2016.

Legislative Council Secretariat – Research Office (2014) 'Individual Visit Scheme', *Research Brief* No. 6.

Legislative Council Secretariat – Research Office (2015a) 'Four Pillars and Six Industries in Hong Kong: Review and Outlook', *Research Brief* No. 3.

Legislative Council Secretariat – Research Office (2015b) 'Social Mobility in Hong Kong: Review and Outlook', *Research Brief* No. 2.

Legislative Council Secretariat – Research Office (2016), 'Challenges of Manpower Adjustment in Hong Kong', *Research Brief* No. 3.

Liu, P. K., K.C.J. Lam and K. Shui (2016) 'Riding on Mainland's Economic Development in a New Era', Hong Kong, *Our Hong Kong Foundation*, www.ourhkfoundation.org.hk/sites/default/files/media/pdf/ChinaHK_Report_English_28.10.16.pdf, accessed 15 May 2017.

Lui, H.K. (2013) *Widening Income Distribution in Post-Handover Hong Kong*, Abingdon: Routledge.

Lui, H.K. and W. Suen, (2005) 'The Shrinking Earnings Premium for University Graduates in Hong Kong: the Effect of Quantity of Quality?' *Contemporary Economic Policy*, 23(2): 242–254.

Lui, T.L. (2011) 'Changing Opportunity Structures: Political Concerns and Sociological Observations', in S.K.W. Chiu and S.L. Wong (eds) *Hong Kong Divided? Structures of Social Inequality in the Twenty-First Century*, Hong Kong: Hong Kong Institute of Asia-Pacific Studies, the Chinese University of Hong Kong, pp. 65–92.

Lui, T.L. (2014a) 'A Profile of Hong Kong's Middle Classes: Continuities and Discontinuities', in M.H.H. Hsiao (ed.) *Chinese Middle Classes: Taiwan, Macao and China*, Abingdon: Routledge, pp. 36–56.

Lui, T.L. (2014b) 'Getting Uneasy: The Changing Psychology of Hong Kong's Middle Class', in M.H.H. Hsiao (ed.) *Chinese Middle Classes: Taiwan, Macao and China*, Abingdon: Routledge, pp. 97–109.

Lui, T.L. and K.W.S. Chiu (2007) 'Governance Crisis in Post-1997 Hong Kong: A Political Economy Perspective', *China Review*, 7(2): 1–34.

Mok, K.H. (2015) 'Enhancing Global Competitiveness and Human Capital Management: Does Education Help Reduce Inequality and Poverty in Hong Kong?' in M. Lau (ed.) *Special Issue: Poverty in a Rich Society – The Case of Hong Kong, The China Review*, 15(2): 119–146.

Noble, J. (2014) 'Economic Inequality Underpins Hong Kong's Great Political Divide', *The Financial Times*, 21 October, www.ft.com/cms/s/0/d123d896-5808-11e4-b47d-00144feab7de.html#axzz3nqc8byR4, accessed 9 October 2015.

OECD (2015) *Population with Tertiary Education (Indicator)*. https://data.oecd.org/eduatt/population-with-tertiary-education.htm#indicator-chart, accessed 31 August 2015.

Office of Student Affairs, The Baptist University of Hong Kong, 'Graduate Employment Survey 2014', https://sa.hkbu.edu.hk/career/f/page/973/2281/ges2014.pdf, accessed 3 January 2016.

Office of Student Affairs, The Chinese University of Hong Kong, 'The Chinese University of Hong Kong A Profile of 2014 Graduates in Statistics', www.cuhk.edu.hk/osa/doc/Survey2015/Profile_2014.pdf, accessed 3 January 2016.

Office of the Careers and Placement Centre (CAPS) (2004–2014), 'Graduate Employment Survey', The Hong Kong Polytechnic University.

Oriental Daily (2015) 'Salaries Starting Points for Fresh University Graduates Drops 17% in 20 Years' 大學畢業生起薪點20年跌17% 難圓中產夢, 28 July, http://hk.on.cc/hk/bkn/cnt/news/20150728/bkn-20150728231553533-0728_00822_001.html, accessed 1 August 2015.

OXFAM Hong Kong (2016) 'Hong Kong Poverty Report (2011–2015)', www.oxfam.org.hk/content/98/content_31062en.pdf, accessed 22 June 2017.

Petit, P. (2010) 'The Systemic Nature of the Rise in Inequality in Developed Economies', in W. Milberg and P. Petit (eds) *Special Issue: Inequality as a Source of Economic Vulnerability: Post-crisis Varieties of Capitalism, International Review of Applied Economics*, 24(3): 251–267.

Piketty, T. (2013) *Capital in the Twenty-First Century*, Cambridge, MA: Harvard University Press.

Sassen, S. (2000) *Cities in the World Economies*, 2nd edition, Thousand Oaks: Tine Forge Press.

Siu, P. (2013) 'Hongkongers' Median Income Grew Only 10pc in the Last Decade', *South China Morning Post*, 1 January.

Siu, P. (2015) 'Salaries of Hong Kong's University Graduates Dropped 20 Percent in Last 20 Years, Study Finds', *South China Morning Post*, 29 July, www.scmp.com/news/hong-kong/economy/article/1844661/salaries-hong-kongs-university-graduates-dropped-20-cent-last?page=all, accessed 3 January 2015.

Steger, I. and K. Hu (2015) 'Fewer Mainland Applicants for Hong Kong Universities', *Wall Street Journal*, 25 June, http://blogs.wsj.com/chinarealtime/2015/06/25/fewer-mainland-students-eyeing-hong-kong-universities/, accessed 5 September 2015.

Stiglitz J.E. (2015) *The Great Divide: Unequal Societies and What We Can Do About Them,* New York, W.W. Norton Company.

Tang, H.W. and H.W.S. Wong (2011) 'The Impact of New Immigration on Native Wages: a Cross-Occupation Analysis of a Small Open Economy', *Centro Studi Luca d'Agliano Development Studies Papers* 308.

Vere, J. (2010) 'Special Topic Enquiry on Earnings Mobility', www.lwb.gov.hk/eng/other_info/Special%20Topic%20Enquiry%20on%20Earnings%20Mobility.pdf, accessed 6 September 2015.

Wong, Y.C.R. (2006) 'Why the Minimum Wage Harms the Economy?' *YC Richard Wong on the Political Economy of HK and China*, 6 December, www.wangyujian.com/?p=1938&lang=en, accessed 24 August 2015.

Wong, Y.C.R. (2013) *Diversity and Occasional Anarchy: On Deep Economic and Social Contradictions in Hong Kong*, Hong Kong: Hong Kong University Press.

Wong, Y.C.R. (2015a) 'The Roots of Hong Kong's Income Inequality', *South China Morning Post*, 31 March.

Wong, Y.C.R. (2015b) *Hong Kong Land for Hong Kong People*, Hong Kong: Hong Kong University Press.

Wong, Y.H.M. (2014) 'The Politics of the Minimum Wage in Hong Kong', *Journal of Contemporary Asia*, 44(4): 735–752.

Zhao, S. (2015) 'Earnings Hit for Those Holding Sub-Degrees', *South China Morning Post*, 5 August.

Zhao, S.X.B. and L. Zhang (2005) 'Economic Growth and Income Inequality in Hong Kong: Trends and Explanations', *China: An International Journal*, 3(1): 74–103.

4 Closing the loop

Oligopolistic Hong Kong – the local economy in the shadow of the Competition Ordinance and taxation policies

In Chapter 3, the authors have shown that Hong Kong's GDP per capita has grown much faster than incomes, which indicates that the gains from the economic growth are unequally distributed within the population. In particular, the close analysis of the evolution of the monthly incomes of fresh graduate seemed to indicate a crowding effect, while the salaries of the lower and middle classes have generally stagnated and even decreased. In this condition, it is unlikely that further development of tertiary education is the right remedy to curb inequality – and it might even lead to the opposite effect. It has also been seen that, due to the open nature of its economy, a reason for this situation is the exposure of the Territory to globalization forces that, in conjunction with the influence of China's economy (which is itself a major actor of globalization), have provoked a certain degree of polarization.

However, Chapter 3 did not cover all the issues at stake. In particular, it remains to be seen how a certain portion of the Hong Kong population was able to seize a disproportionate share of the GPD gains. As this chapter will illustrate, this is linked to the structure of the Hong Kong economy and its evolution since at least the 1960s. This structure favoured local entrepreneurs who were early entrants in the property market. Progressively, they erected barriers to entry in the housing market, while they extended their activities to other economic sectors and created oligopolies. As aptly illustrated by Mark Williams (2005, 2009), Hong Kong economy became dual: the international trade remains relatively free and open (even though the seaport and container business are in reality controlled by a few companies); the domestic economy is now mostly in the hands of just a few firms.

The consequences of this situation are multi-fold for Hong Kong, for the Hongkongers, and especially for the younger generation. In addition to the relative stagnation of their incomes, Hong Kong's youth also face escalating housing prices. Here is not the place to review the property market or the housing policy in Hong Kong in detail – both are actually highly debated topics among the local academic community. Instead, following the steps of Alice Poon (2011) and Edward Yiu (2009, 2013, 2015), the authors will aim to demonstrate the above statements regarding the structure of the Hong Kong economy and show the consequences for the (educated) youth and the middle class. It will also be highlighted that domestic policies have not only played a role in developing this situation since the 1960s, but the government has refrained from trying to redress this imbalance in recent years. Specifically, the recent introduction of a competition law has done nothing to curb or prevent the existence of monopolies and/or oligopolies in Hong Kong, while the proposed, but finally aborted, reform of the tax system (which has already been at the advantage of a tiny minority of Hongkongers for decades, contrary to the claims of government officials), would not have benefited the middle and lower classes.

Therefore, the first section of Chapter 4 will argue that Hong Kong's high housing prices are generated by a combination of political and economic factors, which have laid the foundations for a concentration of land in the hands of the happy few and aggressive speculation (thanks to the peg between the HK$ and the US$). The resulting oligopolistic situation, as well as the concentration of capital, have created the conditions for the advent of oligopolies in other sectors of the Hong Kong economy. In the next two sections, the authors will show how some policies to redress the existing imbalance in Hong Kong's economy were systematically discarded by the government in favour of maintaining the economic organization that has benefited to the élites stable. The section titled 'The introduction of the Competition Ordinance and its limits' will show that despite the introduction of a new competition law, which became effective in December 2015, fundamental changes are unlikely to occur because this law has no power over important issues such as mergers and acquisitions and divestitures. The following section ('A few remarks on tax and inequality') will briefly present the government's attempts to reform the existing tax system (which dates back 1947). The proposed reforms – mainly the introduction of a new goods and services tax (GST) and a simultaneous reduction of the revenue tax – would essentially transfer part of the tax burden from the wealthy to the middle class and poor. The authors then suggest that these two partial or aborted reforms were missed opportunities to address some of the pressing issues that Hong Kong faces, such as inequality and astronomical land prices, and consider Hong Kong's future role in world.

From the concentration of the property market to the oligopolies of the Hong Kong economy

To begin with, a few data will illustrate that housing is increasingly unaffordable for the younger generations, who also cannot rely on the public sector to palliate this situation. The authors will start by examining the situation in the public sector before moving to the private market. Then, after showing the severity of the situation, the authors will analyse the causes for this unaffordability, most notably the existence of Ricardian rents generated by the existence of monopolies and oligopolies. This presentation will follow two steps. The first one will separate the reasons for price fluctuations and volatilities from the ones of high prices. Price fluctuations and volatilities are, at times, causing difficulties to citizens and may lead to price peaks, but are not, in themselves, responsible for the general situation of high prices: they have more to see with the international environment and especially the evolution of interest rates in the United States. In the second step, an historical pattern showing how the Ricardian rent has appeared and was nurtured over the years will be presented. It is this historical evolution which provoked contradictions in the economic system and led to often unaffordable housing prices for many Hongkongers. Finally, the last part of this section will show how the existence of rents in the housing market has allowed developers to extend their domination in other local economic sectors.

A few data and facts will best tell the extent of the problem for young people who wish to become independent. In the public sector, the average length of time in which a general applicant has to wait for a flat is 3.6 years (Hong Kong Housing Authority 2015).[1] However, single young adults do not qualify for the general applicants list and if they are eligible for public housing, the waiting time is generally much longer.[2] In a 2010 interview for *Varsity*, the magazine of the School of Journalism of the Chinese University of Hong Kong,

> Legislator Wong Kwok-hing, who is the chairman of the Legislative Council's Panel on Housing, says: 'A single youth has to wait for an average of 24 years for a public housing unit according to the Hong Kong Housing Authority and Housing Department'.
>
> (Liu and Chan 2010: 24–25)

In November 2016, the situation became so critical that some young people decided to launch a judicial review at the High Court, emphasizing that 'the system effectively stripped people (…) of access to public housing and therefore violated their right to social welfare under Article 36 of the Basic Law'. Their barrister specified that, 'a single person who applies at 18 – the youngest eligible age – would be unlikely to score enough points for subsidized housing before hitting 50' (Lee 2016).

At the time of the *Varsity* article, in 2010, the waiting list for these young adults was 'only' about 19,900 applicants long. Since then, it has grown tremendously to about 70,000 applicants. Overall, by September 2015 there were about 142,500 general applicants for public rental housing, and about 142,800 non-elderly, one-person applicants – a record (Hong Kong Housing Authority 2015). In June 2011, the numbers for these two categories were 'only' 89,000 and 66,600, respectively (Legislative Council Panel on Housing 2013). This represented an increase of more than 60 per cent for general applications and a staggering 114 per cent for 'non-elderly one-person applications' in just a few years. That also meant the latter group grew at almost twice the rate (114 per cent vs. 60 per cent) as the former and most of this increase came from young adults, who personify the difficulties of finding decent lodging in the private sector, especially if they are single.[3] But before elaborating on this point, the authors want to detail some of the supply side reasons to explain why the situation became this way.

In addition to the situation on the private market, the lengthened waiting list is also a result of the current objective of the Hong Kong government to restrict the size of the public sector, including the housing market.[4] One former Hong Kong policymaker-turned-scholar observed that

> in practice, the withdrawal of the government from the housing market proved disastrous for the community. A long-term shortage of accommodation became impossible to avoid. The annual supply of new public housing fell by 62 percent: from an annual average of 38,900 units for the period 1997–2002 to 14,600 for the period 2007–12.
>
> (Goodstadt 2013: 90)

This government pullback has had a quite dramatic effect for Hong Kong's lower-to-middle classes, since a significant portion of its population lives in public housing in one form or another: 49 per cent in 2004, 47 per cent in 2009 and 45 per cent in 2014 (Hong Kong Housing Authority 2015). However, by no means do these data signify that the government has fully retreated from the property market – this is, in fact, impossible due to the city's land ownership system (see below). To make this long story short, although it is difficult for younger (and better-educated) adults to obtain public flats owing to the long waiting list, many of them have continued to submit applications and a significant portion of them are single, under 30, and have tertiary level educations (Wong 2015: 21–22).

Since the public housing waiting list is too long, the alternative for younger people is to try their luck in the private sector: after all, the disengagement of the government from public housing was, in the minds of senior officials like the former CE, Donald Tsang, 'to restore the proper role of the private residential property market' (cited by Goodstadt 2013: 90). Unfortunately, the price-to-income ratio has sufficed to show that obtaining a private flat has become increasingly difficult. In 2011, the ratio of house price to annual household income was 12.6 years (compared to 4.4 years in Singapore), and it grew to around 15 years in 2012 (Yiu 2013). Yvonne Liu added that

> [s]oaring property prices in the past few years have given Hong Kong the title of most unaffordable housing in the world for the fourth straight year, according to a survey of 360 cities by US-based consultancy Demographia. The survey reported that Hong Kong's median home price was more than HK$4.02 million, while the annual median household income of HK$270,000 was nearly one-15th of the home price.
>
> (Liu 2014)

The title of Liu's article ('Hong Kong Ranks World's No 1 for 'Most Unaffordable' Housing') and its headlines ('For the fourth consecutive year, the city is ranked world's No. 1 for unaffordable housing') struck her readers and expressed the reality they faced every day.[5] Other indicators reinforced this unaffordability: the maximum loan-to-value ratio decreased from 90 per cent during the 1970s to around 70 per cent during the 1990s and 2000s and again to 50 per cent by the

2010s. At the same time, the maximum mortgage tenure jumped from 20 years during the 1990s to 25 years during the 2000s and 30 years by the 2010s (Yiu 2013). Clearly, these data sufficed to show why the stated policy objective of Tung, the first CE – to achieve a home ownership rate of 70 per cent by the end of 2007 (Yiu 2013; Yeung 2011: 8) – has failed.

The point, then, is to understand why the property prices have risen to such unaffordable levels. The main idea the authors will present below is that consolidation among developers in Hong Kong, which was facilitated by the lack of a competition law until recently, has influenced the creation of an uncompetitive property market. In turn, this oligopolistic situation prompted the consolidation of other sectors of the economy (utilities, supermarkets, etc.) with equally few competitors. Such a concentration of capital in the hands of a few is an important reason for the growth of inequality in Hong Kong, an issue which is generally absent from the analyses pertaining to inequality in the Territory – but not in other countries, as documented by Piketty (2013).

It should be noted, however, that this thesis remains controversial in the academic community, mainly because of the difficulty of demonstrating the influence of oligopolies over prices (Williams 2005). Some scholars argued that while market concentration cannot be denied, tycoons and developers are not responsible for the situation as other factors such as globalization have also played a role (Wong 2015: 216–217). Such a statement has some pertinence, but does not justify the inaction of the Hong Kong government on this issue (a point to which the authors will return in the conclusion of this book). To complicate things, as rightly pointed out by Wang Shu (2015: 6), very few studies actually relate 'the effects of land policies to the development strategies employed by major real estate firms, which more than often alters the theoretical relationship between land supply and the supply of housing'. A reason for this may be the difficulty of accessing information regarding their decisions. In this respect, Poon's study deserves scrutiny because the author, who has worked for a major developer, is well aware of the strategies implemented by these firms (Poon 2011). Her book is also worth reading because she not only concentrated her study to Hong Kong's property market, but also showed the links it had with other markets. Williams' research (2005, 2009) usefully complemented Poon's by providing a detailed framework and historical background of the discussions related to the need to implement a competition law in Hong Kong, which was finally introduced in December 2015, but with serious limitations. These two bodies of literature provide the core of the discussion below, in addition to other sources that pertain more specifically to the housing market. Taken together, the works of Williams and Poon give some evidence for why prices are higher than they should be and why they remain that way. As the authors will detail below, it can be safely acknowledged that an oligopolistic market provides ample opportunities for companies to extract rent at the expense of consumers.

This is also basically what stated *The Economist*. Actually, it is not without reason that Hong Kong was ranked first in its crony-capitalism index, mainly due to the ability of local tycoons to extract rent.

> But many of today's tycoons are accused of making fortunes by 'rent-seeking': grabbing a bigger slice of the pie rather than making the pie bigger. In technical terms, an economic rent is the difference between what people are paid and what they would have to be paid for their labour, capital, land (or any other inputs into production) to remain in their current use. In a world of perfect competition, rent would not exist. Common examples of rent-seeking (which may or may not be illegal) include forming cartels and lobbying for rules that benefit a firm at the expense of competitors and customers.
>
> (*The Economist* 2014)

In other terms, in the presence of oligopolistic rents, GDP growth does not benefit equally to the whole population: economic growth enlarges the existing inequality – a point that will be addressed again in the conclusion.

However, before the authors explain how this oligopolistic situation has developed, first in the housing market and then has spread to other sectors, they would like to introduce a caveat, in order to separate the structural reasons for high prices from the more short- to medium-term effects generated by price fluctuation. In fact, while the existence of an oligopoly can partly explain why prices are higher than they should be in a supposedly competitive market, it is not in itself sufficient to justify large fluctuations and volatility, which have also characterized Hong Kong's property market. Thus, there should be other parameters to link these two phenomena (price hikes and volatility). As hypotheses that needed to be tested, Edward Yiu assigned two sets of factors to them: an insufficient supply of flats and a low (even, at times, negative) real interest rate (Yiu 2015). Poon added another hypothesis to the first factor, which leans towards her oligopolistic argumentation, by hinting that the short supply was due to government policy and land concentration in the hands of large developers. The rent extracted from this oligopolistic situation, in turn, could be used to create other monopolies or oligopolies (Poon 2011). These different hypotheses are not exclusive of each other and will be introduced successively.

For Yiu, it was difficult to know precisely if supply was inadequate because 'the sufficiency is relative to demand, which is not directly observable'. To overcome this difficulty, he tested the insufficient housing hypothesis (…) by taking vacancy rate as a proxy for sufficiency' in Hong Kong and Macau (Yiu 2015). However, his 'results [could] not confirm the negative effect of vacancy rates on housing price' (ibid.). In addition, there is another ambiguity because the vacancy rate does not fully reflect the conditions of demand and the concept itself leads to different interpretations – and, thus, to different estimates.

This is well-reflected in the definition provided by the Transport and Housing Bureau (hereafter the Bureau): 'if a unit is not physically occupied at the time of the survey,[6] or if a unit is under decoration and pending occupation by the owner or tenant in [the] future, it is treated as a vacant property. According to the latest figures published in the RVD's Hong Kong Property Review 2013, there were about 48,000 vacant private domestic units in Hong Kong as of the end of 2012 representing a vacancy rate of about 4.3 per cent – the lowest since 1997 (Transport and Housing Bureau 2013).[7] However, based on the comparison between the number of households and existing housing units, some scholars estimated the number of vacant flats to be 260,000 (ibid.). But even if the lower figure provided by the RVD reflected the reality, Yiu still concluded that there was no shortage of housing and, thus, the high prices might not have been caused by an imbalance between supply and demand, as the Bureau had claimed.[8] The Bureau, however, insisted that

> if there are [were] still a lot of vacant units in the private market as suggested by some, it would logically follow that there should not be pressure on the supply and the price and rent of private units should not have increased significantly. Therefore, the high price and rent in recent years would support the findings that the vacancy rate of private units is very low.[9]
>
> (Transport and Housing Bureau 2013: 3)

Nevertheless, the views of Yiu and the Bureau may not be as contradictory as they seem if, for example, homeowners or developers decide not to release some of their vacant flats on the market immediately. For example, in the case of speculation or investments (from Mainland Chinese, for example), many flats may be physically unoccupied (at the time of the survey), but not available on the market. In that event, even though there may not be a real shortage of supply, prices can still escalate (see below).

Yiu's second hypothesis (the effect of the real interest rate on housing prices) deserves closer attention. With the peg, domestic interest rates are not fixed in Hong Kong but depend on those in the US, which are, in turn, based on its own economic situation. That eventually generates prolonged periods of relatively high inflation and low – even negative – interest rates in Hong Kong. The consequence was an artificial boost to the property and stock markets because people would not want to keep their money in the bank and also because of intense speculation. This phenomenon was analysed by several local scholars (e.g. Luk 2001; Wong 2015), but Yiu (2009, 2015) offered a new approach to it and contended that if 'the effect of real interest rate on housing price change has long been recognized', there were only a few studies that analysed the situations in which negative real interest rates prevailed (Yiu 2009: 267). 'However, the negative impact [on private housing price change] from real interest rate is almost five times than that when the real interest rate is negative', Yiu reiterated (ibid.: 268). His latest study confirmed the influence of the negative interest rate on housing prices and bubble formations (Yiu 2015).

Thus, it is undeniable that the peg, which permits the existence of low or even negative interest rates for sustained periods of time, has boosted housing prices and has been largely responsible for the formation of speculative bubbles. At the same time, the role of low housing supply seems more ambiguous. Nonetheless, these two are not the only factors for Hong Kong's inflated housing prices, so it is now time to turn to the hypothesis raised by Alice Poon regarding land concentration in the hands of a few large developers. This is all too familiar for Hongkongers and was denounced by the Consumer Council as early as1996:

> A 1996 Consumer Council study revealed that in the period 1991–1994, 70 percent of total new private housing was supplied by seven developers and that 55 percent came from just four developers.[10]
>
> (Poon 2011: 24)

The process by which land came under the control of only a few developers has a long history, which can be traced back to the early 1960s. During the 1950s, Hong Kong's property market was very competitive, with over 1,000 developers operating in the city (Wong 2015: 59). During the 1960s, however, the situation started to change and many developers were driven out of business, as strong barriers to entry were progressively erected by dominant market players. Companies that survived this purge were able to take advantage of the circumstances and policies to expand their businesses. Exploiting political and economic instabilities such as the impact of the Cultural Revolution on Hong Kong (1967), the arduous negotiations that preceded the signing of the Sino-British Joint Declaration (1982–1984), and the implementation of new housing policies (e.g. the development of the new towns in the New Territories), they were able to build up ample land holdings, which currently amount to tens of millions of square feet (Poon 2011: 72–73). More specifically, in the face of political and economic uncertainties, some of the historical British 'hongs' such as Wheelock Marden, Swire Pacific and Hutchison, started to divest their Hong Kong businesses or exit the local property market. That gave the opportunity to rising Chinese firms such as Cheung Kong, Sun Hung Kai, Wing Tai and New World Development to aggressively fill the void by buying up the assets the former left behind, eventually by means of public listings (Poon 2011; Wang 2015: 45–46).

As Lai and Wang reported, from the late 1970s to 1997, the land stocks (or 'land banks') controlled by these developers increased from 1.6 million square metres in 1979 to 11.5 million square metres in 1997 (Lai and Wang 1999: 149, Table 2). By 2009,

> Sun Hung Kai Properties possessed a land bank comprising 41.9 million square feet of developable gross floor area and 24 million square feet (in site area) of agricultural land. Henderson Land held 19.8 million square feet of developable floor area plus 32.8 million square feet (in site area) of agricultural land as at the same date.[11]
>
> (Poon 2011: 25)

As mentioned in its annual reports, in 2012, Henderson 'held New Territories land reserves amounting to approximately 42.8 million square feet in land area, which was the largest holding among all property developers in Hong Kong' (Henderson 2012). This increased to 44.5 million by mid-2015 (Henderson 2015).[12]

The advantages for companies that control these large swathes of land are multiple and this will become clearer after showing the consequences of Hong Kong's land ownership system – the most important part of it being that the government is the final owner of all land (except for that on which St. John's Cathedral in Central sits), which it releases as it sees fit.[13] Since the sales of land rights[14] make up a significant portion of its revenue, the government is balancing the maximization of the public interest with the maximization of its gains through land sales.[15] Budget constraints are often justified to keep land prices high, which contributes to keep housing prices up.[16] To some extent, this strategy can be considered an indirect and hidden tax levied by the government, especially since the Basic Law stipulates that taxes should remain at reasonable levels.[17] In short, when the big developers profit, the government usually does, too. But, at the same time, the artificial scarcity of land boosts the prices of the land banks owned by the developers.

More generally, the control of large pieces of land gives them an edge in the market – despite the costs involved in releasing the land. These costs are usually related to lease modifications, which require negotiations with the government and the payment of a premium. However, this premium is much lower than the market price, in part because the big developers do not need to compete in auctions to buy land rights (Poon 2011: 58–59). Differently stated, their control over large land reserves partly disconnects the land market from the property market. Therefore, a land sale does not necessarily help to curb prices on the housing market – a situation that has been analysed econometrically. Agreeing with the results of a previous study by Tse (1998), Hui noted:

> [Tse] considered that developers might withhold land obtained from auction[s] and tender[s], and pocket it in their land banks. They would not start building until future higher prices are expected. Although a maximum development period is fixed under a lease, they can easily apply for an extension.
>
> (Hui 2004: 146)

This strategy obviously gives a significant advantage to the big developers, who are the only ones who can really benefit from it because it requires considerable financial resources, a good relationship with bankers and investors, and strong knowledge of the local property and auction markets. In addition, the market has become so specialized and technical that only established players can compete in it efficiently. In other words, large developers have not only been able to swallow up or dispatch smaller participants, they have also built strong barriers to entry that limit competition. In recent years, only a few big developers from Mainland China have been able to join this market, owing to their huge availability of capital. However, the effect was just to further aggravated tensions in the market and boost land prices, because these Mainland companies are bidding aggressively, pushing prices up.[18]

In any case, it should be noted that, thanks to their oligopolistic position, Hong Kong's major developers have benefited for years from rents that are extracted from citizens but part of these rents can also be considered, in effect, a form of 'hidden tax' indirectly paid by homebuyers to the government.[19] Their strategy of controlling Hong Kong's rare and very valuable resource (land) has enabled them to behave like middlemen between the land owner (the government) and their customers (flat buyers). While it requests a good knowledge of the market and a sense of anticipation, this strategy is more efficient than, for example, keeping flats empty and waiting until optimal market conditions arrive before releasing them, even though this has happened in a few cases.[20] This is why the reasoning of the Transport and Housing Bureau in relation to the supply-and-demand situation is flawed: vacancy rates and price increases are not sufficient to explain the lack of supply in an oligopolistic market.[21]

The story does not stop there. The surpluses extracted from Hong Kong's consumers since the 1960s have enabled developers to intervene in other markets, where they have also attained oligopolistic positions. Since the 1970s, they have seized control of supermarket chains, utilities and transport providers, which comprise most aspects of the daily lives of Hong Kong people. Plus, they can also reap profits from shop rentals. The lack of competition in Hong Kong's economy – in part due to the absence of a competition law (see section titled 'The introduction of the Competition Ordinance and its limits') – became a policy matter after the last governor, Chris Patten, gave his first policy speech before LegCo in 1992. In his own words:

> Hong Kong is proud of its free and competitive markets. But a more sophisticated and prosperous community has become increasingly unwilling to accept unfair and discriminatory business practices. The public has already begun to voice alarm at the use of market power by suppliers in areas of special importance to the ordinary family's wellbeing (…). I shall ask my Business Council to put at the top of its agenda the development of a comprehensive competition policy for Hong Kong.
>
> (Cited by Williams 2005: 243, from the Hong Kong Legislative Council's Official Record of Proceedings, 7 October 1992, p. 16)

'As a result of this policy initiative the government commissioned the Hong Kong Consumer Council to undertake sectoral investigations including banking, supermarkets, gas supply, broadcasting, telecommunications and private residential property between 1993 and 1996' (Williams 2005: 16). This series of reports, which were released in the mid-1990s, alerted the government to the lack of competition in many sectors of Hong Kong's economy, but often to no avail.

In addition to the housing market, these reports also pointed out, for example, that two conglomerates enjoyed about a 70 per cent market share in the supermarket business.[22] For just two companies to control so large a share of the supermarket pie was not without consequences for consumers: the Consumer Council found that between 2000 and 2002, the two chains 'upped average prices by 3.6% during a period when general retail prices fell 5.6%. (…) In 2000, the French supermarket giant, Carrefour, withdrew from Hong Kong after just four years, having been blacklisted by suppliers for selling products below the minimum agreed re-sale prices' (Pritchard 2006, cited by Williams 2009: 547–548). The same oligopolistic situation applies to electricity (a duopoly), gas (a monopoly business), buses, etc., all owned by the same large conglomerates that often started in the property sector.

Finally, a last element of this puzzle should be added, which concerns the control of the retail sector by, again, the same large conglomerates: as the owners of commercial space through their development of shopping malls, they are also able to wield plenty of clout in Hong Kong's retail sector. Thanks to the growth of tourism, they can exert strong pressure on shop rentals, which reached impressive heights in recent years (see Chapter 2). This explains why many of the businesses that served the local community (in some prime commercial districts especially) were driven out of business – to be replaced by luxury retailers, which could afford to pay such inflated rents. During difficult times, developers prefer to let some of their shops sit empty rather than lower their rents, which would compel them to apply to lower rents in all their other shops: rentals, thus, are relatively inelastic.[23] The conclusion is clear: far from being a free market economy, Hong Kong is typified by monopolies/oligopolies that can extract Ricardian rents. This situation is summarized, in a provocative and somewhat cynical way, by Alice Poon:

> Imagine you are an ordinary citizen who lives in a self-owned flat within a private housing estate. You scraped all your savings to buy the flat from the developer, in return for which you get the right to occupy the flat. Then every month you have to pay the mortgage and property management fee. Every day when you go out to eat in a restaurant or fast food shop in the estate's shopping centre (which, let us assume, is owned by the same developer), you help the tenant of that shopping centre pay his shop rent and fee, which also goes into the pocket of the same developer. On weekends, you go shopping in other shopping centers, owned by other developers. Again you help the shop tenants pay their rents and fees by buying consumer items. At the end of the month, can you figure out how much of your monthly salary goes to paying the developers? The answer might be shocking.
>
> (Poon 2011: 89)

This quote makes it easier for one to understand the disenchantment of Hong Kong's younger generations with its existing economic system: the system is rigged, but thanks to the media and the social networks, Hong Kong's youth have become more aware of it. In 2012, for example, the bi-monthly *TimeOut Hong Kong* published a series of articles under the general title, 'The Men Who Rule Hong Kong'.[24] The headlines summarized its argument in clear fashion: 'how did a small handful of tycoons come to rule over an entire city? Simple: they accumulated your wealth' (*TimeOut Hong Kong* 2012a). In one article of the series ('One Degree of Separation'), the headlines read as follows: 'Forget six degrees, every dollar you earn will eventually filter back into the pocket of the tycoons …' (*TimeOut Hong Kong* 2012b).[25]

In other words, this scattered information leads us to this statement: the extreme concentration of capital has led to the growth of inequality, while investing in education can only curb it marginally. Globalization forces have also played their part directly and indirectly: the HK\$–US\$ peg was influential in generating profits from housing and tourism; in turn, consumption by these tourists (thanks to China's economic boom) partly compensated for the relative stagnation of Hongkongers' salaries by boosting shop rents and revenues. In the end, the profits made by Hong Kong companies are increasingly invested overseas in the face of an apparently saturated domestic market and increased competition from Mainland developers in the housing market: according to the specialized consultancy firm JLL, 'the seven [largest] developers would expect their share of total private completions decrease to 53% between 2017 and 2019, from 84% in 2014 and 77% in 2016' (JLL 2017).[26] In any case, these recent changes do not substantially affect the existence of rents in the Hong Kong economy, which are mostly generated by the way the housing market has been shaped over the years.

The loop has closed: the concentration of capital, in conjunction with globalization forces, has increased inequality, limited choices for ordinary people, and damaged Hongkongers' confidence in their city's economic system and future. Thus, despite sustained economic growth, a low unemployment rate and public finances that most countries would love to have, Hong Kong is a pot about to boil over, given the lack of opportunities for its younger generation. As noted above, the situation bears similarities to other world cities in the context of globalization (which also increased inequality, as Chapter 3 showed), but is also the result of the slow evolution of the domestic economy since the 1960s (with consequences for the housing and land markets).

Therefore, the possible solutions for tackling growing inequality and the extreme concentration of capital and addressing the pressing housing market issues should be a mix of 'generic' (e.g. tax reforms, as promoted by Piketty (2013)) and more specific measures. Since the objectives of this book are to show the economic reasons behind the current unease among the younger generation, the authors do not want to make detailed propositions on how to address these issues – they believe these issues should be discussed by Hongkongers in general. Instead, they want to present some of the policies that have been discussed by the government and in the media, and examine why, in the end, they were abandoned or implemented only with limited scope. Two main policies will be discussed below.

The first concerns the introduction of a competition law. The proponents of such a law see it as a major weapon to limit or even curb the extreme concentration of capital in Hong Kong – especially since changing its tax system is bound by the conditions set in the Basic Law (see above). However, that may be wishful thinking, since competition laws have not prevented the concentration of capital and the formation of monopolies or oligopolies elsewhere in the world.

But it does not mean these laws are completely ineffective, and this is why the business community has, for so many years, resisted the implementation of the Competition Ordinance in Hong Kong. In fact, its recent introduction allows the authors to describe the laborious negotiations over it and suggest that the hopes for the new law to reduce inequality could be unrealistic.

The second policy may even be more fundamental and involves a reform of Hong Kong's tax system. More specifically, within the conditions imposed by the Basic Law, what kind of tax reforms should be enacted to curb the growing inequality? Piketty, in his 2013 book, *Capital in the Twenty-First Century*, strongly advised introducing a progressive income tax. This suggestion is perfectly in line with the Hong Kong situation, as the current income tax is only partly progressive (Littlewood 2010: 267). At the same time, a tax on capital gains (much less radical and controversial than the tax on capital advocated by Piketty), which is notoriously lacking in Hong Kong, could also be suggested. These ideas are totally compatible with the limitations stated in the Basic Law and have been locally debated at length, but they have been finally dismissed by the government, which instead favoured a GST and simultaneous reduction of the income tax, for reasons which will be examined in the section titled 'A few remarks on tax and inequality'. In addition, other mechanisms could be explored to address the imbalances in the housing and land markets. For example, in Hong Kong's case, the two abovementioned measures (especially a tax on capital gains) could be completed by a mechanism that would incite large developers to progressively release (some of) their large land holdings to the market. But, owing to the complexity of the topic, the authors will not present an exhaustive analysis of Hong Kong's budget or even of its tax system (for a recent analysis, see Littlewood (2010)), while they will only introduce some basic facts on it. These two different policies (the introduction of the Competition Ordinance and the reform of the tax system) will be presented successively in the last two sections of this chapter.

The introduction of the Competition Ordinance and its limits

In 2012, Patrick Ho Chi-Ping, the former Secretary for Home Affairs who had since become one of the most vocal critics of the Hong Kong government, clarified, in just a few lines, the lack of competition in the housing sector, which was the result of the concentration of capital in developers' hands and their control of large segments of the city's economy. He linked these three elements to the lack of a competition law, which he supported. His commentary, which was published in the *China Daily*, a Communist Party front, justified examining the conditions behind the implementation of what would become the Competition Ordinance and its consequences. In the words of Patrick Ho:

> [T]he lack of competition in the housing [sector] is transforming this once free-trade paradigm into an oligarchy run by a few real-estate developers. Hong Kong may have a GDP per capita as high as Switzerland's, but its income inequality is worse than the Central African Republic's (...).

> Currently, the economic reins are held by a group of cross-sector corporate giants. These companies – near monopolies for years – operate in sectors with little-to-no competition, and, thus, influence the supply and pricing of many essential goods (…). In most cases, these entities started as property developers (…).
>
> As long as the government entrenches its high land price policy by restricting land supplies and shuns the introduction of a competition law, *the likely outcome is that Hong Kong's business giants will grow into monsters* (…).
>
> (Ho 2012; emphasis added)

Ho's essay echoed the view offered by many undergraduate economics textbooks: monopolistic or oligopolistic markets favour the extraction of rents to the detriment of consumers. The erection of barriers to entry in any business sector helps established companies create or protect such monopolies/oligopolies. Accordingly, a competition law that aims to limit the concentration of capital in the hands of a few should have been enacted in Hong Kong early on to prevent such a scenario.[27] However, that did not happen and by the time there was serious talk about passing the law, the conglomerates had, by then, grown large and powerful and they fiercely resisted its passage. The Competition Ordinance was eventually passed, but it contained no clause that would break the oligopolies already in place and obliged companies to divest. It does not mean it is a toothless piece of legislation, but, as examined below, the lack of divestiture clause singularly limits its scope.

The reasons given by the opponents of a competition law converged from three directions. First, they criticized the results of the 1990s reports published by the Consumer Council. From the economic, sociological and legal viewpoints, an interesting aspect of these criticisms concerned the definition and limits of the market. For example, the Consumer Council gave supermarkets quite a restrictive definition: 'establishments that engage in retail sales of general provisions including foodstuffs as one of the major items that use the self-service method' (Williams 2005: 247). Had a broader definition been used (to include, for example, convenience stores), the market share of the two biggest chains may have been different;[28] similarly the market share of the supermarkets for foodstuffs would have been much smaller if wet markets are to be included (ibid.). In a more recent study in December 2013, the Consumer Council found that the combined market share of ParknShop and health and beauty chain Watsons (both belonging to Li Ka-shing's empire) amounted to 23 per cent, while their respective counterparts, Wellcome and Mannings of Jardine's, commanded 35.9 per cent (Davies 2015). Similarly, in the property market, the market share of Hong Kong's large conglomerates varied, depending on whether one considers the total existing stock of housing or the newly built flats only.

The second source of opposition came from academia, especially Chicago School economists. According to this line of thought, a 'competition law and its enforcement do more harm than good and that bureaucratic second-guessing of the market should not be tolerated' (Williams 2005: 37; Williams does not espouse the position of the Chicago School of economics). Unsurprisingly, this reflects, with some nuances, the basic position of Richard Wong (2015: 255). The position of Leonard K. Cheng, an economist who is now a member of the Competition Commission and the President of the Lingnan University of Hong Kong, also deserves some attention. For Cheng, the state of Hong Kong's economy justified the implementation of a competition policy, but 'he worried that a comprehensive law implied a big new bureaucracy which would be too intrusive' (ibid.: 256). In short, such opposition was related to government intervention in Hong Kong's supposedly free market and, to a lesser extent, to the costs of implementing and enforcing the law.

The last source of opposition came from the government itself. The government noted that Hong Kong had been rated the freest economy in the world by the Fraser Institute and the Heritage Foundation for many years, so it argued that markets are perfectly competitive. Therefore, a competition law would not be useful and could even damage Hong Kong's reputation as a free market economy. It also noted that Hong Kong has few barriers to entry and is a small economy with an open trade policy.

These debates considerably slowed down the passage and implementation of the Competition Ordinance, which was first discussed during the 1990s, enacted in 2012, and finally took effect on 14 December 2015 – nearly a quarter century after Patten's speech. Internal and, more importantly, external pressures allowed for the government's passage of the law. Hong Kong was one of the last developed economies without such a law, as most of its neighbours, including China and Singapore, had all implemented it in recent years. As a Member of the WTO, Hong Kong also had to withstand pressure from the Organization, which was pushing for the law. Domestically, while the level of concentration in each industry and its consequences for consumers were difficult to establish once and for all, the arguments provided by the government can be easily dismissed: the fact that it does not erect barriers to enter Hong Kong's market does not mean that industries and companies that operate in the city refrain from doing it to their competitors, and the existence of such barriers justifies a competition policy. This may even be exactly the contrary, especially for small economies, as stated by Mical Gal:

> When trade barriers are reduced, competition policy plays an important role in facilitating trade by reducing private barriers to the entry of foreign importers ... the freer the trade, the stronger the incentives of firms to re-erect barriers and keep their historical advantage. Competition policy should [allow] foreign producers ... to compete with domestic producers on fair and equal terms ... [which] involves the formal right to compete ... [as well as] the creation and enforcement of rules of conduct prohibiting anti-competitive behaviour ... even in a small market with a liberal trade policy, competition policy has a critical role for increasing efficiency in the market

by reducing or eliminating abuses of dominant position and the incentives of firms to collude.

(Gal 2003: 41–42, cited by Williams 2005: 266)

Therefore, the drafting of a competition law was inevitable and only partly delayed by C.H. Tung's tenure as CE.[29] At the same time, resistance remained strong. The recent editorial in *Ming Pao Daily News* accurately reflects this situation:

> To facilitate the passage of the Ordinance, the authorities suggested that, of the four major issues calling for attention, only two be dealt with at the preliminary stage, i.e. price fixing and abuse of market dominance; while combined market power and mergers and acquisition would not be regulated until later.
>
> (*Ming Pao*, 16 December 2015)[30]

To be clear, the Ordinance was 'designed to prevent individual enterprises which enjoy a "substantial degree of market power" from abusing that power through predatory behaviour toward competitors' (Davies 2015), but it does not aim to limit companies from gaining market power. As was already the case when it was drafted (Williams 2009: 571), the Ordinance does not include any divestiture clause. In addition, it cannot serve as a base to decide which companies have too great a market power, which gave it less power than what was stated in the original draft: 'the Proposals suggest that the threshold for investigation of abuse should be set at the relatively low benchmark of forty percent of the relevant market product' (Williams 2009: 569).

This discussion suggests that while the Competition Ordinance may be able to tackle *some* cartels, price fixing and an abuse of market powers (even though all will be difficult to prove), large family-led conglomerates have been able to weaken it to the point in which its enforcement cannot lead to fundamental changes in Hong Kong's economic organization, which makes it powerless to dismantle existing conglomerates. It therefore comes as no surprise that an article on the *SCMP* stated: 'the Real Estate Developers Association of Hong Kong welcomes the Competition Law, and we are in full compliance with the law' (cited by Lee 2015).

A few remarks on tax and inequality

The issue of tax is unquestionably a sensitive one and deserves a much deeper appraisal than the quick comments the authors will make in this section. The issue is also intricately tied to its counterpart in any budget – expenditures. This discussion is largely beyond the focus of this book and, thus, only the main characteristics of Hong Kong's tax system will be presented below.

Accordingly, the aim of this section is to present the status of the recent discussions on possibly reforming Hong Kong's tax system in relation to the issues of inequality and land price. In Hong Kong, discussions of its tax system take on a special tone for two reasons. First, the Basic Law stipulates that

> the Hong Kong Special Administrative Region shall follow the principle of keeping the expenditure within the limits of revenues in drawing up its budget, and strive to achieve a fiscal balance, avoid deficits and keep the budget commensurate with the growth rate of its gross domestic product.
> (Article 107)

However, according to Littlewood, the article is written in sufficiently vague terms to allow for interpretation. For example, the expression 'shall follow the principles' can be interpreted in various ways; similarly, the four words, 'strive to (…) avoid deficits', leave room to flexibility.

The second reason is the 'spectacular successes' of the Hong Kong's tax system (Littlewood 2010: 2). For 2015–2016, the government recorded a surplus of HK$14.4 billion and fiscal reserves at the end of March 2016 stood at HK$842.9 billion (or nearly two years of expenditure),[31] which further increased since then to reach HK$915 in January 2017 (Van der Kamp, 2017). This huge fiscal reserve (for a territory of only seven million people) is the result of years of accumulated surpluses. From 1945 to 1997, the government almost always operated at a surplus (Littlewood 2013: 247). In fact, every year from 1990 to 1997, aside from 1995, which encountered a negligible deficit, ended with a surplus (Wong 2009: 139). Unfortunately, the handover coincided with a series of economic crises and the government ran a deficit for several years after that – which was not considered a breach of Article 107, as stated above –, which prompted the government to discuss a set of reforms.

Consequently, in 2000, the government explored the possibility of reforming the tax system (which had not experienced drastic changes since 1947) with the stated objective of making its public finances more stable and less vulnerable to external shocks. Reform was considered crucial, as Hong Kong's public finances only relied on limited sources of revenue: mostly the profits and salaries taxes (which garnered about 30–40 per cent of Hong Kong's total revenue during the 1990s) and non-tax revenue such as land premiums, investment income (mainly coming from the fiscal reserve), etc. During the 1990s, the non-tax revenue averaged at least 32 per cent of total public revenue with a peak of 55 per cent in 1999 (Wong 2009: 139–142).

These financial sources are not only limited in number, but also highly sensitive to economic developments. For example, in the context of the 1997 Asian Financial Crisis, land premiums represented 22.6 per cent of total revenue that year, but only 8.9 per cent the next year (Wong, 2009: 141, Table 6.3). More significantly, while total revenue increased from US$26 billion in 1996 to US$36 billion in 1997, it dropped back to US$27 billion in 1998 (ibid.: 140, Table 6.2), which made long-term projections difficult. It is true that to a certain degree, all government income is sensitive to economic developments, but, from the government's viewpoint, diversifying its revenue sources should mitigate this vulnerability.

The government's main propositions and the reactions of the public are outlined in the 2007 'Public Consultation on Tax Reform – Final Report' (Financial Services 2007).[32] In this report, the government acknowledged the existence of a narrow tax base and the need to enlarge it in order to make Hong Kong's public finances more resilient against global crises:

> Our revenue relies heavily on Salaries Tax, Profits Tax and non-tax revenue (including land premium and investment income from our fiscal reserves). Such income is susceptible to the ups and downs of economic cycles, which render our public finances highly volatile.
>
> (Ibid.: i)

In addition:

> the community is also aware that our population is ageing rapidly and the pressure of the government expenditure on health care and social welfare would increase. (…) Moreover, in order to maintain our competitiveness, we have to cope with a number of challenges. These include globalization and the trend that many overseas economies are reducing their direct tax rates to attract capital and talent. In addition, we have to upgrade our human capital.
>
> (Ibid.: ii)

These quotes perfectly reflect the government's position regarding the reform of Hong Kong's tax system. In light of the previous chapters, some of the stated reasons look rather dubious. For example, the need to upgrade human capital may look like an opportunity to introduce the new tax, but there is reason to believe that there are already too many graduates who cannot be absorbed by the labour market while the government has been pushing for more investment from the private sector (e.g. self-financed associate degrees), as shown in Chapter 3. Therefore, the solution may not be to increase investment substantially, but to reallocate existing funds. The same reserve can be made to the necessity to lower direct taxes, as it will be analysed below.

In fact, among all possible options, the government advocated introducing a GST, but in face of the public's negative reaction, as well as the opposition of some influential members of the business community, it gave up this idea. As Littlewood pointed out,

> the government might have been able to legislate against the wishes of the community but, given the composition of the Legislative Council, it could not legislate against the wishes of the representatives of the business. It was essentially for lack of business support, therefore, that the proposal failed.
>
> (Littlewood 2010: 275)

Littlewood refined his argument by adding that it was mainly the 'wise old capitalists' who objected, while the 'brash young capitalists' were enthusiastic about the proposal (ibid.: 275). In addition, with the improvement of the economic situation, the budget started to record large surpluses again, which both lowers the pressure to introduce a new tax and makes it more difficult to justify.

Opposition by the public and the old economic élite to the new tax was, of course, justified by the 'regressive nature of GST, which would widen the wealth gap and add to the financial burden of low income earners', as the government acknowledged itself (Financial Services 2007: ii). To answer these worries, it 'proposed a number of tax relief and compensation measures to address the regressivity of this tax' (ibid.), but its propositions were too general and seemed like empty promises to many Hongkongers. But the issue was more fundamental and related to the ideology hidden behind the implementation of a GST. Again, this is expressed in the most limpid way by Littlewood:

> The net effect of establishing a GST and cutting income taxes[33] would, of course, have been to shift a substantial part of the burden from those who were affluent onto those who were not. (…) [M]any people think that the principal iniquity in Hong Kong's existing tax is that the affluent do not pay *enough* tax. The Hong Kong government, however, took the opposite position: what was unfair about the existing system, it said, was that the burden was excessively concentrated on a relatively small number of taxpayers, who were paying *too much*.
>
> (Littlewood 2010: 252; original emphasis)

This conclusion reached by the government was based on the fact that only 35 per cent of Hong Kong's labour force paid revenue tax. Moreover, the burden 'was even more concentrated on large incomes than that figure suggests: the richest 3 percent of salaries taxpayers contributed 60 percent of salaries tax; and the richest 15 percent contributed 95 percent. Similarly, the top 800 companies paid 60 percent of the profits tax' (ibid.: 252–253).

However, again, the justification was dubious. On one hand, the system had many loopholes and 'permit[ted] avoidance and evasion of kinds and on a scale which in other developed jurisdictions would be considered scandalous' (ibid.: 2). On the other hand, Hong Kong's tax rates were (and remain) very low – much lower than in many other jurisdictions. For example, its profits tax is a flat rate of 16.5 per cent for corporations and 15 per cent for unincorporated businesses, while salaries are taxed at a progressive rate of 15 per cent. This means that in reality, only 1 per cent of Hong Kong's workforce actually pays this rate.[34] Finally, as noted in in the section titled 'From the concentration of the property market to the oligopolies of the Hong Kong economy', the land auction system effectively transfers the tax burden to the middle and working classes (through high private housing prices and rentals).

In light of this, the government's plan to implement a GST and, at the same time, lower revenue taxes, which would 'widen the wealth gap and add to the financial burden of low income earners', according to the government itself, would only increase inequality. The possible redistribution promised by the government would have certainly smoothed out the process *ex post*, but the system would have become even more unequal by then. It is, thus, evident that the fight against inequality did not feature prominently in the government's agenda and this can also be seen in its decision to reject other options and the way the competition law was implemented (on this last point, see the section titled 'The introduction of the Competition Ordinance and its limits').

Yet, what was not taxed may be more significant than what was taxed. The first item was the capital gains tax: gains in the stock and housing markets are not taxed. 'It is often ironic, if not strange, that money made through investment is not regarded as income or profit under the current tax system' (Wong 2009: 148–149). Second, the profits of Hong Kong firms and salaries of Hong Kong residents earned overseas are not taxable, which can lead to tax evasion in conformity with the hypothesis raised in Chapter 2. It seems clear that these taxes could raise substantial revenue and, at the same time, make the system more equitable (Littlewood 2010; Wong 2009).

However, these proposed taxes were rejected by the government with some questionable justifications. For example, the possibility of introducing a tax on capital gains was rejected on the ground that 'the tax may prompt investors to invest offshore in order to avoid tax on their investment gains in Hong Kong' (Financial Services 2007: 17). More straightforwardly, it stated 'imposing such taxes would have a detrimental impact on Hong Kong's status as an international financial and commercial centre. This is because investors would choose or relocate to other jurisdictions which do not impose such taxes (…)' (Government Consultation Paper 2006: 20, cited by Littlewood 2010: 266). But this rationale has a flaw: aligning Hong Kong with international practices would actually result in the introduction of such taxes (Littlewood 2010: 266). In addition, their implementation (or not) should not only be linked to the possible reaction of investors, but should be included in the broader framework of the Hong Kong financial system's role in China and worldwide (this argument was developed in Chapter 2).

The same comment could be raised with regards to the decision of the Advisory Committee on New Broad-Based Taxes to discard the possibility of introducing a worldwide income tax on businesses and individuals:

> The Advisory Committee notes that a complex system of tax credits together with double taxation arrangements are major prerequisites for a tax on worldwide income. Given Hong Kong's low tax rates, the revenue gain is unlikely to be significant. On balance, the Advisory Committee considers that such a tax should not be pursued.
>
> (Advisory Committee 2002: 18)

Again, the government's argument is not fully acceptable because in the current fight against tax havens and for greater financial transparency, countries and territories have developed double tax agreements (DTAs) that also include information exchanges. The main purpose of DTAs is to eliminate the double taxation that would affect cross-border investments and trade. DTAs have existed for nearly 100 years, but Hong Kong only signed its first one in 1998 (Littlewood 2010: 275). It is also doubtful that the tax would raise insignificant returns.[35]

This discussion constitutes an overview of the situation in 2007, when the idea to introduce a GST was shelved for the time being. As explained above, the main justification for a GST was to broaden Hong Kong's tax base, but with the purpose of leaving its overall economic system running similarly to the way it ran in the past. The government and its advisors did not really want to merge tax reform with fundamental changes to Hong Kong's larger economic and social contexts, which had benefited the city's political and economic élites (the incumbents).

However, the authors believe a reform on tax (as well as the introduction of a competition law) could have represented a golden opportunity to rethink some important issues Hongkongers currently face. For example, while the possible consequences of the reforms on the Hong Kong financial system's international role were raised (passive attitude), there was no apparent (or open) analyses on the type of tax reform that would be helpful for building a more competitive international financial system (proactive attitude). As noted in Chapter 2, in a world where most tax havens are on the defensive and have to agree to share information, inaction or simply maintaining the status quo is not acceptable in Hong Kong anymore. In this respect, the implementation of the AMLO (Anti-Money Laundering and Counter-Terrorist Financing (Financial Institution) Ordinance) and the AEOI (Automatic Exchange of Financial Account Information) can be seen as important steps towards such an objective, but the Panama papers have shown that the two reforms are insufficient and still relate to the 'passive attitude': no efforts were apparently made to link AMLO and AEOI to a possible reform of the tax system – which could include, for example, the creation of a worldwide income tax.

Similarly, the important aspect of inequality was at best ignored. There was no apparent effort to make use of the changes in the tax system to reduce inequality. The tax on financial gains, for example, was quickly brushed aside without sufficient justification. Differently stated, the government never intended to modify the tax system to make life fairer for many Hongkongers. On the contrary, as seen in Chapter 3, it has kept the system intact, even if it meant increasing redistributions to avoid too negative a reaction from the public. To the authors' opinion, this is how the rejection of the GST by the old guard of Hong Kong's business community should be read.

It is also in this light that the measures to make housing more affordable in Hong Kong included subsidies and the release of sites for public housing by the government. But here, too, taxation could be an important means to impact the availability and prices of housing. The idea would be to reconnect the land market to the housing market (i.e. pushing developers to release all or parts of their land banks). While the government has been silent on this issue, it has been written by some journalists and commentators in black and white:

> Three of the largest developers in Hong Kong – Sun Hung Kai Properties, Henderson Land and CK [Cheung Kong] Property – together hold about 760-plus hectares in land reserves. Adding those to land banks held by smaller developers would easily take us above 1,000 hectares of empty private land. (…)
>
> Developers should be forced to cough up more land. Impose punitive taxes on those who hoard land beyond a certain size or period. Most developed economies do not allow the indefinite hoarding of land. (…)
>
> Unfortunately, our tycoons and the Heung Yee Kuk, the rural power broker, still enjoy extensive influence. So better destroy the environment and evict the little guy [i.e. homeowners and villagers] (…).
>
> (Lo 2016a)[36]

Alex Lo is indubitably right to insist on this matter: releasing the land banks controlled by developers would have two positive effects. First, that would make more land available and relieve the pressure on the government to find more sites. Second, more land availability should lead to more flats and a decrease in housing prices. On the other hand, this could provoke a decrease in the land premium and a drop in the government's revenue, which could be compensated for by a tax on capital gains and/or a worldwide income tax, as suggested above.

These propositions show that the reform of the tax system and the reform of the financial system should be considered together. In any case, the above suggestions are only stated here with the hope of opening a discussion – any change in Hong Kong's taxation system should be thought through carefully, since spillovers and unanticipated effects are likely. However, in accordance with Piketty (2013), the authors want to emphasize that reforming Hong Kong's tax system can be a major tool for rebalancing the domestic economy, fighting inequality, and providing more opportunities to the middle class and educated youth through reshaping the financial system, including providing more access to lodging, for example. However, so far, the government has only considered the problem from the angle of expenditures. But, as the Education Bureau acknowledged:

> Redistribution helps to lift poverty and inequality and thereby promotes harmony and stability. *It also works well for the rich, because it mitigates economic inefficiencies* that often come with a large income gap.
>
> (Education Bureau 2015: 33; emphasis added)

In conclusion, this chapter documented how Hong Kong's economic evolution, in conjunction with globalization forces (including the opening up of China, the HK$–US$ peg and the growth of tourism), led to its increasingly unpopular oligopolistic situation. Since the 1960s, a handful of local companies, mostly led by Chinese families, have been able to gain control of its property market and, from there, many other sectors of the local economy. The consequences of this are multi-fold. At the most basic level, it has meant that Hongkongers pay for some goods at a higher level than the equilibrium price. More importantly, it explains the extreme concentration of capital in the Territory and its effects on inequality and its evolution. In other words, thanks to Hong Kong's oligopolies, a small number of people have been able to reap most of the benefits of its economic growth. The political situation, in which business interests have a disproportionate say in the government's (economic) decisions, has reinforced the status quo.

Therefore, it is no surprise that support for the existing economic system is declining and the middle class and younger generation feel trapped in a situation they largely do not and cannot control. The situation is not one in which opportunities for average Hongkongers are blossoming, but rather one in which they have become limited with little hope of escaping. Also, despite the existence of a large public housing programme in Hong Kong, many of its people clearly know that access to decent, affordable housing, (which is a basic human right[37]) is jeopardized.

Adequate policies, then, should be adopted to provide more opportunities for Hongkongers – especially if one considers that the capitalist system, which is encapsulated in the Basic Law (see Chapter 1), should provide equal opportunities to all. In this chapter, the authors examined how the government envisaged changing two major policies – the introduction of a competition law and a change in the tax system. Each had the potential to perhaps not provide equal opportunities to the average Hong Kong citizen, but at least to curb inequality to some extent.

However, the government did not seem determined to commit itself to fulfilling the two objectives of curbing inequality and providing equal opportunities to all. The saga of the implementation of the Competition Ordinance showed its resistance to enacting such a law and even when it finally did it, after decades of endless discussions and boggles, it did little to dismantle existing oligopolies or to prevent future ones. With regards to the proposed tax system, the same conclusions can be reached. The aborted reforms – basically, the introduction of a GST – were not proposed with the aim of curbing inequality, but, on the contrary, to create a tax for disadvantaged families that so far paid no tax. Thus, instead of using the tax system to curb inequality, the government preferred to keep intact the economic system that causes it, while trying to limit the resentment and dissatisfaction of its citizens via a limited redistribution programme (which a return to economic growth and budget surplus permitted) – a policy that has been termed 'budget sweeteners'[38] by journalists and commentators.[39] This has generated new debates regarding the use of the fiscal surpluses. Many commentators and journalists are openly criticizing the implementation of short-term sweeteners. They emphasize that sweeteners may just be a waste, while the money could have been used for sounds policies aiming at eradicating poverty and inequality (Lo 2017; Van Der Kamp 2017). Interestingly, even pro-government parties, such as the Democratic Alliance for the Betterment and Progress of Hong Kong, have joined the concert of protests. Its Chairwoman, Starry Lee Wai-king, recently declared:

> We hope the new chief executive will adjust his or her attitude towards our financial reserves and be ready to use the funds to reduce the gap between the rich and poor.
>
> (Cited by Van Der Kamp, 2017)

Thus, the debate over taxes has been partly superseded by new discussions over expenditures and, in particular, the use of the fiscal reserve. Both are two faces of the same coin, but, as shown by Thomas Piketty, a reform of the tax system is necessary to curb inequality and provide more opportunities to Hong Kong people.

Notes

1 The figure has climbed further from 3.6 to 4.7 in 2017 (Housing Authority webpage, assessed in August 2017).

2 There is also an income cap that eliminates most degree holders as soon as they start to work. The income limit was fixed at HK$10,100 on 1 April 2015 for single applicants and HK$16,140 for couples.

3 There was a slight decrease in recent years to 134,000 due to a change in the method of calculation, the famous 'point system' (Lee 2016). But that did not significantly alter the overall situation, as the judicial review showed.

4 For more details of this policy and its (negative) effects, see Goodstadt (2013).

5 The trend did not change in the past two years. As reported in a recent article in the *Guardian*, 'of 10 major metropolitan markets assessed in the housing affordability survey [by the urban planning research agency Demographia], Hong Kong had the least affordable housing for the sixth year in a row' (Davey 2016). And this, despite the recent lowering of speculation in the property market as will be examined below.

6 The Rating and Valuation Department (RVD) conducts a survey every year to provide a snapshot of the year-end vacancy positions of private domestic flats.

7 According to the RVD, in 2014, the number of vacant units decreased further to 43,263 representing 3.8 per cent of the stock. See, RVD, 'Private Domestic – Vacancy at Year End by Class', www.rvd.gov.hk/en/property_market_statistics/completions.html (accessed on 25 March 2016).

8 The difficulty in calculating the number of vacant flats leads to significantly different estimates. Chen Shaoming also agreed with Yiu that the vacancy rates for private housing are still high, but gives different data than the RVD: 5.5 per cent for an area size of 70–99 square metres, 7.3 per cent for 100–159.9 square metres, and 9.4 per cent for 160 square metres or more. See Chen Shaoming 陳紹銘 (2016) 'Housing problems can be solved by money' 房屋問題 錢能解決, *Xinbao*, www1.hkej.com/dailynews/commentary/article/1264802/%E6%88%BF%E5%B1%8B%E5%95%8F%E9%A1%8C++%E9%8C%A2%E8%83%BD%E8%A7%A3%E6%B1%BA (accessed on 25 March 2016).

9 To be complete, it should be added that the government itself has publicized alarming data which contradict those published by the RVD or the Bureau. According to Chen Shaoming, the *Director of Audit's Report* No. 61 (October 2013) indicated that on 31 March 2013, there were only 12,471 public housing units unoccupied. This is insignificant compared to the vacancy rates in private domestic housing. See Chen Shaoming 陳紹銘 (2014) 'To Decode the "[Low] Vacancy Rates" doublespeak of C.Y. Leung' 拆解梁振英「空置論」的語言偽術, *Xinbao*, 17 March.

10 According to Poon (2011: 12), the consolidation has continued: 'Some quarters have estimated that the aggregate residential market share held by the top three developers to be 77%.' However, she did not provide a source for this claim.

11 Sun Hung Kai Properties is controlled by the Kwok Family, which ranked 58th among the world's wealthiest people and fourth in Hong Kong in 2015, according to *Forbes*. This was up from their No. 86 ranking in 2014, despite a scandal in which Thomas Kwok was found guilty of bribing the former Chief Secretary, the number two leader in the Hong Kong government.

12 The same can be said about other big developers. Cheung Kong does not give details of its land bank, but Sun Hung Kai Properties supplies the following information on its website:

> As at 30 June 2015, the Group has a land bank in Hong Kong of 50.8 million square feet in terms of attributable gross floor area, consisting of 28.7 million square feet of completed investment properties and 22.1 million square feet of properties under development. The Group also owns over 30 million square feet (site area) of farmland in the New Territories, primarily along rail lines. The majority of this is in various stages of land use conversion.

It should be noted that 3 per cent of the 'completed investment properties' are residential. See www.shkp.com/Pages/land-bank (accessed on 8 January 2016).

13 After the Sino-British Joint Declaration, it was decided that the Hong Kong government would not put more than 50 hectares of land on the market every year. After 1995, however, this restriction was slightly relaxed as an attempt to cool down the market. See, among others, Augustin-Jean (2004).

14 Technically, the government is not selling the land, but it leases it with specific conditions attached. The government leases the land through several means, but the most common one is by auction.

15

> Since its beginning (1841), Hong Kong has been declared a free port. (…) At the time, the British Government decided that, apart from the military expenses, British taxpayers should not subsidize the running of the colony. Therefore, deprived of taxes on products (because of its free port status) and of resources from London, the government relied on the leasehold system.
>
> (Augustin-Jean 2005: 3–4)

16 As detailed in the next paragraph, there is also a disconnection between the land market and the housing market, due to the existence of developers' land banks.

17 See Basic Law, Cf. Art. 108: 'The Hong Kong Special Administrative Region shall, taking the low tax policy previously pursued in Hong Kong as reference, enact laws on its own concerning types of taxes, tax rates, tax reductions, allowances and exemptions, and other matters of taxation.'

18 As reported by the *SCMP*, Mainland Chinese developers acquired 27 per cent of all residential land sites in Hong Kong in 2016. These acquisitions are mainly in the high-end market, but it is clear that Mainland companies are driving prices up. This can be seen by the record price paid for a site in Ap Lei Chau, which fetched HK$16.86 billion. This amount was about 50 per cent higher than the original market valuation (Sito and Ng 2017). This point will be developed further in the conclusion.

19 Interestingly, in his 220-page book devoted to housing policy, Richard Wong spent only a few lines to address Hong Kong's oligopolistic market without any real discussion. Instead, he denied any influence its major developers had on prices:

> While Hong Kong's property development market is heavily concentrated today, it is not obvious that developers can control the total supply, behaving as if they are in collusion with one other. It is a common mistake to use monopoly power to explain price increases. Prices will rise if a competitive market is monopolized, but this is only a one-off effect. It can only explain why prices are higher, not why they continue to increase.
>
> (Wong 2015: 135)

Moreover, Wong did not discuss the rent effect created by the oligopolistic situation in Hong Kong (even if it were a one-off effect, as he suggested). And finally, there could be many reasons why the oligopolistic market pushed prices up (for example, the 'à la carte' release of the land plots that the major developers effectively control).

20 Another and related, issue, not developed in this book, is the government's claims that housing prices are high because of the scarcity of land. This rationale is flawed by the existence of the large land banks controlled by the developers. In addition, many scholars and commentators have denied that there is a land shortage in Hong Kong. For example, Dr Lam Pun Lee, a former Associate Professor at PolyU, thinks the government of C.Y Leung is exaggerating the problem of land shortage. See Lam Pun Lee 林本利 (2015) 'Does the Government Add Oil to the Already Deformed Property Market?' 樓市畸形政府火上加油？ *iMoney* (issue 389), 9 April, http://topick.hket.com/article/582064 (accessed on 15 March 2016).

21 In addition, the developers maintain control over the flats they build even after they sell them via management fees, which equal 13 per cent to 15 per cent of the flats' monthly rents (Poon 2011: 83).

22 These would be Wellcome, and ParknShop. Wellcome is controlled by Dairy Farm, part of the Jardine Matheson group. Jardine's also owns Hong Kong Land, which itself owns and manages about five million square feet of commercial space in prime locations in Central, as well as other malls in Asia (especially Singapore) and the Mandarin Hotels chain. It also expanded into the (luxury) residential market. ParknShop, as seen earlier, is part of Li Ka-shing's empire, which grew in very typical fashion: from its origins as a plastic flower factory, it entered the property business before expanding into retailing, telecommunications, utilities, etc. That these two local supermarket chains were able to not only limit, but eliminate, the competition from a retailer as big as Carrefour says something about how business is done in Hong Kong and how uncompetitive a market it is.

23 Of course, when the whole economic situation is deteriorating, as it is currently, there is no other solution for many landlords than to lower their rents, as explained in Chapter 2.

24 The authors thank David Herold for providing this reference.

25 Even though some young people may not be fully aware of this phenomenon, many learn it through experience. In some cases, they even express their frustration with it, as shown in the following quote from *Varsity*:

> Study hard, work hard, buy your own home – this is the Hong Kong Dream, the mantra drilled into Hong Kong youngsters from an early age. But many of the so-called post-80s generation are quickly discovering the dream has turned sour. Unable to buy their own flats, some are forced to live in shelters for the homeless; some manage to rent a little flat with friends. Here, four frustrated post-80s people talk about their difficulties in finding a place to call home.
>
> 'I was cheated by the government into studying for a degree! Now I cannot stop working or else I will end up sleeping on the street,' says Candy Ng Yuk-ching, a recent graduate in social work from Lingnan University. 'Even if you earn a degree after three years of university education, it does not guarantee you a job with an income that would allow you to afford an apartment,' she says.
>
> (Liu and Chan, 2010)

26 The seven largest developers are: Sun Hung Kai Properties, Cheung Kong Property, Henderson Land, Nan Fung Group, New World Development, Sino Land and Wheelock Properties. Basically, the developers are losing ground in the land auctions, but they keep their dominant position in the market due to their land banks. They also think the prices in the auctions are out of touch with reality. In his flowery language 'Property tycoon Li Ka-shing has said that the price of 'flour' (or land) now exceeds the cost of 'bread' (apartments)' (cited by Dong and Ying in *The Standard*, 2017).

27 Ho also accused the government of favouritism (almost in the same way as Poon):

> Dangerous and damaging monopolies form, however, when public policy is not impartial toward the market and creates a monopoly through direct or indirect intervention. These can be as government price controls or biased policies, or as

> subtle and discreet as the leaking of confidential data to certain private companies. This is when a monopoly can cause real harm to the economy. The experience of Hong Kong is a typical example.
>
> (Ho 2012)

The lack of concrete proof that the government engaged in favouritism compelled the authors to be careful with such an assertion. But, from what they wrote in Chapter 2, the possibility that the government and conglomerates have colluded was quite high.

28 However, the major convenience store chain in Hong Kong, 7-Eleven, is under the ownership of Dairy Farm – like Wellcome, which is itself under the Jardine Group.

29 The fact that the main business of the Tung Family was shipping – another of Hong Kong's concentrated industries – might have explained Tung's foot-dragging on this issue.

30 More precisely, 'at present, the Merger Rule only applies to mergers involving carrier licence holders within the meaning of the Telecommunications Ordinance' (Competition Commission, 'Guidelines on the Merger Rule'), www.compcomm.hk/en/legislation_guidance/guidance/merger_rule/merger_rule.html.

31 In 2015–2016, expenditures amounted to HK$436.6 billion. See Informational Services Department (2016), www.gov.hk/en/about/abouthk/factsheets/docs/public_finance.pdf.

32 Littlewood provided a complete analysis of the proposed reforms, the government's rationale behind these propositions, and the different steps it took since 2000 before submitting its report. See Littlewood (2010, Chapter 9).

33 For the government, a GST would allow it to lower the income tax, which it saw as necessary to maintain its competitiveness because many developed regions in the world had lowered their income tax rates (Littlewood 2010: 252). However, the argument did not seem valid because, as will be shown below, Hong Kong's tax rate is already quite low. See, also, the above quote from the Financial Services (2007: ii): 'These [challenges] include (…) the trend that many overseas economies are reducing their direct tax rates to attract capital and talent'.

34 For more details on the salaries tax, see Hong Kong government 2016, 'Tax Rates of Salaries Tax and Personal Assessment', www.gov.hk/en/residents/taxes/taxfiling/taxrates/salariesrates.htm.

35 For more details on this point, as well as on the technical issues pertaining to such taxes, see Littlewood (2010: 267, 275–281).

36 The columnist returned to the same topic a couple of months later:

> Here's a question for undergraduate students in public administration: if officials can evict hundreds of residents and villagers to make way for a public housing development, why can't they force developers to cough up idle land reserves?
>
> Actually, we all know why. But in this day and age, you would think it's about time to apply equal justice when it comes to recovering land in the public interest.
>
> (Lo 2016b)

37 See, the United Nations' Universal Declaration of Human Rights, Article 25:

> Everyone has the right to a standard of living adequate for the health and well-being of himself and of his family, including food, clothing, housing and medical care and necessary social services, and the right to security in the event of unemployment, sickness, disability, widowhood, old age or other lack of livelihood in circumstances beyond his control.

See www.un.org/en/universal-declaration-human-rights/.

38 From the viewpoint of policymakers, the best sweeteners are those that are limited in time and do not engage in repeated spending, which would create a long-term burden for the budget.

39 A search done in January 2017 by the authors in the *SCMP* website with two both keywords, 'sweeteners' and 'budget', netted 307 articles.

Bibliography

Advisory Committee on New Broad-Based Taxes (2002) 'Final Report to the Financial Secretary', Hong Kong: The Government of the Hong Kong Special Administrative Region.

Augustin-Jean, L. (2004) 'Intervention publique et développement à Hong Kong: un libéralisme en trompe-l'œil?' *Espaces et Sociétés*, 116–117(1–2): 209–233.

Augustin-Jean, L. (2005) 'Urban Planning in Hong Kong and Integration with the Pearl River Delta: An Historical Account of the Local Development?' *GeoJournal*, 62(1–2): 1–13.

Chen, S.M. 陳紹銘 (2014) 'To Decode the "[Low] Vacancy Rates" Doublespeak of C.Y. Leung' 拆解梁振英「空置論」的語言偽術, *Xinbao*, 17 March.

Chen, S.M. 陳紹銘 (2016) 'Housing Problems Can be Solved by Money' 房屋問題 錢能解決, *Xinbao*, www1.hkej.com/dailynews/commentary/article/1264802/%E6%88%BF%E5%B1%8B%E5%95%8F%E9%A1%8C++%E9%8C%A2%E8%83%BD%E8%A7%A3%E6%B1%BA, accessed 25 March 2016.

Competition Commission (2015) 'Guidelines on the Merger Rule', www.compcomm.hk/en/legislation_guidance/guidance/merger_rule/merger_rule.html, accessed 19 January 2016.

Davey, M. (2016) 'Housing 'Severely Unaffordable' as Sydney Price to Income Ratio worsens', *Guardian*, 16 January. www.theguardian.com/money/2016/jan/25/housing-severely-unaffordable-as-sydney-price-to-income-ratio-worsens, accessed 26 March 2016.

Davies, K. (2015) 'Competition Law Yet to be Tested', *China Daily* (Hong Kong Edition), 18 December, Comments: 10.

Dong, E. and M. Ying (2017) 'Record HK Bids by China Firms Will Continue, Says Developer', *The Standard*, 9 March, www.thestandard.com.hk/section-news.php?id=180536&fc=7, accessed 10 May 2017.

Education Bureau, Personal, Social and Humanities Education Section, Curriculum Development Institute (2015) 'Income Inequality', www.edb.gov.hk/attachment/en/curriculum-development/kla/pshe/references-and-resources/economics/income_eng.pdf, accessed 25 October 2016.

Financial Services and the Treasury Bureau, the HKSAR (2007) 'Public Consultation on Tax Reform. Final Report', www.taxreform.gov.hk/eng/pdf/finalreport.pdf, accessed 25 June 2016.

Gal, M.S. (2003) *Competition Policy for Small Market Economies*, Cambridge, MA: Harvard University Press.

Goodstadt, L.F. (2013) *Poverty in the Midst of Affluence: How Hong Kong Mismanaged its Prosperity*, Hong Kong: Hong Kong University Press.

Henderson Land Development Company Limited (2012) 'Annual Report 2012', www.hld.com/en/pdf/investor/annual/2012/annualreport/BusinessinHongKongLandBank.pdf, accessed 8 January 2016.

Henderson Land Development Company Limited (2015) 'Interim Report 2015', www.hld.com/en/pdf/investor/annual/2015/interimreport/hld_interim_2015_e.pdf, accessed 8 January 2016.

Ho, P.C.P. (2012) 'Monopolies Must Go if HK's Economy Is to Thrive', *China Daily* (Hong Kong Edition), 18 April.

Hong Kong Government (December 2016) 'Tax Rates of Salaries Tax and Personal Assessment', www.gov.hk/en/residents/taxes/taxfiling/taxrates/salariesrates.htm, accessed 19 January 2017.

Hong Kong Housing Authority (2015) 'Number of Applications and Average Waiting Time for Public Rental Housing', www.housingauthority.gov.hk/en/about-us/publications-and-statistics/prh-applications-average-waiting-time/, accessed 4 January 2016.

Hui, C.M.E. (2004) 'An Empirical Study of the Effects on Land Supply and Lease Conditions on the Housing Market. A Case of Hong Kong', *Property Management*, 22(2): 127–154.

Informational Services Department, the HKSAR (2016) 'Hong Kong: The Facts – Public Finance', April www.gov.hk/en/about/abouthk/factsheets/docs/public_finance.pdf, accessed 15 February 2017.

JLL (2017) 'Hong Kong: Top Local Developers Losing Influence in Residential Market', Press Release, 28 February, www.jll.com.hk/hong-kong/en-gb/news/577/top-local-developers-losing-influence-in-residential-market, accessed 10 May 2017.

Lai, N. and K. Wang (1999) 'Land-Supply Restrictions, Developer Strategies and Housing Policies: The Case in Hong Kong', *International Real Estate Review*, 2(1): 143–159.

Lam, Pun Lee林本利 (2015) 'Does the Government Add Oil to the Already Deformed Property Market?' 樓市畸形 政府火上加油？ *iMoney* (issue 389), 9 April, http://topick.hket.com/article/582064, accessed 15 March 2016.

Lee, E. (2015) 'Hong Kong Business Groups Do Not Appear to be Worried over the Competition Law's Impact on Their Dealing with Members', *South China Morning Post*, 14 December.

Lee, E. (2016) 'Single "Barred from Getting Public Housing"', *South China Morning Post*, 16 November.

Legislative Council Panel on Housing (2013) 'Analysis of Housing Situation of Waiting List Applicants as at end-June 2013', LC Paper No. CB(1)184/13–14(03), www.legco.gov.hk/yr13-14/english/panels/hg/papers/hg1104cb1-184-3-e.pdf, accessed 3 November 2015.

Littlewood, M. (2010) *Taxation without Representation. The History of Hong Kong's Troublingly Successful Tax System*, Hong Kong: Hong Kong University Press.

Liu, E. and V.C.H. Chan (2010) 'Housing Dream out of Reach', *Varsity*, 114 (March): 23–25.

Liu, Y. (2014) 'Hong Kong Ranks World's No 1 for "Most Unaffordable" Housing', *South China Morning Post*, 22 January.

Lo, A. (2016a) 'Blinkered View in Search for Land', *South China Morning Post*, 31 October, www.scmp.com/comment/insight-opinion/article/2041715/blinkered-view-search-land, accessed 13 January 2017.

Lo, A. (2016b) 'The Land is There for Housing, if Officials Remove Their Blinkers', *South China Morning Post*, 26 December, www.scmp.com/comment/insight-opinion/article/2057295/land-there-housing-if-officials-remove-their-blinkers, accessed 13 January 2017.

Lo, A. (2017) 'John Tsang – the Most Imperfect of Our Imperfect Leadership Hopefuls', *South China Morning Post*, 14 February, www.scmp.com/comment/insight-opinion/article/2070532/john-tsang-most-imperfect-our-imperfect-leadership-hopefuls, accessed 14 February 2017.

Luk, J. (2001) *An Investigation on the Effects of the Hong Kong Dollar Peg on the Hong Kong Financial and Real Properties* (DBA Dissertation), Dept. of Management, The Hong Kong Polytechnic University, http://theses.lib.polyu.edu.hk.ezproxy.lb.polyu.edu.hk/handle/200/1055, accessed 6 April 2016.

Piketty, T. (2013) *Capital in the Twenty-First Century*, Cambridge, MA: Harvard University Press.

Poon, A. (2011) *Land and the Ruling Class in Hong Kong*, 2nd edition, Hong Kong: Enrich Professional Publishing.

Pritchard, S. (2006) 'A Not-Entirely-Free Economy Needs Some New Rules', *Hong Kong Journal*, www.hkjournal.org/archive/2006_summer/pritchard.html, accessed 16 January 2016.

Rating and Valuation Department, 'Private Domestic – Vacancy at Year End by Class', www.rvd.gov.hk/en/property_market_statistics/completions.html, accessed 25 March 2016.

Sito, S., S. Zhen and N. Ng (2017) 'Chinese Builders Pay Record HK$16.86b for Ap Lei Chau Site', *South China Morning Post*, 24 February, www.scmp.com/property/hong-kong-china/article/2073805/mainland-developers-logan-kwg-win-residential-site-ap-lei, accessed 10 March 2017.

Sun Hung Kai Properties, 'Land Bank', www.shkp.com/Pages/land-bank, accessed 8 January 2016.

The Economist (2014) 'Our Crony-capitalism Index: Planet Plutocrat', www.economist.com/news/international/21599041-countries-where-politically-connected-businessmen-are-most-likely-prosper-planet, accessed 24 July 2017.

'The Basic Law of the Hong Kong Special Administrative Region of People's Republic of China', www.basiclaw.gov.hk/en/basiclawtext/index.html, accessed 17 August 2015.

TimeOut Hong Kong (2012a) 'The Men Who Rule Hong Kong', 15 February, www.timeout.com.hk/feature-stories/features/48820/the-men-who-rule-hong-kong.html, accessed 9 September 2015.

TimeOut Hong Kong (2012b) 'One Degree of Separation', www.timeout.com.hk/extra/one-degree-of-separation/, accessed 9 September 2015.

Transport and Housing Bureau (2013) 'Assessing the Vacancy Situation of Housing Units in Hong Kong' (Follow-up paper), *Subcommittee on the Long Term Housing Strategy, Legislative Council of the Hong Kong Special Administrative Region*, LC paper No. CB(1)194/13–14(01), www.legco.gov.hk/yr12-13/english/panels/hg/hg_lths/papers/hg_lths0927cb1-194-1-e.pdf, accessed 3 October 2015.

Tse, R.Y.C. (1998) 'Housing Price, Land Supply and Revenue from Land Sales', *Urban Housing*, 35(8): 1377–1392.

United Nations (1948) 'Universal Declaration of Human Rights', www.un.org/en/universal-declaration-human-rights/, accessed 15 January 2017.

Van der Kamp, J. (2017) 'The Fiscal Reserves Are Our Money, and They Are Not Being Properly Used', *South China Morning Post*, 1 February, www.scmp.com/comment/insight-opinion/article/2068160/fiscal-reserves-are-our-money-and-they-are-not-being, accessed 1 February 2017.

Wang, S. (2015) *Effects of Land Policies and Development Strategies on Housing: A Case of Hong Kong* (MSC Dissertation), Program in Real Estate Development, Massachusetts Institute of Technology.

Williams, M. (2005) *Competition Policy and Law in China, Hong Kong and Taiwan*, Cambridge: Cambridge University Press.

Williams, M. (2009) 'The Lion City and the Fragrant Harbour: the Political Economy of Competition in Singapore and Hong Kong Compared', *Antitrust Bulletin*, 54(3): 517–577.

Wong, W. (2009) 'The Days after the End of the Asian Miracle: the Budget Crisis of Hong Kong', in M. Sing, *Politics and Government in Hong Kong: Crisis under Chinese Sovereignty*, Abingdon: Routledge, pp. 136–161.

Wong, Y.C.R. (2015) *Hong Kong Land for Hong Kong People*, Hong Kong: Hong Kong University Press.

Yeung, L.S. (2011) *An Analysis of the Policy Making Process in the Hong Kong Special Administrative Region: A Case Study of Subsidised Home Ownership Schemes since 1997* (Master dissertation), Department of Politics and Public Administration, The University of Hong Kong.

Yiu, E.C.Y. (2009) 'Negative Real Interest Rate and Housing Bubble Implosion – an Empirical Study in Hong Kong', *Journal of Financial Management and Construction*, 14(3): 257–270.

Yiu, E.C.Y. (2013) 'Hong Kong Monetary Policy and Housing Affordability', *Alternative Social Projects in the Context of the European Crisis and the Hong Kong Transformation*, International Seminar, 29 November, Department of Applied Social Sciences/China-Europa Centre, The Hong Kong Polytechnic University.

Yiu, E.C.Y. (2015) 'Housing Price Hikes by Negative Real Interest Rate? A Differencing Model Test on the Housing Markets of Hong Kong and Macau', *International Journal of Housing Markets and Analysis* (forthcoming).

Conclusion

This book has focused on the main economic factors that have affected the prospects of many Hongkongers. The emphasis was put on the better-educated members of the younger generations, who are suffering from Hong Kong's existing economic conditions more than their elders, who had better access to affordable lodging and tended to find better jobs when they were the same age. Thus, the younger generations face a difficult task to anticipate and make plans, especially since the role of Hong Kong in the globalization process and in the Chinese economy remains uncertain. Even though the authors did not detail it in the book, the same statement could be made with regards to Hong Kong's political situation: the economic lens that was adopted here should not be regarded as the only angle to analyse the problems described in this book. The handover and gradual integration with China have caused worries for many Hongkongers, who fear losing their unique culture and way of life – not to mention their freedom of expression (i.e. their core values). In other words, the struggle by many Hongkongers for 'genuine democracy' has also been genuine. Put together, these different parameters have created an anomie for a significant portion of its population.

So far, however, this book has not fully linked the Umbrella Movement to these economic conditions. The reality is that the slogans and messages used during the Movement were mostly political and only a few were directed to the economic situation. This conclusion aims to fill this gap and to show how the economic conditions and the call for democracy are two sides of the same coin and are intrinsically tight together.

More specifically, while the actions of the protesters were mostly addressed to the Decision of the 31 August 2014 of the National People's Congress Standing Committee (NPCSC) and the Hong Kong government that insisted on it, the political forces behind this Decision, however powerful, were also buttressed by the local social and economic situation. The thesis presented in this conclusion, therefore, is that the current demands for democracy have also been triggered by the political and social deadlock, which itself was formed by the actions of interest groups since at least the 1980s. This situation, which mainly occurred for economic reasons, also generated contradictions between the economic and political system on the one hand, and the aspirations of a sizable share of the population on the other. The introduction of the Basic Law, while protecting the civil liberties and the way of life of the locals, has contributed to maintain these contradictions by freezing the economic and social system as it was at the beginning of the 1990s. In recent years, the influence of globalization and of China's economy in the Territory have further reinforced this situation, which led to more and more frequent protests. These different points are clarified below.

To start with, the Umbrella Movement is the latest outcome of a long string of demands for democracy that can be dated back to at least the end of nineteenth century. In the 1980s, in relation to the Sino-British negotiations over the future of Hong Kong and the Tiananmen Square protests in 1989, these demands became more pressing and structured, and involved a larger share of the local population. At the beginning of the 1990s, they gave birth to democratic parties – the Democratic Party itself was created in 1994 as a merger of former movements –, in line with the mistrust many people had in the Chinese government in the aftermath of the Tiananmen Square crackdown and the proximity of the handover. As the authors have mentioned in Chapter 1, the same mistrust has regained strength recently: the attempt by the government to enact an anti-subversion law, as requested by Article 23 of the Basic Law, has brought half a million people to the streets. Similarly, in 2010–2011, the proposal to introduce a 'Moral and National Education' curriculum in schools was 'welcomed' by protests from students and their parents, as the teaching materials presented by the government were criticized as biased. This latest event gave birth to new political and social concern groups such as Scholarism, a student activists group that has played a central role during the Umbrella Movement.

The two proposals (the anti-subversion law and the National Education curriculum) have been shelved under the pressure of the street. Nevertheless, they are not abandoned: it is difficult to believe, for example, that the Hong Kong government can indefinitely defer the implementation of an anti-subversion law since it is a constitutional obligation. But, more importantly for the conclusion of this book, these two mass protests can also be seen as direct precursors of the Umbrella Movement. Both showed that people have become very sensitive to any measure that, in their opinion, may jeopardize their civil liberties, and that they are ready to protect them if they feel necessary. The Movement itself arose in the context of the 31 August 2014 Decision from the NPCSC to grant democracy, but under a very restrictive framework (see Chapter 1). It outstripped some previous initiatives, such as the OCLP, launched in 2013 by Benny Tai Yiu-ting.[1]

This historical pattern is well known. It shows the political roots of the Umbrella Movement, in full consistency with the prevailing views of scholars like Ortmann (2015, 2016) and Veg (2015). It also helps to draw major differences between the Umbrella Movement and other movements such as Occupy Wall Street. Protesters during Occupy Wall Street were more radical than their Hong Kong counterparts, as they strongly rejected global capitalism – on the contrary to the Umbrella participants. Hong Kong demonstrators were also more legalistic (Veg 2015: 55–56): even though their occupation could be seen as illegal, they still wanted changes to be implemented within the framework of the Basic Law. According to them, democratic reforms should be conducted in accordance to Article 45 of the Basic Law, and they did not challenge China's sovereignty over Hong Kong – apart from a tiny, albeit growing minority. The two movements, however, shared similar concerns, most notably the desire to build a more equal and fairer society: '[f]or decades, neoliberal ideology in Hong Kong was justified on the grounds that it provides "equal opportunity" ' (Ma 2011: 688), but many Umbrella Movement participants understood that it was not the case: the call for democracy was also an attempt to address this issue.

It is at this level that economic considerations can be reintroduced. As it will be shown, even scholars who insisted on the prevalence of political factors in the motives for the Umbrella Movement, did not ignore economic parameters. Ortmann, for example, acknowledged the 'growing dissent against business interests among young social activists' since the end of the 2000s, in line with the Choi Yuen Tsuen protests (Ortmann 2015: 44). Similarly, Veg, while stating that the 'Hong Kong demands were univocally concerned with formal democracy and the rule of law rather than global capitalism' (Veg 2015: 55–56), also pinpointed that students demanded more fairness in the system, 'questioning the ideology of maximizing profit while leaving politics to a higher authority' (ibid.: 69). Veg also highlighted that the Mainland authorities were relying, as the British before them, on a handle of tycoons to govern the Territory. More broadly, there is an agreement among scholars that the demands of the protesters were not only political, but also social, and that 'students issued critiques of capitalism and productivism, environmental pollution and economic alienation' (ibid.: 71).

The point is clear: it is not possible to separate political demands from existing social and economic conditions. For the protesters, a democratic polity also implied a fairer society with more equal economic opportunities to all. Therefore, the thrust for democracy is intricately linked to changes in the social realm. In Hong Kong, this can be seen from at least two angles. The first is tied to the influence of the business community in governmental affairs. The symbiosis between the government and economic interests undoubtedly benefited business circles, but also generated social instabilities in the long run. To make it short, this first link between democratic and economic issues is provided by the refusal of the business community to accept the implementation of democratic reforms. This attitude, which can be attested since at least the 1980s, can be explained by the fact that business people understood that more democracy would automatically imply social changes, including 'the possible expansion of social redistribution, more powerful unions, and more business regulations' (Ortmann 2015: 39) – which would lead, the authors add, to an increase in taxes. This was a powerful motive, still put forward by the CE during the Movement as the authors will present at the end of this conclusion.

This point leads directly to the second aspect as this motive directly conflicts with the demands of the (educated) youths for a fairer world. The opposition between the demands of the younger generations and the refusal of the economic élites to introduce at least some of them has led to a declining support for the economic system. This is especially the case since these young people have increasing difficulties to find their place in it. These two aspects will be presented in greater detail below.

First, the refusal of the economic élites to introduce democracy in Hong Kong provided a first basis to the rapprochement between the local capitalists and the Beijing authorities (see Chapter 1). Again, there is a strong intermeshing between political and economic affairs that deserves some explanations.

In a well-documented book, Suzanne Pepper raised an important question: she wondered why Hong Kong did not start to democratize before the very end of the colonization era, which ran contrary to the experience of most other former British colonies. For her, an element of answer lies in the fact that Hong Kong always remained special: its 'original status as an integral part of the Chinese empire could never be discounted because the Chinese themselves refused to do so, leaving uncertain the exact nature of its standing as a full-fledged British possession' (Pepper 2008: 27). For Pepper, this factor prevented the colonial and British governments to progressively trigger a democratization process. Ortmann further added to this argument that the 'British abandoned their plan to democratize the colony in 1952', after the Chinese government threatened to take it back by force (Ortmann 2015: 34–35). Besides its ideological stance, the attitude of the Chinese government was also dictated by the risk that democratization could lead to (demands for) independence after 1997. To limit such risks, the Chinese government requested and obtained, in 1972, that Hong Kong was removed from the list of 'Territories to which the Declaration on the Granting of Independence to Colonial Countries and Peoples applied' (United Nations, 1985). The fact is that Hong Kong was by-product of the Opium Wars; it was created first and foremost by, and for, the merchant interests, with the support of the military. Hong Kong was merely thought of as an economic place to trade with China and as a military outpost in the Far East. There was not much desire for the British to develop the Territory beyond these dual functions until a recent date (and under the pressure of the population) and thus they could accommodate, most of the time, the position of the Chinese government, which did not aim to take back Hong Kong before the lease of the New Territories expired.[2]

This historical background explains the existence of the economic bias in political-making and why business people were always over-represented in the government apparatus and in advisory boards. It is then easy to understand the reluctance of the business community to engage in democratic reforms. After all, it managed to develop a system which perfectly suited its interests, thanks to the comprehensive attitude of the government – and it was not so willing to amend it.[3] After the 1966–1967 riots, it understood that minimal social and welfare measures had to be introduced so as to maintain the political and economic order. In the 1980s, the fact that British economic interests were finally superseded by rising Chinese family-led conglomerates did not change the perspective: these groups responded to the growing demands for democracy by a strong rejection of it. In short, while the demands for democracy were stronger, the answer of the economic élites, in conjunction with the authorities in the Mainland, which feared that could either lead to Hong Kong independence or the spread of democracy in China, was a strong rejection – leading to a progressive blockade of the system.

At first, this divorce between the ruling economic class and the newly educated people was not fully visible, because the growing economy and the globalization process required highly qualified people, who then enjoyed relatively high salaries. However, this pattern changed after 1997 because economic crises multiplied and opportunities for the educated youths were on the decline. The economic and social system, as it has developed since the 1960s, generated contradictions that became apparent. The wealth gap, enlarged by the existence of Ricardian rents (see below), not only widened, but also became inacceptable to many.

Thus, this contradiction between a political system that has been frozen by the Mainland authorities and by the economic élites to protect their interests formed the bedrock for the democratic protest of 2014. The demands for democracy and for a fairer economic and social system were two sides of the same coin. As noted above, protesters were not, in their great majority, revolutionary: with no suitable alternative in sight – the only other available model they could apprehend, across the Pearl River Delta, did engender corruption, inequality and environmental problems – they did not search to remove the capitalist system; they just wanted it to provide equal opportunities to all.

Nonetheless, as limited as these demands may have been, if they were effectively tackled by the government, they would lead to deep changes. But, the other way around, if, in the near future, they are not properly addressed, they may cause further turmoil. In this respect, the article published in the *South China Morning Post* by Paul Yip, just a few months before the start of the Umbrella Movement, may be seen premonitory – or, maybe, it only reflected the deep knowledge that the author, who is a Professor of Social Work at the University of Hong Kong, had of the situation: 'Wealth gap will break Hong Kong if we don't change the economic order' (Yip 2014). Since then, such articles proliferated in the media – some of them directly linking the economic hardship of the younger generations and the Umbrella Movement.[4] In this respect, the award for catastrophism goes to Yonden Lhatoo, senior editor at the *South China Morning Post*, who titled one of his chronicles: 'Hong Kong's Appalling Wealth Gap is a Burning Fuse for Revolution' (Lhatoo 2016). One of the issues raised by these newspapers' articles is not only if the situation is as serious as they claim; it is also if the proliferation of such news will not lead to a self-fulfilling prophecy....

This provides us with a direct link to the second issue, for which several elements have already been provided: the way the declining support of the young generation for the existing economic system is articulated with the demand for more democracy. The first point is at the abstract and theoretical levels. The economic theory of the market supposed a conceptual equality between buyers and sellers. In this model, the opposition between suppliers and purchasers, as well as their inherent diverging interests, is resolved by prices: markets have no thickness and are only defined by the equilibrium price. In the real world, this proposition has crystallized in the ideology of the 'Lion Rock Spirit': everyone starts in the same line, and success depends on personal ability. With hard work and acumen, everyone can become a billionaire. But the younger generations, in the face of economic hardship, have more and more difficulties to adhere to this message: they discovered that the market, at least as it is organized in Hong Kong, is not the fair institution which gives equal chance to anyone that is described in economic textbooks and in government's discourses (see Chapter 2).

It is thus no coincidence that a banner was hanged on the Lion Rock on the 23 October 2014 as a support for the protesters and a call for a better future (the banner was removed the next day by the government). The banner read 'I want universal suffrage'. But in an interview, one of the members of the group who climbed to install the banner, wearing a Superman suit, added:

> The chief executive only cares about the rich people living on Victoria Peak (…). We think the spirit of Lion Rock isn't just about money.
>
> The people fighting for real universal suffrage all over Hong Kong have shown great perseverance. This kind of fighting against injustice, strength in the face of troubles, is the true Lion Rock spirit.
>
> (Cited by Lo *et al.* 2014)

The quote is a vivid testimony of the relationship between democracy and the fight for justice. As noted above, more and more people are aware that hard work is just not enough to make a better living; and they believe less and less that the poor are self-responsible for their situation – on the contrary, surveys show that an increasing number of people think that poverty is (also) generated by society. The above quote pinpointed that a fairer society figured high in the demands of the protesters: the demand for democracy was also a demand for more equal opportunities – and a revival of the 'Lion Rock Spirit'. The educated youths do not call for an equal society; they just want a fairer one.

Behind the scenes, then, economic factors were in the backs of many protesters' minds. An exhibition organized by students at PolyU to commemorate the Umbrella Movement a few months after the events (22 March–6 April 2015) fully confirmed this point: aside from photos and paintings made during the Umbrella Movement, most of the artefacts and their captions were related to Hongkongers' daily lives and economic hardships. For example, under one artefact – a simple brick – the caption read: 'in Hong Kong, you need at least four million [Hong Kong dollars] to buy a decent flat'. Another caption under childhood stationaries stated: 'since when the small shops [have] disappeared from our estate malls[5] and [were] replaced by cold unitary chain shops?' The modesty of these artefacts, together with the pictures and the slogans, reinforced the feeling of helplessness for a generation that has difficulty in integrating in the current system. And the same feeling extends to even younger people. In a recent newspaper article, a social worker, Eddie Wong Lok-man, reported on the harrowing discussion he had with a 14-year-old student:

> He told me his biggest worry was that he would never be able to afford a home, and he said he needed to start planning even at this age. [He added that] many [young people] think getting into local universities means nothing unless one can get into the top three. They see tertiary education more as getting [into] huge debt than achieving social mobility.
>
> In short, he sees nothing he can aspire to for life.
>
> (Chan 2015)

Thus, among the two possibilities (voice or exit) raised by Hirschman (1970) and in the face of declining economic opportunities for the younger generations (and for other people as well) in Hong Kong, nearly only the 'voice' option is available to them. Little wonder that many students and young people are demanding more say in the political arena, which is a clear signal that the existing political and economic system no longer works for them.[6]

In the remainder of this conclusion, the authors will show, as a recollection of the analyses presented in this book, that a convergence of factors, including globalization forces, the rise of the Chinese economy, and the structure of the domestic economy and its evolution, explains this situation. They mainly insist on the fact that long-applied solutions, such as boosting the GDP, will not be sufficient, and that more innovative policies must be implemented.

First, on the international side, the difficulties the younger generation and the middle class are facing are far from unique in Hong Kong, and they are shared in many global cities in the world – a point the authors have emphasized in the discussion on polarization. However, whether there is a disappearance, or the development of a new middle class does not really change the perspective, because the opportunities for social mobility are fewer and are further diminishing: as the above citation illustrates, a university degree is now indispensable to get a good job, but, with the proliferation of degree holders and the likely crowding effect, many graduates can only hope to become 'Associate Professional' – and sometimes less. Thus, as already noted, in relation with this gloomy future for young people and fresh graduates, the Umbrella Movement bears some resemblance with other movements that have shaken several global metropolises in recent years such as Occupy Wall Street, or the Indignants Movement in Spain – even though the economic situation in Spain is much more deteriorated than in Hong Kong, especially in terms of employment.[7]

Similarly, in the Epilogue of his book on Hong Kong housing policies, Richard Wong pointed out that the difficulties of the younger generations and the middle class were not unique to Hong Kong, but he also insisted on some of the local specificities. According to him (and the authors have provided evidence of this in this book), globalization created the conditions for an accumulation of wealth for a few and helped push housing prices up. Hong Kong's rigid housing supply, China's economic growth and the HK$'s linked exchange rate to the US$ also helped lead to Hong Kong's current state. In addition:

> Large landlords and property developers in Hong Kong have been major beneficiaries of the four factors I describe [above]. They have become extremely capital rich and able to make major acquisitions within Hong Kong and also abroad. Thus, it is those factors that have resulted in the growing concentration of wealth, not the post-1997 political arrangements.
>
> The creation of a tycoon-dominated economy was largely an accident of the circumstances Hong Kong found itself to be in during the 1980s and 1990s. Those who started with property or were able to acquire [it] reaped a huge windfall gain.
>
> (Wong 2015: 216–217)

Fair enough. But Wong did not propose policies to mitigate the negative consequences of this situation; nor does he analyse the effects of this oligopoly, which inevitably created Ricardian rents: there is an implicit transfer of wealth from consumers (mainly, the working and middle classes) to developers and this rent is further enlarged since developers also control large portions of the retail and utilities sectors. This is exactly the phenomenon described by Stiglitz:

> But economists now apply the term 'rents' more generally, not only to land rents, but also to the returns, say, to a monopolist ('monopoly rents'). If rents – not only land rents or the returns to monopoly power and other forms of market exploitation – increase, there will be corresponding capital gains. Much of the increase in inequality in incomes and wealth is associated with an increase in rents and capital gains, reflecting an increased value of real estate and increased market power (exploitation) in many sectors of the economy.
>
> (Stiglitz 2015: 95)

Since Hong Kong only recently implemented the Competition Ordinance, rent-seeking has been in place for a long time by the structure of its economic system, including the rules and regulations that highlight the contradiction between the principles of a market economy and the historical development of a capitalist system. Plus, even with the Ordinance in place, it is unlikely that this situation will change. As Wong noted, this is also the result of Hong Kong's historical evolution since at least the end of World War II and perhaps earlier: the original decision to make the Hong Kong government the ultimate owner of almost all the land in the city (and thus, a full market player) certainly favoured this interpretation.

However, in the face of growing inequalities which the current system helped cause, the role of the government in managing the economy should be reconsidered, especially in the prospect of ensuring social stability in Hong Kong for the long term. It is unlikely that selling some public housing stocks or expanding access to higher education, as Wong recommended, will suffice to narrow Hong

Kong's enormous wealth gap when in 2014, the wealthiest 10 per cent of its population owned as much as the poorest 77.5 per cent – up from 69.3 per cent in 2007 (Noble 2014).

Similarly, focusing on economic growth is equally likely to be unsuccessful. This temptation – and the assumed strategy – for the government to address the challenges of inequality was directly inspired by the ideas of economist Robert Lucas and merely calls for increasing the size of the economic pie. This idea was once again well-captured by Stiglitz:

> One noted economist, a University of Chicago Nobel Prize winner, Robert Lucas, put it forcefully: 'Of the tendencies that are harmful to sound economics, the most seductive and … poisonous is to focus on questions of distribution.
>
> Like so many conservative economists, he argued that the best way to help the poor was to increase the size of the nation' s economic pie, and he believed that focusing attention on the small slice of the pie given to the poor would detract attention from the more fundamental issue of how to enlarge the pie.
>
> (Stiglitz 2015: 272)

This policy is destined to fail – for the simple reason that it has already failed in the past: Hong Kong's GDP increased by over 46 per cent in real terms from 2004 to 2014 and by nearly 68 per cent from 2000 to 2014, but inequality not only did not decrease, but rather grew! The increased concentration of wealth mentioned above proves such a plan is counterproductive. At the same time, the fact that such a remedy for it is still trotted out by economists encourages the Hong Kong government to avoid making radical changes to its economic policies. To be fair, as explained above, some of the problems resulted from globalization and, hence, are beyond the control of a small and open economy like Hong Kong's. For example, even though a reform of the HK$–US$ peg may be desirable, it is difficult (and risky) to implement it – not least because it would create uncertainty over the future of the HK$. But other issues are directly related to the organization of the domestic economic and political system as the authors will develop below.

Hong Kong's economic (or political and social) policy is controlled by the same group of people who have benefited most from the status quo. Chapter 1 showed how advisory boards are influenced by business interests. At the same time, the Basic Law has been drafted with the purpose to protect the current economic system by guaranteeing the retention of Hong Kong's supposed free market capitalist system. However, that does not mean reforms are not possible altogether. Indeed, some have been implemented, but with a lack of ambition and with the desire to keep the status quo. For example, the authors have shown that the Competition Ordinance, after being delayed for years, was implemented in a way that did not really alter the existing economic system: Hong Kong's oligopolies and monopolies have been left intact. Similarly, the Basic Law leaves room for significant changes to be made to the tax system. But here, too, the government preferred to introduce a GST rather than, for example, to tax idle lands (e.g. a tax on land banks) or the profits on capital gains – or to create a worldwide income tax that could reach Hong Kong's interests located in tax havens such as the BVIs. Of course, while a GST can only increase revenue, a tax on idle land or one on financial profits may have deeper consequences on Hong Kong's budget. However, in the face of the city's current economic and political situation, as well as its changing (and unsettled) relationship with China and the global economy, a modification of the tax system and its consequences should be at the heart of the government's considerations, especially since Hong Kong's tax system is particularly unfair and since Hong Kong's role as a tax haven has to evolve. But the hostility of Hong Kong's business community and economic philosophy of its government have thwarted such reforms, starting with an overhaul of its tax system, while the Competition Ordinance has so far been little more than a cosmetic measure at least regarding the reduction of inequality. Both cases represent missed opportunities to head off future civil unrest in Hong Kong.

The final element is the control of the election process through the existence of the Functional Constituencies in LegCo and the 1,200-member panel that selects the CE. In a recent interview, Stiglitz indicated that the cost for each candidate during the last presidential elections in the US amounted to over US$1 billion, which he called an 'investment', rather than a donation (Chavagneux 2015). Hong Kong's system of control is much less costly for its élites, as it suffices for a CE candidate to secure a majority of the Election Committee's votes and to have enough allies on the advisory boards to influence the CE's political and economic decisions.

Thus, in this context, the possibilities for Hong Kong's youth to influence the system are very few. Their chances of securing good jobs, salaries and housing – even after they have received good educations – are equally slim and they can feel the negative effects of globalization on their daily lives. Thus, they have every reason to fight for democracy (an objective stated in the Basic Law). There is little wonder why 'Hong Kong People Feel Powerless in Politics', as a *South China Morning Post* article proclaimed (Cheung 2016). As the people know too well, their chances of success are low because the political system is rigged: the control of the business élites over the economic and political system was reaffirmed and reinforced by the NPCSC decision. By no means can protests lead to fundamental changes in the system – the 'incumbents' are too entrenched to be challenged by protests, at least in the short term. In both a naïve and cynical way, this is exactly what the current CE, Leung Chun-ying acknowledged to the foreign media:

> if you look at the meaning of the words, 'broadly representative,' it's not numeric representation.
>
> You have to take care of all the sectors in Hong Kong as much as you can … and if it's entirely a numbers game and numeric representation, then obviously you would be talking to half of the people in Hong Kong who earn less than [US]$1,800 a month.
>
> Then you would end up with that kind of politics and policies.
>
> (Cited by Bradsher and Buckley 2014)[8]

These consequences are exactly the ones raised by the business community since the 1980s: the implementation of democracy would automatically lead to the satisfaction of social demands, which would imply changes in the economic system. For Leung, who has been serving local economic interests in addition to the Mainland government, that was absolutely not acceptable.

Consequently, the Umbrella Movement ended with no major achievement for the protesters and the NPCSC's 31 August Decision was voted down by LegCo in June 2015. But that does not mean the Movement was an entire failure: in the 2016 LegCo elections, seats went to some of the protesters and their supporters. In the colourful language of Suzanne Pepper: 'The Kids Are Alright: Hong Kong's latest elections are proof the Umbrella Movement did not fail' (Pepper 2016).

Even though some of these seats are currently jeopardized by a court decision, it is noticeable that several of these pro-democracy lawmakers are also fighting for social and economic issues. A remarkable example is provided by Eddie Chu Hoi-Dick, who played a prominent role in the Choi Yuen Tsuen protests and is now aiming to preserve agricultural land and the environment. Together with another legislator, Edward Yiu Chung-Yim, he is also strongly involved in housing issues. In the same way, Lau Siu-Lai has tried to protect the interest of the hawkers.[9] These actions constitute another piece of the puzzle, showing that the fight for democracy is not only for the sake of it, but it is also for building a fairer and more sustainable society: the political, social and economic elements are tightly intertwined.

Then, the economic conditions that triggered the protest are still there and the disenchantment of the youth was exacerbated by the unsuccessful conclusion to the Umbrella Movement. Strong reforms are urgently needed to change this pattern, but this is not likely to occur. On the one hand, the economic and political bias that favours the developers will still remain in place. On the other hand, the hopes of a change in the economic structure are slim. There are strong possibilities that the relative influence of local conglomerates will diminish domestically because of the age of the patriarchs who are often well over 80 and because the groups they created are diversifying their activities overseas. However, the declining influence of local groups is to be compensated by the increasing level of investments from the Mainland, including from State-Owned Enterprises. And, while this trend deepens the worries of local people in the face of the growing (economic) influence of China in the Territory, it also participates in the reinforcement of the existing system in favour of economic interests. In the last few years, the only new companies which have been able to overcome existing barriers to entry and to actively participate to the land auctions were Mainland developers. They have sufficient liquidities and are pushed to intervene in the Hong Kong market by the decreasing opportunities in the main Chinese cities. In the words of Li and Sito, 'Chinese developers [were] driven away by market-cooling restrictions on the mainland and a desire to get their deteriorating currency out of the country' (Li and Sito 2016). This drives the land price up further and, therefore, 'Chinese Developers, Hong Kong Government Says Xie Xie [i.e. thank you]' (ibid.).[10]

In any case, the Central government has made clear that economic achievements should come first and that status quo should be maintained. This preference is strongly encapsulated in the Basic Law (see Chapter 1), and Chinese leaders have reinstated it constantly during and after the Umbrella Movement. The composition of the delegation who visited China at the invitation of the Central government after the 31 August 2014 Decision (and which was composed of businessmen only) is another proof of it. More recently, Chinese leaders equally assert that 'street politics' should be avoided:

> Hong Kong should avoid politicization of its economic problems and resorting to 'street politics' as it will tarnish the city's image and scare off foreign investors, the state leader overseeing Hong Kong affairs warned (…).
>
> National People's Congress Chairman Zhang Dejiang (…) said [Hong Kong people] understood the city's economic success was built on its economic achievements and proximity to the mainland.
>
> (Cheung and Fung 2016)

However, as this book has emphasized: it is not possible anymore to avoid the politicization of economic problems because resorting to 'street politics', as Zhang Dejiang put it, is, in part at least, due to existing economic hardship (and it is one of the biggest tools ordinary people still have to make their voices heard). The traditional policy to boost economic growth so that the overall population may benefit from it to a certain extent clearly shows its limits. Similarly, as seen in Chapter 2, the proximity to China is seen both as an opportunity and as a threat, in the absence of perceived role for the Territory in China and in the world – and the overuse of C.Y. Leung favoured catchword, 'super-connector', to qualify Hong Kong is clearly not enough to dispel existing ambiguities. The launch of the Belt and Road Initiative by President Xi Jinping, in 2010, just adds to this general sentiment. Even though, in his 2016 policy address, C.Y. Leung used 48 times the expression 'One Belt, One Road', it was mainly in vague terms that did not appeal to most Hongkongers (G.K.W. Cheung 2016).

Thus, the failure of the government to address the concerns of Hong Kong's youth, as well as the relative sclerosis of its economic and political systems, may very well lead to further and more radical movements. Unless major changes occur in Hong Kong's economy, superficial and piecemeal policies such as distributing 'sweeteners' to the poor and middle class or increasing land supply will not be enough to alleviate their grievances. A more comprehensive policy that aims to arrest the city's inequality and reverse its extreme concentration of wealth – similar to what Piketty proposed – is more urgent than ever. This would need a strong action by the government; but, even if it is willing to do so, it remains to be seen if the Beijing authorities, its business community and, increasingly, the Mainland companies which also benefit from the system would let it engage in deep reforms.

Notes

1 This is, of course, a very short summary, which neglects other important events. Among them, the Choi Yuen Tsuen (Choi Yuen Village) controversy may have played an important role in raising the social awareness among the younger generation. The Choi Yuen Tsuen was a village located in the New Territories that has been demolished to give way to a section of the Guangzhou–Hong Kong high-speed rail under construction. Important mass protests occurred from November 2009 to February 2010 to oppose the planed destruction, but did not manage to save the village. Interestingly, the data collected at the same time by the Hong Kong Transition Project indicated a

> shift toward elevated dissatisfaction quite suddenly, particularly among those under 30, and must be related to the government's conservative proposals for constitutional reforms since no other significant event has occurred between the Policy Address survey in late October 2009 and the survey in mid-January 2010.
>
> (Hong Kong Transition Project 2010: 3)

Thus, the report explained the change in attitude by the release of a government proposal related to the (lack of) constitutional reforms for the 2012 CE election and not by the Choi Yuen village controversy, but the concomitance of the change in attitude of the young generation and the protest related to the dismantling of the village is troubling. For example, Ortmann linked directly the rise of the anti-capitalist movement at the end of the 2000s and the movement to protect the village (Ortmann 2015: 44). While this point should be discussed prominently for a political analysis of the Umbrella Movement, it remains somewhat secondary to the main theme of this book.

2 This was even the case during the 1966–1967 riots. Gary Cheung carefully described how Zhou En-lai, the then-Prime Minister of China, tried to protect the colony from leftist actions. The colonial government itself stated that the disturbances during the events – which caused 51 deaths – were minimal (Cheung 2009, Chapter 9).

3 The old cliché during colonial times, 'power in Hong Kong resided in the Jockey Club, Jardine and Matheson, the Hong Kong and Shanghai Bank and the Governor in that order' is an exaggeration, but it is still illustrative of the dominance of economic interests in the Territory.

4 E.g. Sophie Yan, for CNN during the Movement: 'Hong Kong's growing wealth gap fuels protests'. In her words:

> At the pro-democracy protests – where student-led groups are calling for free elections – complaints over housing costs are frequent.
>
> 'We cannot afford [an apartment], we could not have a shelter [even though] we work all the time,' said protester Kaley Lau, 25, who works as a nurse.'
>
> (Yau 2015)

If even nurses, which, as presented in Chapter 3, have relatively higher wages than many other young graduates, are facing such type of difficulties, it shows the seriousness of the situation.

5 These are the shopping malls located in all public housing estates. Below is a comment criticizing the decision of the Housing Authority to sell the 'ownership and rights of management' of these malls. Other artefacts addressed food safety issues, MTR (local metro) fares, and free TV licences.

6 'Exit' would imply emigration from Hong Kong – a strategy that is not available to most Hongkongers. It should be noted, however, that the demand for foreign visa has surged in recent years by 15 to 20 per cent. The title 'I Want to Be in America: Despondency in Hong Kong Fuelling Rush for US Visa, Says Immigration Experts'

and the headlines 'Poor career prospects in the city and rising social tensions make the move an appealing prospect for growing numbers' of a recent newspaper article are perfectly illustrating the 'exit' trend (see Karacs 2016).

7 For example, like in Hong Kong, the Spanish movement is composed of a weak alliance of several associations and organizations, such as 'Youth Without a Future' (*Juventud Sin Futuro*). But, as the authors have shown, there are also major differences – namely, the importance of the political factors, the desire to keep, for the majority of the protesters, a legalistic perspective, and the fact that they do not wish to replace the existing economic/capitalist system since they cannot see suitable alternatives.

8 Article was from the *New York Times*, but the sentences were reprinted and commented on by all major media overseas and in Hong Kong. Leung later apologized for his comments.

9 Both Lau Siu-lai and Edward Yiu, who were initially academics, have lost their seat at the LegCo. The reason is the way they took their oath of office. The oaths were declared invalid. The LegCo president decided to allow them to retake their oath, but the decision was contested in court by the government. Four other lawmakers are concerned by this action, all of them having also lost their seat.

10 According to another newspaper article, Mainland Chinese developers acquired 27 per cent of all residential land sites in Hong Kong in 2016. These acquisitions are mainly in the high-end market, but it is clear that Mainland companies are driving prices up. This can be seen by the record price paid for a site in Ap Lei Chau, which fetched HK$16.86 billion. This amount was about 50 per cent higher than the original market valuation (Sito and Ng 2017).

Bibliography

Bradsher, K. and C. Buckley (2014) 'Hong Kong Leader Reaffirms Unbending Stance on Elections', *New York Times*, 20 October, www.nytimes.com/2014/10/21/world/asia/leung-chun-ying-hong-kong-china-protests.html?_r=0, accessed 8 August 2015.

Chan, S. (2015) 'Suicides on Rise among Hongkongers', *South China Morning Post*, 10 September.

Chavagneux, C. (2015) '"Le 1% les plus riches met tout en œuvre pour maintenir des sociétés inégalitaires" – Interview with Joseph Stiglitz', *Alternatives Economiques*, 350 (October), www.alternatives-economiques.fr/le-1-nbsp-25-les-plus-riches-met-to_fr_art_1391_73617.html, accessed 5 October 2015.

Cheung, E. (2016) 'Hong Kong Youth Feel Powerless in Politics', *South China Morning Post*, 1 September, www.scmp.com/news/hong-kong/article/2012375/hong-kong-youth-feel-powerless-politics, accessed 25 November 2016.

Cheung, G.K.W. (2009) *Hong Kong's Watershed: The 1967 Riots*, Hong Kong: Hong Kong University Press.

Cheung, G.K.W. (2016) 'We Get It, CY … One Belt, One Road Gets Record-breaking 48 Mentions in Policy Address', *South China Morning Post*, 13 January, www.scmp.com/news/hong-kong/politics/article/1901017/we-get-it-cy-one-belt-one-road-gets-record-breaking-48, accessed 25 July 2017.

Cheung, T. and O. Fung (2016) '"Street Politics" Could Tarnish City's Image', *South China Morning Post*, 7 March.

Hirschman, A.O. (1970) *Exit, Voice, and Loyalty: Responses to Decline in Firms, Organizations, and States*, Cambridge, MA: Harvard University Press.

Hong Kong Transition Project (2010) 'Protest and Post-80s Youth. Sources of Social Instability in Hong Kong', the Baptist University, February, http://hktp.org/list/protest_and_post_80s_youths.pdf, accessed 12 July 2017.

Karacs, S. (2016) 'I Want to Be in America: Despondency in Hong Kong Fuelling Rush for US Visa, Says Immigration Experts', *South China Morning Post*, 26 March 2016, www.scmp.com.easyaccess1.lib.cuhk.edu.hk/news/hong-kong/politics/article/1931043/i-want-be-america-despondency-hong-kong-fuelling-rush-us, accessed 28 March 2016.

Lhatoo, Y. (2016) 'Hong Kong's Appalling Wealth Gap is a Burning Fuse for Revolution', *South China Morning Post*, 13 October, www.scmp.com/comment/insight-opinion/article/2027778/hong-kongs-appalling-wealth-gap-burning-fuse-revolution, accessed 17 April 2017.

Li, S. and P. Sito (2016) 'Chinese Developers, Hong Kong Government Says Xie Xie', *South China Morning Post*, 29 December, www.scmp.com/property/hong-kong-china/article/2057278/chinese-developers-hong-kong-government-says-xie-xie, accessed 10 March 2017.

Lo, C., P. So and E Tsang (2014) 'Pro-democracy Banner Hung from Lion Rock Has Officials Scrambling', *South China Morning Post*, 23 October, www.scmp.com/news/hong-kong/article/1622971/climbers-hang-giant-banner-lion-rock-calling-real-universal-suffrage#comments, accessed 25 April 2017.

Ma, N. (2011) 'Value Changes and Legitimacy Crisis in Post-industrial Hong Kong', *Asian Survey*, 51(4): 683–712.

Noble, J. (2014) 'Economic Inequality Underpins Hong Kong's Great Political Divide', *The Financial Times*, 21 October, www.ft.com/cms/s/0/d123d896-5808-11e4-b47d-00144feab7de.html#axzz3nqc8byR4, accessed 9 October 2015.

Ortmann, S. (2015) 'The Umbrella Movement and Hong Kong's Protracted Democratization Process', *Asian Affairs*, 1: 32–50.

Ortmann, S. (2016) 'The Lack of Sovereignty, Umbrella Movement and Democratisation in Hong Kong', *Asia Pacific Law Review*, 24(2): 108–122.

Pepper, S. (2008) *Keeping Democracy at Bay. Hong Kong and the Challenge of Chinese Political Reforms*, Lanham: Rowan & Littlefield.

Pepper, S. (2016) 'The Kids Are Alright: Hong Kong's Latest Elections Are Proof the Umbrella Movement Did Not Fail', *Hong Kong Free Press*, 11 September, www.hongkongfp.com/2016/09/11/the-kids-are-alright-hong-kongs-latest-elections-are-proof-the-umbrella-movement-did-not-fail/, accessed 15 June 2017.

Sito, S., S. Zhen and N. Ng (2017) 'Chinese Builders Pay Record HK$16.86b for Ap Lei Chau site', *South China Morning Post*, 24 February, www.scmp.com/property/hong-kong-china/article/2073805/mainland-developers-logan-kwg-win-residential-site-ap-lei, accessed 10 March 2017.

Stiglitz J.E. (2015) *The Great Divide: Unequal Societies and What We Can Do About Them,* New York, W.W. Norton Company.

'The Basic Law of the Hong Kong Special Administrative Region of People's Republic of China', www.basiclaw.gov.hk/en/basiclawtext/index.html, accessed 17 August 2015.

The United Nations Department of Political Affairs, Trusteeship and Decolonization (1985) 'Twenty-Five Years of the Declaration on the Granting of Independence to Colonial Countries and Peoples,' www.un.org/en/decolonization/pdf/decolonization/decon_num_26-1.pdf, accessed 15 June 2017.

Veg, S. (2015) 'Hong Kong's Umbrella Movement: Legalistic and Utopian', *New Left Review*, 92: 55–73.

Wong, Y.C.R. (2015) *Hong Kong Land for Hong Kong People*, Hong Kong: Hong Kong University Press.

Yau, C. (2015) 'Official Use of English Being 'Neglected' by Hong Kong Government', *South China Morning Post*, 8 June.

Yip, P. (2014) 'Wealth Gap Will Break Hong Kong if We Don't Change the Economic Order', *South China Morning Post*, 5 June, www.scmp.com/comment/article/1525874/wealth-gap-will-break-hong-kong-if-we-dont-change-economic-order, accessed 17 April 2017.

Index

Page numbers in **bold** denote tables.

For Product Safety Concerns and Information please contact our EU representative GPSR@taylorandfrancis.com Taylor & Francis Verlag GmbH, Kaufingerstraße 24, 80331 München, Germany